EDITED BY
Harriet Harriss, Rory Hyde,
Roberta Marcaccio

DESIGNED BY
Studio Folder
(Marco Ferrari, Elisa Pasqual,
Letizia Bernardelli)

First published 2021 by Routledge,
52 Vanderbilt Avenue, New York, NY 10017

and by Routledge
2 Park Square, Milton Park, Abingdon,
Oxon, OX14 4RN

Routledge is an imprint of the
Taylor & Francis Group, an informa
business

ISBN: 9780367441227 (hbk)
ISBN: 9780367441210 (pbk)
ISBN: 9781003007753 (ebk)

This book has been prepared from
camera-ready copy provided by the editors.

Library of Congress
Cataloging-in-Publication Data

Names: Harriss, Harriet, editor. | Hyde, Rory,
editor. | Marcaccio, Roberta, editor.
Title: Architects after architecture: alternative
pathways for practice / edited by Harriet
Harriss, Rory Hyde, Roberta Marcaccio.
Description: New York, NY : Routledge, 2020. |
Includes bibliographical references and index.
Identifiers: LCCN 2020030120 (print) |
LCCN 2020030121 (ebook) | ISBN
9780367441227 (hbk) | ISBN 9780367441210
(pbk) | ISBN 9781003007753 (ebk)
Subjects: LCSH: Architecture. | Architecture-
Vocational guidance. | Architects.
Classification: LCC NA2540. A575 2020 (print) |
LCC NA2540 (ebook) | DDC 720.92--dc23
LC record available at
https://lccn.loc.gov/2020030120
LC ebook record available at
https://lccn.loc.gov/2020030121

ARCHITECTS AFTER ARCHITECTURE

Alternative
Pathways
for Practice

EDITED BY

Harriet Harriss
Rory Hyde
Roberta Marcaccio

PLUS

BEYOND

PREFACE

As we make the final edits to this book, the world is on lockdown. Covid-19 has exposed the fragility of our current condition and inability to prevent the spread of this deadly virus. In London, where Rory and Roberta are based, close to 1,000 deaths per day have been recorded; while in New York, Harriet has focussed on converting Pratt's model workshops to produce personal protective equipment for frontline healthcare workers.

Architecture has lost some greats in these first few weeks of grappling with the disease. Our friends, colleagues and mentors Michael Sorkin, Bill Menking, Lou Goodman and Vittorio Gregotti are among those who have died, with, tragically, many more likely to come. This book is dedicated to them.

Many architects are out of work, as construction sites close down, and the economy grinds to a halt. We don't yet know what other social, political, environmental or technological shocks may be coming over the horizon. What is certain is that the recovery – if we can call it that – will be slow, and the world we return to will not be the same one we left.

It is not the time for optimism. And yet, we believe we must find hope in what is to come. We must work together to rebuild the way we live, to strike a new social and ecological contract, to support those who are most vulnerable, and to defend against other crises.

Many of the people and practices presented in this book also forged their paths in times of crisis. Faced with great challenges, they were forced to reevaluate their priorities, and to reinvent the way they work in order to move forward.

We hope that in these stories you might find the tools to overcome whatever challenge you may find yourself facing at the moment you choose to read this book.

Editors
April 2020

Architects After Architecture

INTRODUCTION

HARRIET HARRISS
RORY HYDE
ROBERTA MARCACCIO

The image of the architect as a singular hero is a stubbornly persistent one. The most famous instance of this stereotype is Howard Roark, the uncompromising genius conceived by Ayn Rand in her 1943 novel *The Fountainhead*, and played with singular intensity by Gary Cooper in the 1949 film. Roark is determined to make his mark on the world, to create great works of art, in fulfilment of what he perceives to be his life's destiny. But beneath this narrative of purpose and ambition lies a far darker philosophy of individualism and greed. When the client changes his design, Roark chooses to destroy the building rather than see it built imperfectly. In his defence, he argues that 'The first right on earth is the right of the ego'.

If you thought that the stereotype of Roark was just that, with little bearing on the reality of the architect today, you would be mistaken.[1] The Fountainhead is a libertarian fantasy, a dreamworld where the architect's individual genius, authority and control is held up high above the meddling clients who commission them, and the little people who occupy their buildings. This fantasy is given form today in the guise of the 'starchitect', the globe-trotting superstar designer, creating lunging forms for the covers of magazines, and often working for unscrupulous clients.

It's what many students have been pedagogically primed to become, and the clearest expression of what success in architecture looks like, reinforced by the awards system, media attention, and commissions, in a self-preserving cycle.

What's so unhelpful about this image of the Randian starchitect is that it perpetuates the idea that architecture is about form rather than use, about the individual rather than the collective, about perfection rather than constructive compromise, and about artistry rather than social purpose. It contains within it a whole set of assumptions about how architects are supposed to work, where, and for whom.

It also couldn't be further from reality. The most effective architects are not those who seek to control every detail, but who are open collaborators in a productive process. They are professional generalists, who know a little bit about a lot of things, able to ask the right questions to get the best out of a team. They are good hosts, able to invite the right people around the table, in order to better define the brief, and to consider it from multiple perspectives. They are synthesists, able to process this often contradictory information, to satisfy multiple goals and stakeholders. And they are propositional, able to transform this raw material of people, perspectives and ambitions into an actionable vision for the future, something which can spark excitement, garner support, and show the way forward. They are microscopes and macroscopes, able to operate at the scale of a glazing detail, at the scale of the city, and all that lies between. Architecture requires a unique combination of pragmatism and emotion, of technical problem-solving and imaginary vision. In this version, the architect is recast as a creative mediator, bridging between different forms of knowledge, seeking clarity amongst complexity, bringing together disparate communities, building and combining emotional power with pragmatic potential. The form-making for which the starchitect is known is only a small proportion of the job, and far from the most important aspect.

This version of the architect as mediator may not sound as glamorous as the starchitect, but it is a more useful one. And, in our experience as educators, despite much latent hero-worship, we find many students would prefer it this way.

Architects After Architecture

Increasingly, architecture schools seek to imbue students with a practical idealism and social purpose, setting students the task of designing libraries and museums, social housing and public transport systems. They are motivated by a desire to improve the city and positively impact society, rather than to build their own reputations. This is where students want to be. And yet despite this civic education, the unquestioned assumption of many schools of architecture is that upon graduation the natural destination is to enter a private practice, in an urban centre, to work on projects commissioned by those who can afford it. It is the aim of this book to expand this horizon of possibility, to reveal alternative pathways for architects.

PLUS AND BEYOND   *Architects After Architecture* draws together the people and practices who are collectively expanding this horizon, by questioning what can be considered architecture. They have gone beyond the conventional notion of practice, to redefine who they work for, where they work, what kinds of questions they ask, and what kinds of answers they can give. Together, these examples point toward a version of architecture that is plural and diverse, with many paths toward reclaiming broader relevance to society.

These people and practices fall roughly into two groups. The first, gathered under the heading of 'Plus', are those who consider themselves to be still working within architecture, but who are stretching the boundaries, redefining what is possible. These are architects who are working with the public sector, designing social housing, enabling communities, designing with nature, tackling the climate emergency, advocating for LGBTQ+ rights, working in post-conflict zones, and more.

The second group, under the heading of 'Beyond', is made up of those who have 'left' architecture to apply their skills in other disciplines. They have recognised the broad applicability of the architect – as integrator, as professional generalist, as practical idealist – and applied these skills in service of other questions beyond the building. These people have studied architecture, but now find themselves in technology, in politics, in advocacy, in videogames, in property development, in design thinking, in art, in museums, and more.

By bringing these two groups together in one volume, we can create a broad and inclusive definition of what architecture is; by neither turning our backs on those who leave, or pigeonholing those who stay. We can acknowledge that making a videogame, a policy, or a legal case, is simply architecture by other means, thereby legitimising the work of those who leave – they are not 'abandoning' architecture, but expanding its relevance into other adjacent territories. And on the other side of the same coin, we hope this expanded definition also offers permission for many others to stay, particularly those who may not see themselves in traditional practice, and who are reaching for other business models (or role models) with which to apply their training.

The number of architects who either leave or redefine what they do is surprisingly high. In the UK, data from the Royal Institute of British Architects (RIBA) show more than half of the students who have completed the undergraduate bachelor of architecture degree, known as Part I, do not go on to complete the post-graduate Part III, a requirement for registration as an architect, representing a gap of around 1,600 students per year.[2] With some claiming the ratio of those who become registered architects versus those who embark on the degree is as low as one in 14.[3] In the US, the gap between graduates and those registered is narrower, with 37 percent not ultimately registering as an architect, or about 2,500 per year.[4] This is perhaps due to the far greater total cost of a US education, at an average of $190,000 for a four year professional degree.[5]

It's unclear where these students go or what they end up doing, as their pathways are not captured in the research. Anecdotally, we know that many graduates of architecture continue to work in architectural practice while never registering as architects. Many will go elsewhere. We are hesitant to place too much emphasis on the statistics, as few professional bodies or schools have set out to specifically capture the professional destination of those who have left.

OVERLEAF   A conceptual map of *Architects After Architecture.* At the centre is ARCHITECTURE as it is traditionally conceived. Around this body is PLUS, the ambiguous zone of those who are stretching the boundaries of the discipline from the inside. BEYOND represents those who have left architecture behind, to apply their skills in other fields.

SARAH WIGGLESWORTH

WORKAC

AL

CULTURE

CLIMATE

JEREMY TILL

ANT FARM

ANDRÉS JAQUE

JUDIT

PASCALE SABLAN

INCLUSION

JOS BOYS

PARLOUR

MUF

ELSIE OWUSO

JOEL SANDERS

PLUS

ARCHI

INTERBORO

AAA

COMMUNITY

PETER BARBER

WE MAD

SIB TRIGG

PUBLIC WORKS

JACK SELF

TAKESHI HAYATSU

ASSEMBLE

PRACTICE

ROTOR

MAKING

ROGER ZOGOLOVITC

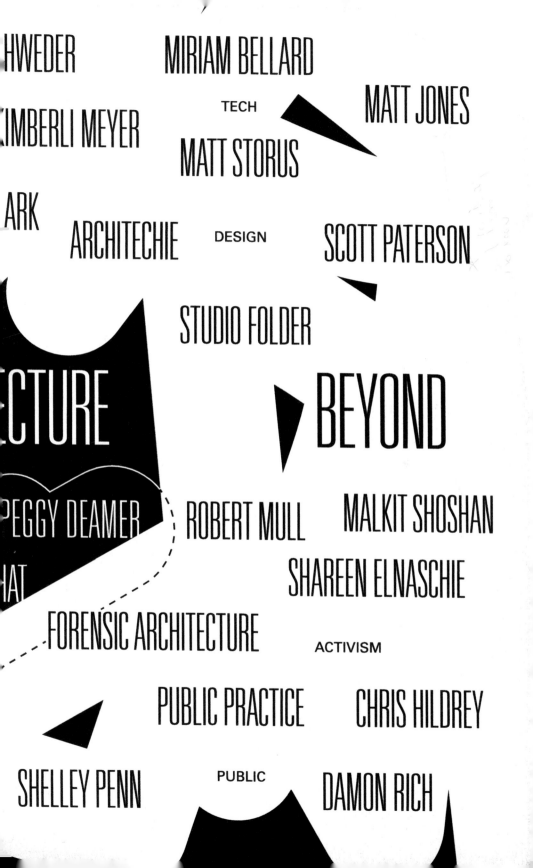

It's simply not in their interests; what's the point of five years of vocational training if you don't even become an architect? This is not the sort of thing universities write in their prospectuses.

But rather than sweeping this cohort under the carpet, pretending that they don't exist, and letting them find their own way, what if we were instead to acknowledge their diverse roles and pathways as a sign of success? The broad applicability of architectural thinking beyond the building is surely a strength rather than a weakness, it suggests a flexibility of mind, and a high level of transferable competence. What if architecture were promoted as a generalist degree, a way of thinking about the world, rather than a step toward professional accreditation?

THE EXPANSION OF THE DISCIPLINE AND THE EXPERIMENTATION WITH ALTERNATE FORMS OF ARCHITECTURE PRACTICE IS NOT SIMPLY A NEW TREND, BUT A SURVIVAL TACTIC.

It is this flexibility of mind that society needs most of all today. The great challenges we face, from the climate emergency to the housing crisis, the rise of the right to global pandemics, do not conform to neat disciplinary silos, but cross over into the messy space between politics, economics, culture, and – critically for architects – spatial thinking. These challenges are defined by their interconnectedness and by change. They cannot be solved with the old processes, but require new forms of thinking and working, combining a planetary consciousness with a responsible humanism that respects and enables local expertise. As Bruce Mau has said, 'If you think about architecture as a methodology – independent from the outcome – you would see that architecture has a deep culture of synthesis informed by civic values. If you have that capacity, that's the most valuable capacity of this time in history.'[6] We find this to be hugely encouraging, a reminder that the architect's combination of skills is what is needed now, if only we were brave enough to free these skills from the constraints of the building.

But why should architects apply their skills elsewhere? 'Stay in your lane!' you cry. 'Focus on designing buildings, on what you're good at!'. A fair point perhaps, but it overlooks two things: the broader obligation of the profession to society, and the state architecture finds itself in today.

Firstly, to this obligation. Academics Richard and Daniel Susskind define the purpose of the professions – law, medicine, accountancy, teaching, and architecture, among others – as to regulate the way in which specialist expertise is made available in society.[7] This asymmetrical relationship is governed by what is known as a 'grand bargain', a social contract that grants exclusivity over a domain of knowledge in exchange for agreeing to apply this knowledge for the benefit of all. So architects are granted protection of title, preventing anyone who can use a pencil from calling themselves an architect, with the expectation that they will then serve society as a whole. This is not the case however. In the UK for instance, while doctors have the National Health Service and lawyers have Legal Aid, architects have their private practices, working for whomever can afford to pay them, a vanishingly small proportion of the public. By neglecting the vast majority of people, architects are arguably in breach of this grand bargain.[8]

You would think that given they're having their cake and eating it, things would be looking up for architects. Unfortunately, that's not the case. A recent article in *The Architect's Journal*, citing research from the Federation of Master Builders and the Office of National Statistics, states that 'Brickies earn more than architects'.[9] There is no reason why a brickie shouldn't be paid more – it's a hard job, and you should be rewarded for doing it –

THE GREAT CHALLENGES WE FACE DO NOT CONF[
BUT CROSS OVER INTO THE MESSY SPACE BET[
CULTURE, AND — CRITICALLY FOR ARCHITECTS -

but given the time and expense it takes to train as an architect, this should be a harsh wake up call for the perceived value of architecture today.

This state of affairs, we contend, requires a radical rethink. By applying architectural knowledge beyond the policed boundaries of the profession,[10] there is an opportunity to recast who architects work for, how they work, where they work, what kinds of questions they can ask, and the answers they can give. All of which can help them to get back on the path to rebuilding relevance to the public, and with it, their value.

PRECEDENTS   In this attempt to recapture architecture's public relevance by redefining the boundaries of architecture, we build upon the work of many thinkers and practitioners before us. Here we compile an incomplete list of quotes and projects.

Our title is a riff on Bernard Rudofsky's *Architecture Without Architects*, a book and exhibition at MoMA in 1964 which celebrated the ingenuity of vernacular building across the globe, which he termed 'non-pedigreed architecture'.[11] By looking far beyond the western canon, Rudofsky radically recast the boundaries of what was considered architecture.

We were inspired by a quote from Charlotte Perriand, who in 1936 wrote to Pierre Jeanneret, 'If I abandon the "profession of architecture" in order to focus on problems more directly connected with life, it is to be able to see more clearly

into these problems.'[12] Perriand steps blithely over the disciplinary boundary of architecture, to form a practice comprising
art, photography, furniture, graphic design, urban planning,
exhibitions, and architecture for extreme environments.

Christopher Alexander and his colleagues at Berkeley's
Center for Environmental Structure in the 1970s, developed a
series of manuals to enable the democratisation of architectural
knowledge, placing it into the hands of citizens. 'Without the
help of architects or planners', Alexander writes, 'if you are
working in the timeless way, a town will grow under your hands,
as steady as the flowers in your garden.'[13]

Lina Bo Bardi, who was first honoured with an exhibition of her work when she was 74 years old, dismissed architecture's 'traditions' as a 'set of classical rules that were codified
in books and erudite treatises,' and placed emphasis upon the
need to 'forge another "true present" that could not be found
in books, but rather expresses a need.'[14]

The critic Reyner Banham disapproved of the architectural guides to Los Angeles that came before him, noting they
included 'neither hamburger bars and other Pop ephemeridae
at one extreme, nor freeway structures and other civil engineering at the other.'[15] By examining non-canonical and infrastructural forms such as these, in his *Four Ecologies*, Banham is
able to connect architecture back to larger forces of landscape,
ecology and culture.

Architects After Architecture

Similarly, when Cedric Price said that 'The quality of air conditioning is more important than the shape of a building', he effortlessly upended the assumed priorities of architecture, looking beyond form to technological systems, and clearing the path for a mode of practice that asked more questions than it gave answers.[16]

For Sharon Egretta Sutton pushing beyond architecture began with a direct confrontation of the inherent power imbalances within education. She recounts the bold cohort of ethnic minority students who earned degrees from Columbia University School of Architecture during the Civil Rights Movement in the 1960s, in the face of much institutional resistance.[17] This episode shows that architecture's domain extends well beyond the spaces it shapes, encompassing struggles for racial, social and economic equality.

Denise Scott Brown first invited Robert Venturi, and then their students from Yale, to Las Vegas, a place so far off the orthodox architectural map that it was actively despised. By suspending judgement, and seeing it through fresh eyes, they were able to glimpse a new form of American urbanism, writing that 'We believe a careful documentation and analysis of [Las Vegas'] physical form is as important to architects and urbanists today as were the studies of medieval Europe and ancient Rome and Greece to earlier generations.'[18]

Frank Duffy, with his consultancy DEGW, developed a mode of practice as a flexible form of knowledge, using scientific methods to address broad questions from organisational change to the adoption of new technologies. Writing in 1997, he defined architecture as 'an inherently idea-hungry, project-based, solution-oriented discipline, open-ended and systemic, capable of connecting anything with anything'.[19]

Rem Koolhaas describes a similar epiphany in the founding of AMO, a think tank directed to providing answers to architectural questions that may not result in a building. 'Liberated from the obligation to construct', he writes, 'architecture can become a way of thinking about anything – a discipline that represents relationships, proportions, connections, effects, the diagram of everything.'[20]

These architects, and many others like them, saw the arbitrary limits of the profession for what they were and stepped right over them. By seeing the world through new eyes, by redefining the canon, by subverting the exclusive hold over architectural knowledge, and by empowering the public to participate, they opened up productive new territories for the expansion of the discipline, and suggested new pathways for reclaiming architecture's public relevance.

CRISIS AND REINVENTION   This questioning of the arbitrary limits of architectural practice received a considerable boost in the wake of the financial crash of 2008, the aftershocks of which continue to be felt today. Architecture was one of the hardest-hit professions, with a huge proportion of the workforce being laid off, and a substantial cohort of graduates unable to find work in the first place.[21] The recession revealed how architecture's close dependency upon real-estate and speculative development left the profession in a precarious position. It's no surprise then that architects went looking for 'other ways of doing architecture'.[22]

Viewed in purely economic terms, the expansion of the discipline and the experimentation with alternate forms of architecture practice was not simply a new trend – the next stage in architecture's parade of styles – but a survival tactic. As Paul Nakazawa, professor of practice at Harvard, remarked at the time, 'let's be clear, the foreseeable future only requires about half of the pre-recession workforce in architecture. Those who remain in the profession need to augment their knowledge.'[23]

For many, this has meant throwing away the inherited business model of architecture, where upon graduation you hang up your sign and wait for the phone to ring, and striking out in new entrepreneurial directions. For others, it has meant seeking out greener pastures. A number of contributors to this volume made the jump to technology, an industry in exponential expansion over the past decade, while architects have struggled to get back on their feet.

The need to develop new ways of working existed long before the economic crisis. The conventional architectural practice – with its masochistic culture, expectation of long working hours, limited flexibility, vast gender pay gap, and cult of the 'master' – has proven stubbornly resistant to adaptation, leading many to leave. In the UK, US and Australia, men and women graduate from architecture degrees in roughly equal numbers, and yet on average 72 percent of registered architects are male.[24] With this in mind, it is not surprising that a number of the contributions to this volume come from a feminist position. As Parlour co-founder Justine Clark discusses here, the reasons for leaving are many, and not all women feel pushed out, but many are pulled toward greater opportunity.[25]

THROUGH THE ACCUMULATION OF THESE STORIES, WE HOPE TO ILLUSTRATE A VERSION OF ARCHITECTURE WHERE THE LIMITS ARE NO LONGER FIXED.

This story is also true of those from diverse backgrounds. In the US 30 percent of new architects identified as non-white, compared to 60 percent of the population as a whole. In the UK, only 11 percent of all architects are Black, Asian or Ethnic Minority (BAME), despite comprising 19 percent of the population, with the Mayor of London's Supporting Diversity initiative reporting that BAME architects 'continue to face discrimination in the workplace or on site'.[26] Leaving one to wonder, what does architecture need to offer in order to achieve better representation?

For those architects still nurturing their social purpose, the hollow centre of architecture had become all too apparent. Rather than following commercial developers meekly in tow, these architects sought to recapture architecture's civic responsibility. They went far outside of the urban centres to apply their knowledge in refugee camps; they challenged the 'standardised' design solutions, to create space for the full spectrum of gender and cultural identity; and they sought to reinvent building to address the climate emergency.

A number of the contributions here take the form of the personal narrative, the journey from architecture to their ultimate destination. It is our hope that through these individual stories, of pursuing passion and opportunity, the reader may recognise their own ambitions, and discover a path which they may learn from. But more importantly, through the accumulation of these stories, we hope to illustrate a version of architecture where the limits are no longer fixed, but able to be designed and redesigned, making the most out of the unique form of intelligence that architecture can offer.

RESET   It is no coincidence that Ayn Rand's creation of Howard Roark is an architect. His individualism, ego, arrogance, confidence and self-regard at the expense of all others, is merely a distillation of how architects saw, and continue to see, themselves. Roark's 'virtue of selfishness', as Rand has described it, is made all the more believable by simply playing to type. This poisonous vision is now taking over the world. *The Fountainhead* has become a touchpoint for conservative politicians in the US, the UK, and beyond, offering validation for the shameless pursuit of wealth and power at any cost. The UK's former chancellor of the exchequer, Sajid Javid, claims to read *The Fountainhead* twice a year; the Republican speaker of the US House of Representatives, Paul Ryan, is famous for giving every new member of his staff a copy of *Atlas Shrugged*, Rand's door-stopping follow up. And, naturally, the commander in chief himself, president Donald Trump, has declared *The Fountainhead* as his favourite book, saying 'it relates to business, beauty, life and inner emotions. That book relates to... everything.'[27]

If, in a way, this ideology begins in architecture, does architecture hold some responsibility for setting things right?

It is our hope that these stories of architects as collaborators, as integrators, as enablers and listeners can stand as a powerful alternative to the stubbornly resilient image of the architect as a singular hero. It is by charting these many alternate pathways that we can begin to reset this perception, and discover the unrealised potential of architects after architecture.

1   To make this point, Jeremy Till cites a regular feature in *Building Design* magazine, which asked architects 'what is your favourite book?' Over 12 weeks, four architects named *The Fountainhead*, leading Till to suggest – only half jokingly – that one in four architects think it is the greatest book ever written. Jeremy Till, 'Beyond *The Fountainhead*', lecture at Columbia GSAPP, Studio-X Rio, 16 September 2014

2   *RIBA Education Statistics, 2015/16*, published April 2017. This data shows 2,925 students completing Part I in 2014/15 – the latest year studied – and 1,309 students completing Part III.

3   Bob Sheil, 'The After Life', in Harriet Harriss and Daisy Froud (eds.), *Radical Pedagogies*, RIBA Publishing, 2015, p.106

4   The National Architectural Accrediting Board, '2018 Annual Report on Architecture Education', accessed January 2020

5   US Department of Education, IPEDS Survey 2017-2018

6   Bruce Mau, 'The Massive Changer' (interview), in Rory Hyde, *Future Practice: Conversations from the Edge of Architecture*, Routledge, 2012, p.26

7   Richard Susskind and Daniel Susskind, *The Future of the Professions: How Technology will Transform the Work of Human Experts*, Oxford University Press, 2015, p.9

8   This argument is developed further here: Rory Hyde, 'Architecture is in Breach of the Social Contract', in Rob Hyde and Alan Jones (eds.), *Defining Contemporary Professionalism: For Architects in Practice and Education*, RIBA Publishing, 2019

9   Greg Pitcher, 'Brickies earn more than architects', *The Architects' Journal*, 6 March 2018

10 Frank Duffy has forcefully questioned the role of these professional boundaries, writing: 'The classical hallmarks of professionalism – restricted entry, standardized and visible qualifications, fixed fees, the publishing and policing of codes of conduct – are more concerned with keeping things as they are than with developing an intellectual programme.' Francis Duffy with Les Hutton, *Architectural Knowledge*, Routledge, 1997, p.viii

11 Bernard Rudofsky, *Architecture Without Architects: A Short Introduction to Non-Pedigreed Architecture*, University of New Mexico Press, 1964

12 This quote was printed as a wall text in the exhibition 'Charlotte Perriand: Inventing a New World', at the Fondation Louis Vuitton in Paris, 2019

13 Christopher Alexander, *The Timeless Way of Building*, Oxford University Press, 1979, p.8

14 Lina Bo Bardi lecture at the Architecture and Urbanism College of University of São Paulo (FAU-USP), 14 April 1989. Transcript by the Instituto Lina Bo e PM Bardi (ILBPMB)

15 Reyner Banham, *Los Angeles: The Architecture of Four Ecologies*, University of California Press, 1971, p.22

16 Cedric Price, quoted by Andrea Branzi, in Hans Ulrich Obrist *(ed.)*, *Re:CP*, Birkhauser Verlag, 2003, p.42

17 Sharon Egretta Sutton, *When Ivory Towers Were Black: A Story about Race in America's Cities and Universities*. Fordham Univ Press, 2017, p.1

18 Denise Scott Brown and Robert Venturi, *Learning from Las Vegas,* MIT Press, 1972

19 Francis Duffy, *Architectural Knowledge*, Routledge, 1997, p.xiv

20 Rem Koolhaas, *Content*, Taschen, 2005, p.20

21 Christopher Sell, 'Number of Architects Claiming Benefits Rises by 760 Percent', *The Architects' Journal*, 20 March 2009

22 Nishat Aswan, Tatjana Schneider and Jeremy Till, *Spatial Agency: Other Ways of Doing Architecture*, Routledge, 2011

23 Paul Nakazawa, 'Embrace the Change', *Architect* magazine, January 2011

24 According to the RIBA, in the UK, 51 percent of architecture graduates are male, and 49 percent are female, while 72 percent of registered architects are male. In the US, NCARB data shows 52 percent of architecture graduates are male, and 48 percent female, while 70 percent of registered architects are male. In Australia, research group Parlour has drawn upon data from the national census, as well as professional bodies, to show 56 percent of graduates are male, and 44 percent female, while 76 percent of registered architects are male.

25 See Justine Clark's chapter 'Spaces to Speak' at p.49

26 US figures are reported by NCARB, in their 2019 'NCARB by the Numbers' report. UK figures are reported by the *RIBA Journal*, 'Drop in BAME architects across UK's top practices, new data reveals', 14 June 2019, and by the Mayor of London's 'Supporting Diversity Handbook', 2019. Data for ethnic minority architects in Australia is incomplete (Yvonne Meng, 'Cultural diversity in architecture', Parlour, 8 June 2016), but anecdotal evidence suggests BAME people are similarly underrepresented.

27 Jonathan Freedland, 'The new age of Ayn Rand: how she won over Trump and Silicon Valley', *The Guardian*, 10 April 2017

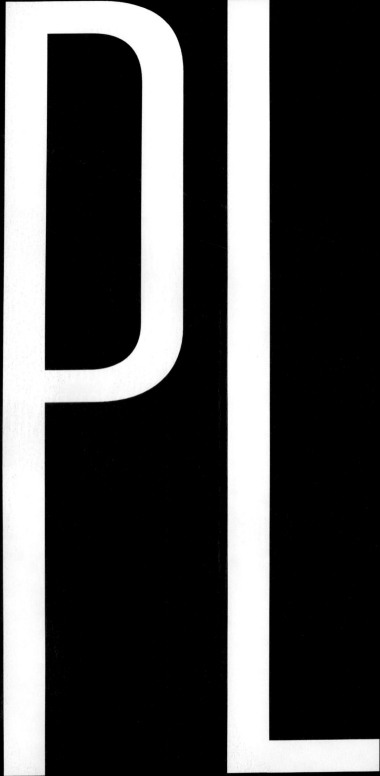

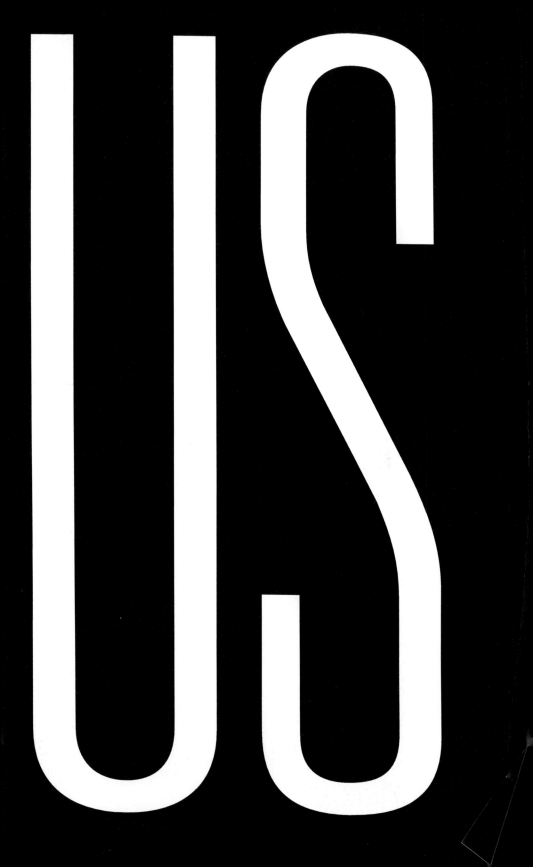

ARCHITECTURE AFTER ARCHITECTURE

JEREMY TILL

Architecture and construction are a massive contributor to carbon emissions. And while the profession makes the right sounds – sustainability, zero carbon, LEED – is it doing enough? Jeremy Till, architect, writer, and head of Central Saint Martins, takes a swing at those virtue-signalling architects who trumpet their environmental credentials while continuing to build airports. Instead, Till argues, tackling the climate emergency will require a fundamental restructuring of the profession, the seeds of which he sees in the empathetic and critical work of his students.

It has been a conflicted few weeks for me, architecture, and the climate emergency. First, Sarah and I have just finished a major retrofit of our house,[1] doing all the things we wished we could have done when we built it, and also preparing it for our older age. When we conceived the house 25 years ago, sustainable design was in its infancy. The kit available back then (boilers, solar things, whole house ventilation and so on) was incredibly primitive in relation to today's technology. So, we have upgraded all that. But the main failing of the house – despite it being widely feted as a sustainable pioneer – was its airtightness, or rather lack of it. We designed it when a sealed box was not the norm in environmental design, before Passivhaus was a widely known term. Now our environmental engineers brought along a wind machine, sucking air out and blowing it in. We held our hands up against the gusts of air coming in and out, and looked at each other in despair. The retrofit has therefore involved ripping materials out and taping up all the joints. It feels very fragile to confront the future ravages of the climate emergency with lengths of sticky tape, however expensive it might be.

At the same time that our project was underway, all the architects who had won the Stirling Prize declared a climate emergency. This felt like a powerful move of solidarity and potential action. However, the whole initiative quickly unraveled as one after another of these famous architects announced major new airport projects, in each case wrapping a major engine of carbon production in a soft eco-wrapping. First, Grimshaw's Heathrow Terminal Five declared itself to be 'carbon neutral', in an astonishing sleight of truth. Zaha Hadid Architects' Sydney Airport did not match this false hubris, merely saying that they will integrate 'extensive use of daylight, natural ventilation and water recycling' as part of their 'sustainable' approach. Meanwhile in Saudi Arabia, Foster + Partners raised the sustainability stakes by announcing that a new resort was going to be 'eco-friendly'. As if! For an 'ultra-luxury tourist destination', a car crash of environmental rights? As I shouted down the phone to a bemused journalist the other day: 'build their bloody airports if they must, but then don't virtue signal. They can't have it both ways.'

Finally, I went to a lecture by the revered architectural historian, Kenneth Frampton. He opened with strong statements about capitalism, commodification and climate, and then (as in his seminal essay on critical regionalism) he finds resistance to these conditions in a very particular strain of architecture: poetic tectonics, Semper's earthworks and roofworks, a thoughtful engagement with context. At the end he got all but a standing ovation. The audience had luxuriated in the belief that the continuation of a stylised canon of architecture is going to be enough to resist the environmental, political and economic ruptures that we face. The reality is that this version of architecture represents too comfortable an avoidance of the scale of challenges we face.

These are but three small examples of the conflicted nature of architecture's engagement with the climate emergency. First, the fragility of design, sticking tape over much larger societal cracks. Second, the duplicity of phony words and declarations which deny the reality of the environmental crisis. Third, the retreat from engaging with external issues to the perceived safety of internalised values. In all, there is a clinging to the emollience of the term 'sustainability' in the face of a crisis that confronts the very basis of the word. We cannot sustain our current modes of consumption and growth, and so to continue to use the word 'sustainability' holds out a false promise. In a way these reactions are understandable, but they are not acceptable. They are understandable because the climate and biodiversity emergencies demand systemic change, and this includes architecture and its value systems. The current approaches (technical, ethical and cultural) are simply not capable of effecting the change required, and so tend to divert from it. But this is not acceptable, for the simple reason that the emergencies are just that, and we all need to enact radical action as both citizens and experts.[2] To do this, we need to break architecture's attraction to certain systems and values.

It is not surprising that the twentieth century was a golden era for architecture. It was an era driven by the twinned paradigms of progress and growth. Progress is signaled by growth, and when one speaks of progress one assumes growth. As the extractive industry par excellence, architecture was the perfect vehicle for the announcement of growth, turning anonymous earth into pillars of constructed matter. These were then wrapped in various sheens to demonstrate progress, an endless advance of style, form, aesthetics and techniques that became ever more hysterical as the old century turned to the new. We should have called out the architectural writhing of this period for what it was – the spatialisation of an out-of-control capitalism – but too much money was being made, and the pictures were too good. *Dezeen* boomed.

The problem is that the endless production of buildings is also tied to all the traits that have led to the climate emergency: a reliance on a technocratic regime fuelled by the carbon state; extraction of raw materials and fossil fuels; growing consumption; dependency on the orthodoxies of neoliberalism. To say that architecture is complicit in the climate emergency is not to apportion blame, it is a statement of fact. What happens, then, to architecture when we think seriously about the systemic change that the climate emergency demands? Can architecture in its current guise be either acceptable or viable? If architecture is so firmly identified with images of progress and growth, what happens when those conditions are no longer tolerable? And what happens to the identity of the architect when the continuing production of buildings is questioned? How might we reframe our value to be knowledge, rather than the production of novelty?

I ask these questions not because I have the answers, but because the climate crisis fundamentally disrupts the value system, and with it the cultures and identities, on which architecture has thus far been founded. The emergency demands we come to provisional answers, and soon;

it forces the condition of *architecture* after architecture, in which previous assumptions and operations are replaced with new ones. This might sound like a negative scenario – the dismantling of a discipline – but I suggest otherwise. Of course, new buildings will be built in the future, and we need to take every measure to ensure that they are as carbon reducing as possible; this should be the primary value system through which any new *architecture* is produced and judged. Beyond this, the climate emergency presents new opportunities for spatial agents, *architects,* spatial activists, or whatever we might all become. As Rebecca Solnit notes: 'inside the word emergency is emerge; from an emergency new things come forth. The old certainties are crumbling fast, but danger and possibilities are sisters.'[3] The danger of the crisis is twinned with potential. If the climate emergency demands systemic change to our economies, values, behaviours and relationship to non-humans, then all of these changes bring with them new spatialities, and these need to be co-designed by expert citizens and citizen experts.

Unfortunately, much of what passes as architecture's engagement with alternative futures relies on notions and images of utopian technologies: floating islands, hydroponic facades, self-flowering desert cities and so on. These approaches align with the techno-boosterish end of the ecology spectrum, those who persuade us that the solution lies somewhere in the future through technological intervention, and in the meantime it can be business as usual. Too often these speculations repeat the mistake that created the emergency in the first place, namely an unfettered command of nature, splitting humans from the world we are part of. They suggest solutions, but the climate emergency is not a problem that can be solved, it is a predicament that we have to make best sense of. In this light, buildings are not solutions but the new architecture is a means of making spatial sense of the new societal conditions that will emerge. To live in the Anthropocene, the geological era in which the effects of the emergency are unfolding, needs a shift in sensibility from humans as distanced beings in the pursuit of freedom and progress to humans embedded in, and responsible for, a non-human world of interconnected systems.

Architects After Architecture

This responsibility turns the project of *architecture* after architecture into a profoundly ethical one.

In 2019, one remarkable statement from the Royal Institute of British Architects (RIBA) elided ethics with sustainability. The RIBA Ethics and Sustainable Development Commission of 2019, opened their final report with a recommendation for 'an unequivocal commitment to placing public interest, social purpose, ethics and sustainable development at the heart of its activities.' It is remarkable in placing social purpose and ethics at the centre of all architectural activity. But maybe the claim was too bold to be accepted, for little positive action has followed. This is why it is difficult to have complete confidence in the current generation of architects adapting to the new world. While there are numerous architects with good intents and doing good work, in the main there are too many vested interests in play and it is always difficult to abandon values that have been inculcated from the start of architectural education.

HOW MIGHT ARCHITECTS REFRAME THEIR VALUE TO BE KNOWLEDGE, RATHER THAN THE PRODUCTION OF NOVELTY?

I therefore place my hope in the next generation of designers, with some of whom I am in the privileged position of working with on a daily basis at Central Saint Martins. For a number of reasons, my sense is that design is well positioned to engage with the predicaments the crisis throws up. First, the open-ended nature of creative practice, in which fixed solutions are not predetermined at the start – lends itself to engaging with the openness of future developments.

A handsome new heat recovery unit, installed
as part of sustainable upgrades to Stock
Orchard Street, the home and office built by
Sarah Wigglesworth and Jeremy Till in 2000.

The scale and complexity of the climate emergency is such that assumptions of certainty and prescription are found wanting. While it is certain that we are facing climate change and accompanying ecological crises, the social and systemic implications are much less clear. It is here that the contingency of creative work has a key role to play, if one follows the definition of contingency as the fact that things could be otherwise than they are.

Second, is the condition of empathy that should lie at the heart of all design. Creative work never emerges from a social vacuum; it is always located in relation to others both human (users, viewers, participants, citizens, audiences) and non-human (biosystems, sites, climatic conditions). This in turn asks that the creative act is imbued with empathy, because without that empathetic engagement the creative work becomes an abstraction removed from the worldly conditions in which it will eventually be located. This empathy extends beyond the human to the non-human, meaning we should see the world, nature, atmospheres, animals, geology, as interconnected living agents, and so treat them all with equivalent empathy. Creative practice is exemplary in understanding connections, operating iteratively and laterally (where the scientific method, for example, is more linear and deductive). The creative citizen/expert is thus well placed to think through and act on the networks of the climate emergency.

Third, is the combination of hope and criticality that this generation of designers have. The creative act is one of transformation, taking a chunk of the world and changing it for the better. (Why would they ever set out to make the world a worse place?) Confronted with the devastating evidence of climate change and ecological collapse, it is all too easy to be paralysed. Distribute the pockets of hope of the next generation, and transformative acts follow. This hope is not naively constructed (and so doomed to failure) but founded on a criticality which excavates the construction of current conditions and power structures in order to understand the way things have turned out the way they have, and then use creative practice to move forwards in a transformative manner that does not avoid past failings or systems of power.

Hope is not
v real!

Finally, and perhaps most importantly, is the central role of design and the new architecture to envision new futures, not in an ungrounded or merely speculative manner but in a way that materialises and spatialises revised social conditions and relationships. The creative act is here a form of storytelling, in which alternative narratives might be imagined. The climate emergency demands that we discover new ways of living; designers and the new architects after architects can be the agents of envisioning them, always in partnership with others.

1   This project is explored in the
    next chapter.
2   See Jeremy Till, 'The Negotiation
    of Hope', in Peter Blundell Jones,
    Doina Petrescu, Jeremy Till (eds.),
    Architecture and Participation,
    Routledge, 2005
3   Rebecca Solnit, Hope in the Dark,
    Canongate, 2016, p.13

Architects After Architecture

DESIGNING FOR THE CLIMATE EMERGENCY

SARAH WIGGLESWORTH

CASE STUDY

OPPOSITE   Upgrading the walls and windows
to the 'library tower' of Stock Orchard Street.
TOP   Insulating the steel structure to prevent
cold bridging.

The most sustainable building is likely
to be the one you keep. In this case study,
Sarah Wigglesworth of Sarah Wigglesworth
Architects returns to the home and office
she designed in 2000, outlining the recent
adaptations made to improve its performance.
The modest set of changes reveal the care
and attention required to enable buildings
to adapt to changing needs for decades to
come, adding maintenance and custodian-
ship to the architect's toolkit. A slow process,
at odds with the extractive practice that
is addicted to building more and more.

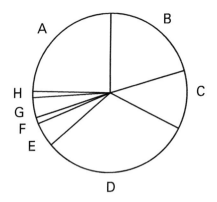

Heat loss from building, pre renovation:

A   Infiltration 25%
B   Walls to Exterior 21%
C   Suspended Floor 12%
D   Windows and Doors 31%
E   Roofs 5%
F   Solid Floors 1%
G   Thermal Bridges 4%
H   Ventilation 1%

When they were finished in 2000, the house and offices at Stock Orchard Street – where Jeremy Till and I currently live and work – represented a radical change in thinking about green design. The project reinvented the live/work typology, extended green technical knowledge to an urban context, and included responsible sourcing (incorporating waste streams) in the specification of materials.

But in the past 20 years the green movement in architecture has evolved, and techniques of analysis have improved, while the evidence of climate change makes green design responses more urgent than ever. Today, our two much celebrated buildings perform just a little better than average.

In this light, we have recently undertaken a major refurbishment of the buildings, a process informed by a wealth of knowledge about the pleasures and pitfalls of living there, and supported by new scientific data measuring the building's performance. In the process, almost every part of the project has been touched, yet to the casual observer it appears broadly the same as before: a testament, perhaps, to the appropriateness of some of the early design decisions.

A poorly-performing polycarbonate roof has been replaced by a set of skylights, improving insulation and drainage.

Key areas the refurbishment focused on:

- Improved airtightness by installing tape at floor-wall junctions and around incoming services;
- Reduced thermal bridging by increasing insulation;
- Replaced underperforming components such as roof lights and windows to reduce heating demand;
- Improved ventilation by replacing mechanical ventilation and heat recovery units with latest technology;
- Installation of new boilers in both home and office;
- New ventilation provision in the office for night-time cooling;
- Added external shading to the south west elevation to reduce glare and overheating.

In all, we have made more than 60 improvements to the buildings to prepare them for the next 20 years of living. Through this careful attention to the way a building is put together, and how it is shaped by the climate, it is our hope that it can show a modest path forward for designing in a period of ecological emergency.

Architects After Architecture

'WHOSE VOICE COUNTS?'

Interview with LIZA FIOR, MUF

Whose voice counts in the making of a city? By foregrounding the needs of children, refugees, social housing tenants, the disabled, and other minority groups, the practice of Muf has been asking this question over and over, in various ways, for more than 20 years. Operating at the ambiguous intersection of public art, participatory practice, urban strategy, and masterplanning, Muf have developed processes that enable these voices to come to the fore, in an implicit critique of the power and priorities of urban development today. We started by asking co-founder Liza Fior what led her to start the practice.

EDITORS   Can you talk about the foundation of the practice, what led you to start Muf?

LIZA FIOR   One of the reasons we created Muf was as a way of making a space to make work. We each had different motivations at that moment. As a student I had a fantasy of something between an office, a place of research and a studio; when I was pregnant we started doing things together – I kind of knew that my life in architecture was over without that space. Juliet Bidgood and I met as diploma students at PCL (now University of Westminster), Kath Shonfield was a friend, and I had met Katherine Clarke at the Architectural Association. In 1994 we entered a competition for the South Bank, sending off our four sheet submission in an amazing act of youthful arrogance. Richard Rogers won, but we were off and working together. We had the name, and around the same time we had been commissioned by the Arts Council to do a feasibility study for the Museum of Women's Art. Our recommendation was not to build a building, and not to enclose a female oeuvre again. There was a paradox there. So that showed a lack of business planning from the off, and that the answer to a brief is not necessarily a building.

EDITORS   In *This is What We Do: A Muf Manual*[1] – the founding document for the practice – you talk about 'widening the scope beyond the limits of the building', which I read as both literally – looking beyond the building line – but also looking to other forms of knowledge.

LIZA FIOR   I ran a seminar at Yale called 'The Extended Building', which was talking about the fuzzy edges of the expansion of effect of the building as artefact. Manfredo Tafuri describes the building as sitting between two positions: the building as an object, and the building as a thing that affects a wider site. So in the seminar the students took buildings and described the networks of what comes into it and its effect beyond it.
     I use the example of Brunelleschi's Ospedale degli Innocenti (Hospital of the Innocents) in Florence (1419-1427), built as a foundling hospital, with a hole in the wall where you can leave a baby if you couldn't care for it, and a charm in the

Architects After Architecture

hope that you could get it back. So the building housed the orphans, but also the clerks who meticulously recorded the wet nurses who nursed the babies spread throughout the country-side around Florence. The physical building itself has a loggia and a set of steps, which Alberti writes about as a place where the nursemaids sit and watch the children playing in the piazza. So you start with the building, and when does the building stop? And what is this fuzzy territory between buildings as arte-facts, and buildings as urbanism?

It's not exactly a radical idea, but even now, we've just finished some design guidance where we take this phrase 'active frontages' and really interrogate it, trying to ensure buildings give due consideration to the impact they will have on the street. So this notion of the fuzzy edge is one aspect of what we mean when we talk about looking beyond the limits of the building.

> EDITORS It's one of those things that's just so obvi-ous when you say it like that, but which has gone so long unchallenged. I feel in the way architecture is still largely talked about as objects contained within a frame, rather than shifting that frame to look at how the object relates to its context.

LIZA FIOR It is basic, but it has implications for a lot of what architects do. We talk about density as if it's just this benign force of good, but if a load of tall buildings are built up around the hospital, who's thinking about whose wig will be blown off on the way to a chemotherapy appointment? This is a very crude way to explain it, but we also need to think about the dis-torted relationships between those who pay for large projects and those who have to use them. This is particularly the case in so-called 'regeneration' projects, where the poorer the area, the more it tends to be subjected to other people's ideas.

> EDITORS This ties in to another phrase of yours I'm going to quote back to you: 'Each occupied chair represents another interested party who is not there'. It seems to me a big part of your work is speaking for the people who aren't in these chairs, whether it's

Inclusion

children, the residents of public housing, or the pensioner whose wig is to be blown off.

LIZA FIOR   Now, we can look back at then, now we have 'intersectionality' or a 'checking of privilege'. Ideas span decades – for example our contribution to the Royal Academy Summer Exhibition. Here it is. [Liza holds up a timber door stop] 'If you're invited into the room, stay long enough to wedge the door open for others', which is something we try to do in different ways that are particular to place. For instance, in Ruskin Square, a privately owned public space, each phase in the project comes with attempts to expand our client beyond the tenants of the office buildings, to stretch each stage of the design process and build. This has included the Festival of Toil, a second occupation of the site, a chance to work with a group of young refugee leavers (and pay them) to explore the site before construction.

A commission developed by us as part of a quite conventional public realm scheme. It followed on, from the temporary garden on the same site which included cricket practice nets, chosen as the sport of choice of both our client and the young Afghani men who the Refugee Council worked with.

EDITORS   What are the points of resistance you find in working in this way? What are the bottlenecks to advocating for people who are not formally represented?

LIZA FIOR   One of our strategies is what we call 'brief obedience'. It's a kind of literal mindedness, where we work through a brief very closely, and hold it to account. We examine the gap between the stated ambition and what is proposed. This can be quite painful. You're not meant to point out that the council have stated they want an inclusive borough, and yet they're demolishing existing workspace to make way for a masterplan.

And in a way, it's just what you're doing now, in the way you're asking us these questions, by holding us to account for the things we've written or said before. It's interesting that we started by writing a book and by stating a series of ambitions. It's an example of how you can talk something into being, painfully, word by word. I suppose it took us all that time because it is complicated and continues to be, not just because we were bringing together conceptual art practice, which is necessarily open-ended, with architecture, which is more fixed. We had built almost nothing when we wrote the Muf manual of a 'how to' as both ambition and statement of intent. And so now we remain true to the ideals, we have a body of knowledge, and what are we going to do with it? And I think the ambition now is to avoid the cosmetic.

EDITORS   What do you mean by 'avoid the cosmetic'?

LIZA FIOR   Katherine is designing public realm structured around SUDs (sustainable urban drainage). These are drainage systems for roadsides which reduce flooding and help stop polluted rainwater runoff damaging natural watercourses. They look attractive, little gardens along the road, but the bit that costs money is the below ground engineering and contouring of the road so that it directs water into the gardens. In this case, avoiding the cosmetic means we wouldn't build the garden if we weren't also able to adjust the road.

EDITORS   This relates to something which I feel is critical to your work, the jump between the urban and the material. That you can be equally focused on the materiality, on the craft, and on the masterplan.
That these two things are somehow tied together.

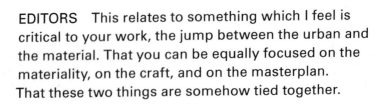

LIZA FIOR   That's been there from the beginning, that we're continuously thinking of those two scales.[2] The impact at a city scale, and whatever it is you're doing there, and then what you're going to touch or vice versa. In health they talk about this, what you touch – the sheet, the nurse, the hook to hold your hat. People's experience of hospital is at that one-to-one scale. But then there's this mega thing in the UK called the National Health Service, and those two realities have to sit together. The connection between strategy and detail experienced at one to one is lost, in the anxiety around risk in construction, developers or project managers replace the designers once they've got

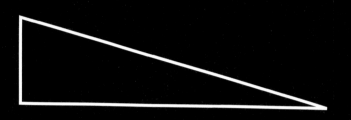

IF YOU GET INTO THE ROOM,
WEDGE THE DOOR OPEN FOR OTHERS

TOP   Muf's contribution to the Royal
Academy of Arts' Summer Exhibition in 2019.
BOTTOM   The folly in Barking Town Square,
a peculiar fragment made up of salvaged
ornament, creating new stories.

planning permission, and in doing so, they have lost the people who are going to ensure these different scales are linked up. But when you can see things through you have the opportunity to operate at both. There are few disciplines who can jump between scales in this way.

EDITORS   To finish off, I'm going to throw another quote at you, again from the book, because I feel it's relevant to this point. You write, 'We realised the work was not defined by its medium'. I like that a lot.

LIZA FIOR   And why do you like it?

EDITORS   Well, it implies that architecture is not about its products but about its processes. That this is a way of thinking that is so core to what architects do, and yet it remains so under-articulated. I think it's a huge failure in how architecture is defined, which is that the most valuable part – the analysis and strategy, bringing together stakeholders, and writing the brief, is almost done as a kind of free bit at the beginning.

LIZA FIOR   Yes, it's either done as a free bit at the beginning, or to a consultant other than the designer. We refuse to do the 'prep' unless we get the job to see it through. We almost always refuse to do consultation or brief writing unless we're going to see it through because we believe it's essential to be accountable. You need to be there at the end to be accountable to your initial research. The two are connected.

1   Muf (eds.), *This is What We Do:*
     A Muf Manual, Ellipsis, 2001
2   This idea of operating at two scales
     simultaneously is further explored
     in Kath Schonfield, 'Premature
     gratification and other pleasures',
     in Muf, ibid, p.63 and reproduced at
     www.morethanonefragile.co.uk

SPACES TO SPEAK

JUSTINE CLARK, PARLOUR

Men and women graduate from architecture degrees in roughly equal numbers, but at each stage in a career – registration, progression, leadership – this ratio tips further out of balance. Australian advocacy group Parlour: women, equity, architecture was established in 2012 both to understand why, and to try and effect change. Co-founder Justine Clark discusses the group's work providing a platform for women and women's stories. Ultimately, Clark argues, making the discipline more accommodating will require the redefinition of architecture itself, to celebrate and legitimise unconventional paths and roles.

Perched on a stool in Hobart one autumn evening, Jude Abell describes her career as like 'throwing spaghetti against the wall to see what sticks.' The audience chuckles, intrigued by tales of a life that moves back and forth between architecture and fine art, between Hobart and London. Reflecting on being an active part of the architectural community yet unable to use the title 'Architect', Jude explains that, as public art coordinator for Hobart, the whole city is her site. She is on stage with Liz Walsh who, a decade after graduation, is already a high achieving registered architect. Expecting her first child, Liz is optimistic, if somewhat apprehensive, about what the future might bring. They share stories of growing up in small rural towns, surrounded by people inventing and making – designing in all but name.

In Brisbane, academic Kelly Greenop shares her story with Christina Na-Heon Cho, recently appointed director at one of Australia's largest architecture practices. They talk about extraordinarily full and busy lives that encompass architecturally informed contributions well beyond the workplace. 'I don't like to be bored,' declares Kelly.

On a visit from the UK, Jos Boys describes her overlapping cross-disciplinary work – the early days of Matrix Feminist Design Collective, journalism, periods within academia and on its edges, and work in disability activism. Throughout her conversation with scholar Karen Burns, Jos reiterates the importance of critically engaging with how spaces can work to include or exclude.

A few months later, Linda Kennedy reminds her Melbourne audience that in Australia we always build on unceded Aboriginal land. She challenges her conversation partner, accomplished practitioner Meaghan Dwyer, to consider what it means to work in a discipline that consistently erases or ignores the knowledge of her community. It is not an easy or comfortable conversation, but it proceeds with generosity and goodwill. The audience concentration is intense.

These conversations, and many others, took place as part of Parlour's Seasonal Salons. With no chair, each pair simply take the microphone to exchange stories of lives in and around architecture, of commitments pursued and connections made, obstacles faced and opportunities found, all with humour and humility. Enthusiastic audiences see myriad possibilities in the tales told.

Parlour: gender, equity, architecture is a research-based advocacy organisation, which seeks to improve gender equity in the discipline.[1] The Salons are just one of many initiatives developed to expand the opportunity for women and gender diverse people within the discipline, and to help create a more inclusive, robust and sustainable profession. At the time of writing, 32 Salons have been held in six cities across Australia. They were established as both a venue for public storytelling and a means to facilitate new networks. The only constraint is that conversation partners should be from different generations, and the only rule is those who attend must make an effort to talk to someone they don't already know.

Individual Salons are engaging because each conversation is so personal and particular, but the events are especially powerful in aggregate. Month after month, city after city, conversations are held for burgeoning audiences. Together they reveal the extraordinary range of possibilities within, beyond and after architecture.

These conversations show that the line between conventional architecture practice and 'alternative' careers is blurred, ragged and, in places, indistinct. This reflects the boundaries of the profession itself, which are at once tightly defined through the regulation of the title 'Architect', and made permeable via the day-to-day activities and work of the architecturally educated.

Architecture has long given graduates the skills, knowledge and modes of thinking to work in many contexts. The factors that lead the architecturally trained into other fields

Architects After Architecture

51

are as diverse as the places in which they find their *métier* – circumstance, educational experiences, economic cycles, aptitude and opportunity, social and cultural background and connections all play a role. Gender – the effect of gender-based bias and socio-cultural expectations – is part of this, interacting with other factors to influence opportunities presented and withheld, career paths taken and destinations found. Parlour's interest in these is two-fold – our project of increasing visibility includes those working in non-traditional ways, and we believe that there is much to learn by better understanding their experiences.

Parlour strives for inclusion. We build spaces for exchange among many, varied participants. We complement informal advice with rigorous analysis and the collection, examination and dissemination of demographic data. This data captures broad patterns of participation and reveals great diversity within architecture – diversity of people, diversity of modes of practice, diversity of roles. All of this is fundamental to creating new futures – and there is a clear consensus among our constituency that architecture needs to be more broadly framed. Charity Edwards sums up the attitude of many: 'I think it should be a lot more fluid, less restricted in scope, more engaged in politics and local economies, and with about a million more options than currently exist in mainstream practice.'

One of Parlour's earliest projects assembled demographic data and individual stories to increase knowledge of those working within, across and beyond the traditional limits of the profession. In 2012 Parlour, then a fledgling website associated with a substantial research project, conducted two large-scale surveys – 'Where Do All the Women Go' and 'What About the Men?' Initially, we wanted to know what had happened to the women who had been graduating from architecture programs in significant numbers for decades. Analysis of data from the Australian Census had revealed that twice as many women were active in architecture than were registered architects, and we knew anecdotally that graduates were working in myriad ways. But very little was known about what they did, or – for that matter – about the women working within private practice. 'Where are you, and what do you do?', we asked.

Women

Parlour's Spring Salons bring together
women to exchange stories of lives
in and around architecture.
TOP   Cath Hall and Hannah Webber.
BELOW   Jos Boys and Karen Burns.

We cast our net wide. The survey gained rapid momentum. It was forwarded on and on – some women tell of receiving it three, four, five times from different directions. This 'snowball' method was particularly effective in reaching those outside the conventional confines of the profession, or marginalised by existing professional structures. It also brought limitations – the results cannot be used to make population-wide assumptions – nonetheless, the survey captured the experiences of a larger group than any prior academic study of women in architecture. In all, twelve hundred women responded.

SINGLE-CATEGORY DESCRIPTIONS RARELY CAPTURE THE REALITY OF WORKING LIFE, AND THAT PARTICIPATION EXTENDS FAR BEYOND PAID EMPLOYMENT.

Many men also expressed a wish to document their own experiences. We launched a second survey, which garnered 918 responses. Comparing the results is instructive. There are many similarities – long working hours, poor remuneration and worries about the current state and future of the profession were major concerns across both surveys – but the broad patterns of careers, and engagement with professional structures, were quite different.

As a group, the women were more likely to have 'atypical' career paths, with multiple breaks, different levels of intensity and changing roles over the course of a career. They were more likely to work in allied fields, and to move in and out of private practice. In contrast, men, as a group, were more likely to follow a 'traditional' path and be active in conventional areas of influence and power.[2] These patterns are reiterated in credentials and connections. Half the women were registered architects, and three-quarters of the men. One quarter of the women were neither a member of Australian Institute of Architects nor registered architects, compared to only eight percent of the men.[3]

The surveys asked respondents to identify principal, secondary and previous fields of activity. Just over half the women identified architecture as their principal field. Others worked in interior architecture, urban design, heritage, project management, in design and film, in craft and fine art practice. The list goes on. They worked in government, in media, in education, client side, or for construction companies. Secondary roles covered an extensive range of activity, and numerous and varied roles. This reminds us that single-category descriptions rarely capture the reality of working life, and that participation extends far beyond paid employment.

These surveys demonstrated diversity already present within and on the edges of architecture. They also revealed a clear interest in broadening the idea and role of the profession. As one respondent observed, 'Architecture is too narrowly defined at present. This limits its impact in Australia and on Australian cities and also limits the ability for all graduates to engage well and be well paid.'

Eight years on, the Parlour community encompasses people working across many fields. Motivations for moving sideways vary widely. For some, it was a result of frustrations within the architectural workplace, untenable conditions or constricted roles – this group moved to gain more flexibility, less overtime, better remuneration and greater opportunity.[4] For others the rationale is broader – further professional challenges, social objectives, or more control over outcomes. Many simply saw more opportunity in other fields, or express the desire to get involved earlier – at planning, feasibility, briefing and/or procurement stages – as a way of having more positive influence on the built environment.

Architects After Architecture

Many observe that they use their architectural background every day. Further, they suggest that experiences beyond the studio might offer meaningful insight back to the profession and its future development. Indeed, those on the edges of architecture are often among the most thoughtful in considering architecture's potential and possibilities.

The challenge is to ensure that these careers are seen and these voices are heard. As Annmarie Adams and Peta Tancred explained in 2000, all too often the profession's self-image and priorities preclude such visibility. They described a large cohort of women who had moved into the wider field and were 'ignored by the profession, but nevertheless extending and elaborating upon the core areas of architectural practice.'[5] Visibility is slowly increasing, but as conditions in mainstream practice deteriorate there is a tendency to recede and draw the boundaries more tightly, perhaps inadvertently restricting access to new knowledge and diverse skills.[6] If the profession is to benefit from these experiences, they need to be understood as a vital extension of the professional landscape, rather than positioned as 'atypical' or 'alternative'.

Commentators have long argued that the varied modes of practice pursued by many women – often from necessity – have the transformative potential to reshape the future and field of architecture. In 1989, Rochelle Martin urged architects to envisage new kinds of professionals, and argued that it would be those in the margins who would lead that new vision.[7] In 1996, Francesca Hughes observed that women who are architects potentially occupy the liminal position necessary for critical engagement: 'Insider by her education, her adoption by and of certain professional institutions; outsider by her difference, her gender-related experience contains grounds for her resistive reading of certain architectural operations. She is able, almost obliged, to invent her practice and to do so critically, in order to test certain accepted aspects of the production of architecture.'[8] In 2000, Adams and Tancred identified the 'fusion track' pursued by women as a place of innovation and creativity.[9] In 2010, Naomi Stead asked: 'What if women's career patterns in architecture, rather than being seen as aberrant or unconventional, instead encouraged us to rethink the definition of what is an architect, what are the characteristics of architectural 'success,' and what other models of architectural practice might be possible?'[10] In 2012, Sarah Wigglesworth argued that architecture needs new business models: 'As people who tend to have portfolio careers, juggle competing needs, diversify their experience and make do financially, women are well placed to invent these new forms of practice.'[11] In 2015 Sarah Treadwell described architecture as practiced by those on the Architecture + Women database as 'porous and mutable ... with an ability to expand and transform its practice.'[12]

This reframing of women's careers as inventive responses to complex situations is empowering for many.[13] It is invigorating to think that all the juggling, ducking and weaving might actually place them in a position to contribute knowledge back to the profession. It is encouraging to imagine the edges as places of insight and invention rather than near-exile. But sharing diverse accounts of lives in and after architecture has effects beyond invigorating individuals. It increases the presence and influence of those who may be unseen within mainstream architectural narratives and professional structures, and thereby shifts the collective image of the profession. It helps develop more inclusive understandings of the roles pursued by the architecturally trained and what might be learned from this.[14] This in turn opens up the possibilities for architecture itself, and extends the idea of what the profession is and could become.

Parlour is a 'space to speak' (from the French, *parler*), but it is also a space of encounter. These encounters are fundamental to the development of the discipline. As Sarah Treadwell observes in her introduction to *Architecture in an Expanded Field* 'The edges of architecture are productively shaped, or frayed, by such engagement with other, other people, other points of view and other practices.'[15] We work hard to multiply sites for exchange – online, through events, on social media – and to engage people with many differing connections to architecture. It is in these aggregating interactions that architecture will find its futures.

1   Parlour originated as the communication and engagement component of a scholarly research project funded through the Australian Research Council's Linkage Grant scheme and titled: 'Equity and Diversity in the Australian Architecture Profession: Women, work, leadership', 2011-2015. This involved three universities, five industry partners and an interdisciplinary research team. Led by Naomi Stead, researchers were Justine Clark, Gill Matthewson, Karen Burns, Amanda Roan, Gillian Whitehouse, Julie Willis and Sandra Kaji-O'Grady. The Parlour website, archiparlour. org, was conceived and developed by Justine Clark and launched in 2012. In 2015, Parlour became an incorporated association. Co-founders were Clark, Stead, Matthewson, Willis, Burns, and Susie Ashworth. In 2020, it is led by Clark, Stead, Matthewson, Ashworth and Willis, along with new directors Alison Cleary and Sarah Lynn Rees.

2   These are broad patterns, and they will not neatly align with individual experiences – of course, many men pursue hybrid roles, and many women maintain successful careers within traditional practice.

3   This differential is also expressed in the way people knew about the surveys. Nearly 60 percent of women were alerted by Parlour communications, whereas the majority of male respondents heard about it through the Australian Institute of Architects.

4   This reiterates earlier research which found that architects from under-represented groups had more satisfying careers when they 'escaped the traditional arena of private practice.' See Kathryn H Anthony, Designing for Diversity: Gender, Race and Ethnicity in the Architectural Profession, University of Illinois Press, 2001, p.180

5   Annmarie Adams and Peta Tancred, Designing Women: Gender and the Architectural Profession, University of Toronto Press, 2000, p.3

6   Julia Evetts argues that, at best, the professions are a useful and 'uniquely desirable method of regulating, monitoring and providing complex services to the public' and, at worst, a biased ideology that leads to 'market closure and monopoly control of work.' See Julia Evetts, 'Sociological Analysis of Professionalism: Past, Present and Future,' Comparative Sociology 10, no.1, 2011, p.10

7   Rochelle Martin, 'Out of Marginality,' in, Ellen Perry Berkeley and Matilda McQuaid (eds.), Architecture: A Place for Women, Smithsonian Institutional Press, 1989, p.233

8   Francesca Hughes, The Architect: Reconstructing Her Practice, MIT Press, 1996, p.xv

9   Annmarie Adams, Peta Tancred, Designing Women: Gender and the Architectural Profession, 2000, p.110

10 Naomi Stead, 'Redesigning Practice,' Parlour, 15 March 2012

11 Sarah Wigglesworth, 'Higher fees would not only improve architecture's status, but crucially give women freedom,' The Architects' Journal, 19 January 2012

12 Sarah Treadwell, 'Preface' in Sarah Treadwell and Lucy Treep (eds.), Architecture in an Expanded Field, Architecture + Women • NZ and Aalto Books, 2015, p.vi

13 Sonia Sarangi, 'Who's Afraid of Ethnic Diversity,' Parlour, 14 July 2016

14 There is substantial and growing interest in this. At the recent symposium 'Transformations: Action on Equity', a lunchtime network session on 'Alternative Practice Models' attracted the largest number of participants, many of whom were currently working within traditional architectural practice or academia, and were looking for other options.

15 Treadwell, Architecture in an Expanded Field, p.vi

ON MIS-FITTING

JOS BOYS

Who is welcome in architecture? Whose perspectives are valued? And how are these perspectives represented in the built world? In this essay, Jos Boys, architect, researcher, and senior lecturer at The Bartlett, explores the productive side of feeling like a 'misfit'. Not fitting in revealed the ways in which architecture excluded particular people and perspectives, and led her to co-found the influential feminist architecture collective Matrix. Boys continues to advocate for underrepresented groups, through projects such as DisOrdinary Architecture, which shows how starting from disability can be a powerful creative force for the design of the built environment.

MISFIT

verb
(used with or without object), mis·fit·ted, mis·fit·ting.
to fit badly.

noun
1 something that fits badly, as a garment that
is too large or too small.
2 a person who is not suited or is unable to adjust
to the circumstances of his or her particular situation.

I became an architectural student in 1974 and loved it from the start. But – maybe like many others – I always felt something of a misfit. The stories I was being offered for what architecture was *about* and what an architect was *like,* never quite made sense. I was endlessly confused by the disjuncture between what my clever, passionate, thoughtful modernist tutors said about designing, and the bleak mechanical qualities of many of their design solutions; between the deliberately obscure languages proffered as 'obvious' within the academy and the inability of my family and friends to talk about architecture in anything but the most banal way; and in beginning to study what seemed centrally a social art, yet had strangely dislocated and abstracted methods of working, where the messiness of actual people's lives became placeholder 'users' and somehow disappeared down the gaps.

Then, later, into the 1980s, stumbling into Marxist and feminist politics looking for models which more effectively explained the relationship between the social and architecture; there seemed to be similar gaps between what was being offered as 'proper' political action and architectural design as an activity; and between what was constituted as the feminist problem (the isolation of the white middle class housewife)

(Dis)ability

and the much more complex and problematic experiences of my own suburban upbringing. Despite being a relatively conventional product of my generation – those white middle-class women who went into British higher education in such numbers post Second World War – it continued to feel as if I was, as Sheila Rowbotham put it about women's experiences more generally, 'lumber[ing] around ungainly-like in borrowed concepts which did not fit the shape we feel ourselves to be.'[1]

In the 1980s, my sense of mis-fitting found a home, as part of a much larger group of women who co-developed a feminist architects' design and research practice called Matrix Feminist Design Collective, one of the first in the UK to bring issues of gender centre-stage to the design of the built environment.[2] Contemporary scholars looking back on the work of Matrix sometimes make it seem very deliberate in its attitudes and methods. Many of the Matrix women seemed very clear-minded, but for me it was much more a creative 'floundering', as we tried to find new ways to think and practice, to work through our diverse and often contested engagements with the difficulties in even talking about what constituted a feminist critique of architecture. This at a time when the word sexism had still to be invented and architecture assumed itself to be unproblematically 'neutral' in designing for social encounters. Co-writing the Matrix book *Making Space: women and the man-made environment* (1984) took several years, as we tried to make sense of things, with participants fitting such work in and around other commitments, blurring normative definitions of what 'proper' work was (paid, status-linked), and its assumed separation from 'hobbies', 'leisure' or the 'normal' women's reproductive work of domestic life; what Sara Ahmed calls 'sweaty concepts':

> A sweaty concept might come out of a bodily experience that is trying. The task is to stay with the difficulty, to keep exploring and exposing this difficulty. [...] Not eliminating the effort or labour becomes an [...] aim because we have been taught to tidy up our texts, not to reveal the struggle we have in getting somewhere.[3]
> In such 'tidying up' of many years effort into the

Architects After Architecture

concrete result of a single book, that difficult, interesting, creative, curious and particular work can cease to be acknowledged,[4] as can the complex and uneven processes through which emergent forms of practice turn out, over time, to inspire change and achieve impact beyond a circumscribed notion of architecture.

In opening up issues of gender and space, Matrix's activities also came to involve many layers beyond the research about gender and space that led to the book. This included creating feminist design guidance and support through informational booklets; working towards enabling more women into construction and architecture through co-creating access courses; designing building projects for and with women; co-exploring new building types ignored by a male-dominated profession, such as women's centres and nurseries; and developing participatory tools which could involve women in designing, for example by using models and building visits rather than orthographic drawings. Matrix also aimed to be a collective, with a non-hierarchical management structure and cross-disciplinary multi-layered ways of working. In this we were part of a much wider range of emerging radical architectural practices such as Community Technical Aid Centres (CTACs)[5], which grew up around resistance to re-development (such as through slum clearance and the creation of urban motorways), as well as related forms of public participation and direct action such as squatting and alternative community plans.[6]

Matrix's impact is still being felt, not only through the important ongoing work of the many women who worked there, but also for more recent generations of students and practitioners keen to find alternatives to the 'starchitect' system by better understanding how buildings can meet the needs of all users, and by challenging conventional architectural approaches and assumptions. By being explicitly feminist in approach, Matrix refused professional 'neutrality' by actively combining research and practice to better understand how gender roles operate through their actual (or attempted) mapping into built space and articulated through everyday social, spatial and material practices. It aimed to empower women as clients of buildings, equally involved in design processes.

(Dis)ability

And it wanted to change the built environment to better suit the diverse lives of different women, both through co-creating building types that did not already exist, and by challenging and redesigning the 'norms' of architectural practices and of the spaces it produces, both material and attitudinal.

Meanwhile, my continuing sense of mis-fitting within architecture as a discipline (mainly as a teacher and researcher) has not gone away – rather it may even have become worse, as the profession was increasingly captured by neoliberalism with its demands for profit extraction through real estate development, cut-throat design-and-build production methods, and concentration on formal and spectacular image-making. But at the same time, I began to find work – particularly by queer, critical race and disability studies scholars – that engages directly with the 'problem' of mis-fitting and critically explores its conceptual, social and spatial dimensions. As Rosemarie Garland-Thomson succinctly puts it, 'a misfit occurs when world fails flesh in the environment one encounters.'[7] Through intersecting feminist and other social and environmental concerns with dis/ability (disability and ability), and by bringing disabled artists, scholars and activists into architecture, I saw that we could begin to recognise how different kinds of bodies come to fit or misfit in built space (and in architectural attitudes and practices). We could ask what kinds of bodies are valued and which are misrepresented, ignored or marginalised. Garland-Thomson again:

> A fit occurs when a harmonious, proper interaction occurs between a particularly shaped and functioning body and an environment that sustains that body. A misfit occurs when the environment does not sustain the shape and function of the body that enters it.[8]

Out of this energising and vital work grew The DisOrdinary Architecture Project, co-founded with disabled artist Zoe Partington. DisOrdinary Architecture is a platform bringing together disabled artists and built environment students, educators and practitioners for creative and positive actions and dialogue that can demonstrate how disability is a valuable and generative force in design, rather than a technical and legalistic 'problem'. Its mission is 'to promote activity that develops and captures models of new practice for the built environment, led by the creativity and experiences of disabled artists.' The group, in various iterations, has been building its expertise in co-developing dis/ability and architecture activities since 2008. It has a committed network of about 15 disabled artists, together with a larger group who get involved in particular projects; as well as a similar number of architectural students, educators and professionals who support the work.

DisOrdinary Architecture often plays with ideas of fitting and mis-fitting. We argue that whilst finding yourself made a misfit in a particular encounter or setting is frustrating and often demeaning, it can also richly inform creativity. This is because moments of mis-fitting can be unpicked to reveal the worst of normative practices, where 'what is normal' acts to continually make some people's lives harder and others' easier. DisOrdinary Architecture instead explores what happens when we start from difference in design, by valuing the rich bio- and neuro-diversity of our human and non-human world; and by challenging building design that starts unthinkingly from current social norms. This means it is also important to ask why architecture does not yet have a body of work around dis/ability equivalent to that exploring gender and sexuality, or race and post-colonialism. That this invisibility is reflected across other academic and professional disciplines is an indictment of cultural and critical theory and practice more generally, and illustrates just how deeply disability remains avoided, compared to other disadvantaged identities.

This, in turn, leads to bigger questions about how architecture is inculcated as a discipline and as a form of practice; who or what gets valued and what is invisible, simply not up for discussion or engagement? Just as the seemingly simple question Matrix asked – 'how is space gendered and what can we do about it?' – opened up aspects of both architecture's failings and its radical potential, another question – 'why has dis/ability somehow remained consistently stuck as a boring, regulatory and mechanical add-on to 'proper' architecture?' –

also turns out to have multiple, expansive and deeply relevant critical fields to develop.[9]

For me, there remains a continuing need to explicitly connect the social and the spatial – to better understand what it is built space, as well as architectural theories and practices, are doing socially to enable some and disable others; to work directly with those who most often get left out; to challenge conventional disciplinary and academy boundaries (who is allowed in, who is excluded); and to co-create forms of debate, shared knowledge and design processes with the widest range of publics, underpinned by a multitude of different voices and forms of communication. I still want to know and better understand the diverse ways people make sense of, and survive in, the world, and what role architecture has in these processes. This has inherently become an engagement between and across academic writing and architectural activism, that wants to expand who counts in architecture, who gets to be involved as equal participants with architectural 'professionals', and how the existing discipline needs to change. This is also inevitably an endlessly 'sweaty' process about always exploring and about staying with the difficulty.

In 2019 the Disability Visibility Project started an online campaign called Access is Love.[10] As they write: 'We believe access should be a collective responsibility instead of a sole responsibility placed on a few individuals.' They go on to outline ways in which we might think about access and inclusion as a shared, emergent, never-finished act of love, of caring for and with each other. This is not just about 'the disabled', rather it aims to make alliances beyond identity categories that stay with the trouble and find connections as well as tensions and contradictions. It is about social, spatial and material *justice*, not merely functional access solutions. This sense of working together, of starting from difference – but also understanding that difference cannot be contained in a single consensus or solution – as a means to co-develop new forms of practice, gives me renewed hope. It offers a way of being and working that refuses the limitations of normative society. It does this by valuing the misfits, by taking notice of, and believing in, the messiness of our many diverse lives, and using these

(Dis)ability

WOMEN'S REALM
A WEEKEND EVENT on WOMEN, BUILDING and THE ENVIRONMENT

on JANUARY 31 and
FEBRUARY 1 1987
to 6pm in the
Department of
Environmental Design,
the Polytechnic of North London,
Holloway Rd,
Holloway, N7 8DB.

WORKSHOPS will include:
Design, Planning,
Building, Art,
Architecture, Landscape
and Furniture.

FACILITIES available include:
Creche, Disabled access,
and also
Evening entertainment.

FEE'S for the weekend:
£10 for the waged.
£5 for the unwaged.
Concessions are available

for FURTHER INFORMATION
contact:
'WOMEN'S REALM'
18, Woodlea Rd,
N16 0TH.

ALL WOMEN ARE WELCOME.

SPONSORED BY THE POLYTECHNIC OF NORTH LONDON AND THE GREATER LONDON COUNCIL *as the very grounds* on which to develop collaborative actions towards social, spatial and material equality. Imagine what such an approach could bring to the education and practice of architecture...

1   Sheila Rowbotham, *Woman's Consciousness, Man's World*, Pelican, 1973, p.35

2   For more about Matrix see Julia Dwyer, Anne Thorne, 'Evaluating Matrix: Notes from Inside the Collective,' in Doina Petrescu (ed.), *Altering Practices: Feminist Politics and Poetics of Space*, Routledge, 2006, p.239-56

3   Sara Ahmed, *Living a Feminist Life*, Duke University Press, 2017

4   For more on this see Jos Boys and Julia Dwyer, 'Revealing Work. Interrogating Artifacts to (Re)View Histories of Feminist Architectural Practice,' in *Architecture and Culture Journal, Special Issue: Architecture and Feminisms*, Taylor & Francis, 2017

5   Source: 'Community Technical Aid Centres,' Spatial Agency, accessed April 2020, www.spatialagency.net/database/community.technical.aid.centres

6   See Peter Blundell Jones, Doina Petrescu, and Jeremy Till (eds.), *Architecture and Participation*, Routledge, 2005

7   Rosemarie Garland-Thomson, 'Misfits: A Feminist Materialist Disability Concept,' *Hypatia: A Journal of Feminist Philosophy 26*, no.3, 2011, p.600

8   Rosemarie Garland-Thomson, 'The Story of My Work: How I Became Disabled.' *DSQ: Disability Studies Quarterly 34*, no.2, 2013

9   See for example, Jos Boys, *Doing Disability Differently: An Alternative Handbook on Architecture, Dis/ability and Designing for Everyday Life*, Routledge, 2014; Jos Boys (ed) *Disability, Space, Architecture: A Reader*, Routledge, 2017; and Jos Boys, 'Invisibility work? How starting from dis/ability challenges normative social, spatial and material practices,' in Hélène Frichot, Catharina Gabrielsson, Helen Runting (eds.), *Architecture and Feminisms: Ecologies, Economies, Technologies*, Routledge, 2017

10 The Disability Visibility Project was set up by Mia Mingus, Alice Wong and Sandy Ho. For the Access is Love project see: www.disabilityvisibilityproject.com/2019/02/01/access-is-love/

'ARCHITECTURE IS A WAY TO CONSTRUCT SOCIETY'

Interview with ANDRÉS JAQUE,
OFFICE FOR POLITICAL INNOVATION

 Where is the edge of architecture? Can a line be drawn around it, to decide what's in and what's out? Andrés Jaque, visiting professor at Princeton University and founder of the Office for Political Innovation, is dedicated to transgressing this boundary. Through his work in theory, practice, and education, Jaque reveals connections between architecture and sexuality, identity, ecology, technology, real estate, climate change and more. In Jaque's hands, architecture is reconceived as a 'constellation', a field of vectors reaching beyond building into the culture of life.

EDITORS   What was your journey from studying architecture to setting up a practice that challenges the very definition of architecture?

ANDRÉS JAQUE   My work originates from an insatiable curiosity for the way contemporary existence is constructed. As a student in the 1990s, I was very much interested in how buildings articulated the social. An aspect which, although clearly part of architecture's DNA, was not at the centre of mainstream professional discourse. I wanted to explore forms of practice which, rather than just designing the containers – the buildings and the envelopes to accommodate the social – could directly shape the processes through which relationships were forged. These processes were not purely about space: they relied on many different technologies, required a deep understanding of relational and performative practices, as well as the control of several scales at once. When you consider all these aspects together, architecture reveals itself as a rather complex phenomenon, one which is much more relevant to society than we think today. The professional crisis described in this book is, I believe, the result of a process of simplification of the disciplinary ecosystem which, starting in the 1990s both in Europe and the US, has slowly eroded architecture's cultural and political agency.

EDITORS   What is your advice to young students and disillusioned professionals?

ANDRÉS JAQUE   One of the issues is that architecture is never a given. Every generation has had to build its own foundations and define its own questions. This is why I would argue that the phenomenon you describe, of contemporary practices operating outside the boundaries of conventional practice, is not a new condition. Even the champions of modernity were not perceived as doing 'proper architecture'.
    Take for instance Robert Venturi and Denise Scott Brown's seminal reading of Las Vegas in the early 1970s. They focused on aspects perceived as 'too ordinary' to be worthy of an architect's attention. Yet, in doing so, they managed to point precisely at what was relevant at the time.

Identity

Today the so-called 'conventional practices' dedicate themselves to solving problems in relation to this or that office building or condominium tower, ignoring the way platforms like Grindr or Tinder are redefining social relationships and the way we use the city. Therefore, as architects give up on trying to understand how technology is reconfiguring our lives and how critical that is to bring a civic dimension to these realities, our profession falls more and more into irrelevance.

To revert this process we should start asking questions which are inherently political, such as: how do we turn Grindr into a space where civic relationships can flourish? How can we take over real estate and turn it into a space for queerness where otherness is celebrated? We should take the front page of a newspaper and use every single headline as the premise for an architectural project, because architecture is a way to construct society through material, relational and performative means.

project! [handwritten annotation]

> EDITORS How can architects produce a more inclusive architecture that, for instance, brings queer space to the foreground and activates the social agency of urban environments?

ANDRÉS JAQUE Architecture is often wrongly described as the product of a single mind which has a vision and imposes it onto reality. This is very inaccurate as architecture doesn't happen in a vacuum and is always a collective endeavour: the result of interactions between many entities, both humans and non-humans – architects, regulations, social movements, environmental factors, etc. The question is how can we, as architects, insert ourselves in this existing process of collective production and influence it? There are many ways and they often involve a process of diplomacy: of introducing an idea, advocating for it and bringing other people on board. This is why we named our studio Office for Political Innovation, persuaded as we were, that any architectural intervention requires political action to engage with and mediate between different players. It is precisely this process of negotiation, where diverse interests meet, ideas are slowly transformed

THE DEFINING ISSUES OF OUR AGE CALL FOR A CO WHICH DRAWS KNOWLEDGE, FROM DIRECT EXPE THIS IS THE ONLY WAY TO LEARN TODAY.

and power is shifted, that I find exciting and which needs to be celebrated as something very different from the idea of architectural design as the product of an absolute genius mind that gives shape to our built environment.

> EDITORS   One of the things which distinguishes your practice is perhaps the ability to simultaneously engage with audiences other than the commissioning clients typical to contemporary architectural production. If this is true, who is the ultimate audience of your work?

ANDRÉS JAQUE   I would say that what we do is not intended for an audience in the sense of a somewhat detached and distant observer. We always insert ourselves within a given situation and craft images and messages (often manipulating existing documents), in order to participate in the wider processes of social change and rearticulation within a particular milieu. There is no distance.

This is also true in a more general sense, because what contemporary crises such as climate change have exposed is that there is no 'outside' anymore: we are all affected by what is happening. This is why architectural accounts of reality need to be wide-ranging. For instance through our project COSMO, developed for MoMA PS1 in 2015, we sought to intervene in a particular situation which had been ongoing in New York City

Identity

since Michael Bloomberg was elected mayor in the early 2000s. At the time architecture was mobilised at many different scales – infrastructure, policy design, apartment design, strategic design – in order to transform New York into a repository of wealth and boost the city's economy, which had been suffering since its harbours were relocated in the 1970s. All this at the price of producing rampant inequality and social segregation.

At first, in 2003, a new interpretation of air-rights law came into being, allowing air-rights between lots with at least a ten-foot adjacency to be traded. This measure, in conjunction with tax deductions for high end apartments and the use of limited liability companies as shell companies to hide the identity of real estate owners, inaugurated the architectural typology of the 'high-end tower' and attracted the desired investments. A few years later, as demand for natural gas for heating continued to grow in parallel with concerns for public health, huge infrastructural investments, such as the New York City Clean Heat Project, sought to reduce the levels of pollution within the city, particularly by lowering the levels of nitric oxide that render skies into gradients of yellow to brown. For the same reasons fracking was also banned in New York State, moving the industry to Pennsylvania. COSMO sought to make visible the city's hidden urbanism of pipes and its inherent toxicity, exposing that, in order to make the sky over Manhattan blue, pollutants needed to be shifted onto the sky above Pennsylvania.

Architects After Architecture

So, to go back to your question about the audience, we are all together in this situation, but our role as architects is to expose the whole socio-technological apparatus to mobilise and rearticulate the elements at play. This is a crucial endeavour because, although we are largely aware of the extent to which architecture has pervaded every aspect of contemporary existence – from our daily lives and the organisation of our cities through to its effects on wider biological and territorial networks – in order to remain functional members of society, people need to ignore all this information, to avoid being paralysed by it. This phenomenon – which was studied in the 1960s by Harold Garfinkel, the founder of ethnomethodology – has huge implications for both architectural practice and education, as today it is key for architects to learn how to mobilise this knowledge.

> EDITORS   How do you think schools should operate in order to facilitate the necessary transformations within practice that you advocate for?

ANDRÉS JAQUE   For me there is no division between practice and pedagogy. Alongside practicing, I have been teaching for many years, at Princeton and now with a formal engagement at Columbia University, and I have greatly enjoyed the energy that emerges from a group of people that are willing to explore uncharted territories together.

The defining issues of our age – from inequality to climate change through to the possibility offered by technology to rethink democracy – are very practical ones and, as such, they can't be addressed through theoretical speculations or utopian visions. They require us to actively reshape those realities from within and call for a collective learning process which draws knowledge, rather than from the past, from direct experience, first hand observation and experimentation. This is the only way to learn today, and it is taking place within academia, where, increasingly, knowledge is being co-produced, rather than just handed over to a group by an elite. Moreover pedagogy has the power to detach ourselves from the miseries of professional practice: like the real or perceived need to be aligned with the dominant forms of powers; the tendency to over-simplify problems; the recurring issue of not having enough time to do things, and so on. This is why I am so passionate about pedagogy as I do not think it can be decoupled from practice.

EDITORS   Which one of your projects best encapsulates your thinking around the role of pedagogy?

ANDRÉS JAQUE   Possibly all of them, as I see all my work as a constellation, rather than isolated episodes. We could take for instance, Ocean Space for TBA21–Academy; PHANTOM. Mies as Rendered Society; the Colegio Reggio in Madrid or Island House in Corpus Christi – one of the islands on the south coast of Texas, which is home to many endangered species – and we would see that all these projects are somewhat talking to each other. They are all looking at the cracks within a given system to rearticulate its social relationships.

Ocean Space is very exciting in this sense. We are working in the Mannerist church of San Lorenzo, in Venice, which is an impressive building where religion and engineering come together within architecture to mediate the relationship between humans and the ocean. Civil society used to gather here to pray for economic prosperity and protection from the sea, while a catalogue of ingenious solutions used to give the community access to drinkable water while keeping them safe from the dangers of the sea.

Today the situation has changed. We can no longer separate ourselves from nature, as to survive we have to stop global warming and protect biodiversity. Our role is thus to reconfigure the existing architecture and develop a different alliance with the ocean, allowing humans to sense themselves as part of it. This is a very exciting architectural challenge, but again, it is an experiment – much like the ones which are carried out within academia – and it requires us to operate across different mediums, scales, and slowly over time.

OVERLEAF   COSMO, a towering water purifier created for MoMA in 2015, exposed New York's inherent toxicity.

DESIGNING WITH CHILDREN

INTERBORO

The Nature Playscape in Saint Louis presents eight different areas in accordance with the site's ecologies. Their features were developed in collaboration with local children.

CASE STUDY

Image labels: Upland Prairie, Upland Forest, Spring, Gravel Bank, Garden, Wetland, Mounds, Meadow, Bottomland Forest

To make a successful playground, you need to consult the experts. No, not architects, but the children who will use it. Interboro have done just that for a new playscape for Saint Louis, even appointing a 'Youth Advisory Committee' of engaged children. Working in this way requires getting out of the office, and embracing a new set of tools and tactics, such as workshops, activities, and exercises, opening up the design process to new kinds of voices and perspectives.

Forest Park is a sprawling, nineteenth century park in Saint Louis, Missouri. Since 2017, Interboro leads a multi-disciplinary team of landscape architects, artists, engineers and ecologists to design a 17-acre Nature Playscape within the park; once completed, it will provide a place where families and children can escape the city and actively explore, discover, and learn in an accessible, freeform natural environment.

In order to design the playscapes, we enlisted the local experts for whom they are ultimately meant to serve: the children of Saint Louis. The first step was to visit schools and youth centres across the city. Through a series of workshops that included a custom 'mobile engagement station,' collage activity games, and hands-on models, we gathered many inventive designs for the park by kids. Next, we translated their work into preliminary design sketches, and presented them to what we called the 'Youth Advisory Committee' (YAC) – a group of children we had met during our school visits and who cared enough about their ideas to come back and evaluate our responses. After incorporating the YAC's feedback, we tested a handful of full-scale prototypes, using found material from throughout the park.

The final design for the Nature Playscape is based on this feedback loop between the design team, hundreds of kids and, in particular, a committed group of youth 'advisors'. This dialogical approach to design also built a constituency for the project. We made it a point to collaborate with children from neighborhoods across the city to ensure the Nature Playscape felt like a place for them.

The project speaks to our belief that good public spaces are the product of a design process where many different voices are involved, especially those who are typically excluded, thus opening up temporary spaces of meaningful public conversation.

A custom-built activity table travelled to community spaces around the city to engage youths of all ages and backgrounds in the design and the evaluation of the proposals. Among other things, the table hosted collage workshops inviting participants to visualise 'a place that looks like fun'.

The Youth Advisory Council – a team of young
play experts – contributed to workshops, tested
the prototypes, and provided critical feedback
for the design of the playscape.   83

FROM EXCLUSION TO INCLUSION

JOEL SANDERS

The seemingly innocuous principle of 'design standards' – so foundational to architectural education and practice – conceals a series of difficult questions: Who is 'standard'? Whose needs matter? Which bodies count? Joel Sanders, professor adjunct at Yale and principal of Joel Sanders Architecture (JSA), examines the public restroom as a contested site of social and political struggle. Drawing upon historical and participatory research, Sanders proposed new bathroom typologies which respect individual needs, while also bringing different people together.

Since antiquity, Western architects have presumed that the user of the designed environment is a prototypical body, one that is by default white, able-bodied, cis-gender, heterosexual and male. From Vitruvius to Le Corbusier, architects have thus designed buildings based on the proportions of an 'ideal' male body, one that people could aspire to but only ever approximate. In the nineteenth century, spurred by developments in science and medicine, the notion of the ideal body eventually gave way to a new conception: the 'normal' body. This body could be studied and measured and would form the basis of ergonomic design standards that have become encoded in architectural guidelines and regulatory codes that are still in use to this day. This putatively objective criteria has at many moments in history, including our own, been used to justify which people are allowed and which people are denied access to public space based on variations of a recurring argument: the unfounded claim that women, people of colour, immigrants and the disabled possess innate physical or mental defects that render them unfit to enter the public realm.

To reshape this legacy of exclusion in architecture to one of inclusion, in 2016 I established MIXdesign, a consulting and design practice associated with my architecture studio JSA in New York. We work with key stakeholders across a range of public buildings, including museums and educational institutions, to offer inclusive design solutions as alternatives to the limited and often problematic design standards and building codes that shape the spaces of our everyday lives. MIXdesign is a think tank and design consultancy dedicated to creating safe and accessible public spaces that meet the needs of 'non-compliant bodies,' people of different ages, genders, races, religions and abilities who fall outside of the cultural mainstream.

Architects After Architecture

A key focus is Stalled!, an extensive research and design project to develop inclusive public restrooms. In this essay I will use Stalled! as a case study to describe MIXdesign's evolving design methodology in which we use cross-disciplinary research and analysis as a critical design tool to reimagine built environments and to question and ultimately offer alternatives to architectural standards that perpetuate the status quo.

PHASE ONE: RESEARCH   Stalled! was sparked by the moral panic surrounding the question of transgender access to public restrooms in the US. On both sides of the debate the issue has been framed as a matter of safety. While advocates cite high rates of violence faced by trans people, and trans women of colour in particular, opponents claim transgender women pose a threat to cis-gender women and portray trans women as predatory men masquerading in dresses to stalk fresh prey in ladies' rooms. Stalled!, with a cross-disciplinary research team consisting of myself, trans theorist Susan Stryker, and legal scholar Terry Kogan, attempts to shift the debate by exploring this complex issue from a cultural, political, legal, economic and design perspective.

Our design methodology begins with research and analysis. First, drawing from insights gleaned from gender, race and disability studies, we question heretofore accepted everyday building 'types.' These formulaic spatial configurations associated with specific activities distribute bodies within formulaic spatial configurations that shape the way humans interact with each other and the world around them. Restrooms are a good example. We presume that the configuration of restrooms reproduced in architectural manuals like *Time Saver Standards* and transmitted through the legal regulations that specify design and construction standards are shaped by seemingly objective functional requirements dictated by ergonomics and waterborne infrastructures. All these documents depict public restrooms in the driest of formats – austere black and white annotated plans and elevations accompanied by line-drawings of robotic cis-gender men and women. The only concession to non-normative bodies are Americans with Disabilities Act (ADA) diagrams illustrating a person in a wheelchair. However, restrooms, when interrogated through a socio-political lens, exemplify the way typologies and building codes are historically relative, social constructions that reproduce and naturalise problematic assumptions about human identity and embodiment.

We quickly discovered that bathroom debates are not new. At different moments in American history, the public bathroom has registered social anxieties triggered by the threat of previously marginalised groups moving into mainstream society. Milestones include the creation of the ladies' room when women threatened to enter the work force in the 1880s, the fight to abolish 'coloured' bathrooms during the Civil Rights Movement of the 1960s, and the unfounded fear that straight men would be infected with HIV by sharing restrooms with gay men during the early years of the AIDS epidemic in the 1980s. Disability rights advocates' campaign for accessible public spaces included restrooms and led to the passing of the ADA in 1990.

Today's 'transgender restroom' debate is the latest and perhaps loudest episode in this long history of exclusion. Yet again restrooms are portrayed as dangerous spaces that put the health, morality and well-being of 'normal' citizens at risk by forcing them to physically interact with 'abnormal' people. In addition, they add a new fear to the list – gender nonconformity. Stalled! believes that what some people find so threatening about trans people is that they question the idea that gender is determined by anatomy. Trans, non-binary, intersex, and other gender-non-conforming individuals demon-strate that there are many ways of expressing one's gender independent from biological sex, and that don't conform to the binary of sex-segregated bathrooms.

After exploring American restroom debates from a political and historical perspective, our next step was to exam-ine an important aspect of the bathroom that has been over-looked in the volumes of commentary generated by politicians, lawyers, and journalists: the physical space of the sex-segre-gated restroom itself. Rather than limit our investigation to contemporary examples, we mapped the historical evolution of the western bathroom design from antiquity to today. Our discoveries challenged preconceptions. While we take for granted that bathrooms combine in one space two activities,

AT DIFFERENT MOMENTS IN AMERICAN HISTORY HAS REGISTERED SOCIAL ANXIETIES TRIGGERED MARGINALISED GROUPS MOVING INTO MAINST

washing and eliminating, history shows that until the nineteenth century, they were separated from one another in two different but communal unisex facilities. From antiquity to the Middle Ages, washing took place in public baths, while urination and defection occurred in streets, latrines and even in holes cut into the roadway of bridges. Attitudes changed during the Enlightenment with the emergence of bourgeois values about shame and privacy. For the first time, body parts needed to be concealed and abject body fluids were considered disgusting. Nevertheless, it was not until the advent of underground sanitation systems and mass-produced plumbing fixtures in the mid nineteenth century that puritan Victorian values were spatially manifested through the first sex-segregated restrooms that combined sinks and toilets in one room.

Design history proved liberating for our work. It encouraged us to seek alternatives to the most common and code compliant all-gender bathroom solution which supplements sex-segregated restrooms with a single-occupancy ADA-compliant toilet labeled gender-neutral. Although a step in the right direction, the single-user solution exemplifies two ways the conventions of architecture perpetuate a problematic bias about non-conforming bodies. First, like other sex-segregated building types including locker rooms, prisons and military barracks, it naturalizes the gender binary, separating 'men' and 'women,' which reinforces the notion of gender identity

HE PUBLIC BATHROOM
Y THE THREAT OF PREVIOUSLY
M SOCIETY.

as an effect of biology. Second, it exemplifies the prevailing 'separate-but-equal' approach to accessibility that caters to people with 'special' needs through separate accommodations – entries, ramps and in this case isolated rooms – that end up stigmatising and separating those with non-compliant bodies. These include trans and gender-non-conforming people and also people with disabilities as individuals who deviate from the norm and thus are prevented from mixing with 'normal' men and women in public space.

PHASE TWO: ANALYSIS   Stalled! advocates an alternative model that abolishes the binary: we are in favour of getting rid of typical gender-segregated facilities characterised by American-style stalls whose revealing gaps, at floor, ceiling and doors compromise visual privacy. We recommend a multi-user solution that treats the restroom as a single open space with floor-to-ceiling partitions and communal areas for washing and grooming. This solution has two advantages: by consolidating a greater number of people in one rather than two rooms, restroom users can visually monitor one another, reducing the risk and fear of violence and it ensures that gender-non-con-forming people aren't stuck between two options that don't align with their identities. This multi-user type meets the needs of the trans community but also a wide range of non-normative bodies traditionally neglected in public restrooms including caregivers, the elderly, mothers needing a place to nurse, Muslims who perform bathroom ablutions, and people with disabilities. Rather than focus on gender alone, Stalled! leverages trans visibility as a point of departure to design prototypes that promote the mixing of all people regardless of ages, gender, religion or ability. A democratic society cultivates respect for human difference by encouraging a spectrum of bodies to safely mingle in public spaces, like restrooms.

But how can we reconcile social mixing and human difference without lapsing into reductive one-size fits all solutions? Our approach is to register the affinities and differences of differently embodied people, and then find creative design solutions that can be shared between them. Working in collaboration with students and faculty at the Yale School of Public Health, we conducted surveys, interviews and a comprehensive literature review to gain an understanding of the specific cultural, psychological and medical needs of end-user groups. We organised them into overlapping categories including gender (trans and non-binary, pregnant and breastfeeding women, cis-gender and trans-men who menstruate), disability (people with mobility, sensory and cognitive impairments including the deaf and hard-of-hearing, blind and low-vision, and autistic), medical and psychological conditions (bowel and bladder conditions such as shy bladder syndrome), religion (Muslims and Orthodox Jews with particular rituals) and caregivers for children and adults. We knew from the outset that creating a bathroom with zones dedicated to each user group would be spatially and economically inefficient. Instead, we conducted a comparative analysis that allowed us to come up with design recommendations for shared spaces that would allow the maximum number of various users to mingle while also providing the option for those who prefer or require privacy.

This end-user research, conducted by Antonia Caba of the Yale School of Public Health, brought a new dimension to Stalled! While our previous work drew from the humanities, law and social sciences to advocate for inclusive restrooms as a social justice issue, Caba's work demonstrates that bathroom access also impacts physical and mental health. It convinces us that future collaborations between architecture, medicine and public health have the potential to productively explore the correlation between environmental design, social equity, health and wellbeing.

PHASE THREE: DESIGN   The next step in our process was design. We applied our end-user findings to develop prototypes that take the multi-user approach one step further by eliminating the ineffective walls and partitions that sort humans into a series of enclosed zones that ultimately reproduce problematic binaries that oppose clean and abject, male and female. Instead, drawing inspiration from pre nineteenth century historical precedents, we created two prototypes which reconceive the public restroom as an open agora-like precinct that encourages a spectrum of human users to mix.

The first project is a collaboration with Gallaudet University, a school for the deaf that has been meeting the educational needs of non-conforming bodies since its founding by Abraham Lincoln. On the upper level of the Field House, we are working within constraints imposed by the modest footprint of existing men's and women's rooms, to retrofit typical sex-segregated bathrooms into a multi-user facility that treats the restroom as a porous extension of the corridor.

The second project is a speculative prototype for larger high-traffic spaces like airports. Located adjacent to the main concourse, it is animated by three parallel activity zones, dedicated respectively to grooming, washing, and eliminating. Slip resistant sheets of diamond plate, tile and rubber differentiate each of the three activity zones which are painted a different shade of blue for the visually challenged. Immediately adjacent to the concourse, a mirrored wall reflects the bodies of the diverse users who groom at a multi-level dry counter that serves people of different heights and abilities. Those who want privacy can retreat into curtained alcoves for breastfeeding, administering medical procedures such insulin injections, meditation and prayer.

Adults, children, and people in wheelchairs wash at a communal water wall. Inset floor lights indicate the location of motion-activated faucets that allow water to flow into an inclined splash plane placed at different ergonomic heights that is then collected and cleaned in a remediating planter before being recycled.

Architects After Architecture

The scent of plants and the ambient sounds of flowing water mask bodily sounds and odors, factors that inhibit some people including those with shy bladders. Located at the back, the elimination station consolidates rows of bathroom stalls of different sizes that offer acoustic and visual privacy. Larger stalls are equipped with a sink, toilet, mirror, changing tables, and a foot shower to give the option of privacy to caregivers as well as to Muslims who perform bathroom ablutions. As users circulate from one station to the next, passing from the outermost grooming station to the innermost toilet wall, they experience a multi-sensory gradient that takes them from public to private, open to closed, smooth to coarse, dry to wet, acoustically reverberant to sound absorptive, ambient to spot lighting.

PHASE FOUR: IMPLEMENTATION   Researching and proposing innovative design solutions has been only a first step. MIXdesign has also addressed the practical realities of building codes and has successfully sought to change those governing restroom design which until now have mandated sex-segregated restrooms. We joined forces with the American Institute of Architects, National Center for Transgender Equality and the law firm Bryan Cave Leighton Paisner to amend the International Plumbing Code (IPC) – the model code governing most construction in the US – to make multi-user facilities code compliant. Our efforts succeeded and the amended code will appear in the 2021 version of the IPC and be available for adoption by state and local governments.

We view our inclusive design methodology for Stalled! as a work in progress. We are now applying it to other building types, including college campuses and workplaces. Our latest project, MIXmuseum assembles an interdisciplinary team of inclusive design consultants and museum stakeholders (curators, educators and administrators) to collaborate with partner

Gender

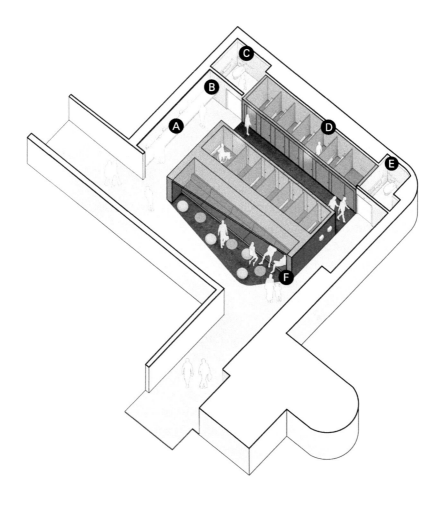

A   Washing Station
B   Grooming Station
C   ADA Wheelchair Accessible
D   Toilet Stalls Occupancy Lights
E   Caregiving Rooms
F   Lounge Area

museums in the US, UK, Sweden and Finland to develop and implement a Toolkit of Design Guidelines and Engagement Practices to transform the key areas of the visitor experience – entry, circulation, restrooms, galleries – in a way that meets their goals to expand and diversify their audiences. Our team also includes collaborators at the Yale School of Public Health and the Perelman School of Medicine at the University of Pennsylvania to add a new component to our process, participatory design. This involves using surveys, interviews, workshops, and focus groups to generate and test design solutions using input drawn from the lived experience of a cross section of museum visitors.

MIXdesign will continue to elaborate and refine our inclusive design approach through cross-disciplinary typological research. However, we cannot do this work alone. Designers must join forces and engage in design activism by exploring the spatial consequences of inclusion and diversity at a time when the human rights of non-compliant bodies are in jeopardy both in the US and across the globe. This means rethinking the structure of architectural education and the protocols of professional practice that silo architecture, landscape and interiors into separate fields. Blurring the boundaries between the design disciplines invites us to think across multiple scales from the overall configuration of buildings to interior room types to the dimensions that govern the design of smaller scale architectural components including doors, windows, furniture, fixtures and equipment.

We must no longer turn a blind eye to the way the seemingly innocent conventions of design reproduce and perpetuate problematic cultural assumptions about standard and deviant bodies. Instead we must form alliances with lawyers, code consultants, politicians, and environmental engineers to cast off outmoded standards and replace them with new and innovative design alternatives that register the complex, fluid and intersectional nature of embodied human identity. The process of looking at architecture through the lens of non-compliant bodies promises to be a catalyst for creativity that will allow interdisciplinary teams to generate unforeseen formal solutions that have potential to transform how all of us experience the built environment.

PRACTICE AS PROJECT

PUBLIC WORKS with ANGHARAD DAVIES

☆ Public Works is a London-based art and architecture practice whose members include Andy Belfield, Hester Buck, Matt Brown, Tom Dobson, Torange Khonsari, Andreas Lang, Rhianon Morgan Hatch and Carlotta Novella. All of their projects use playful tactics to involve local users, residents and passers-by in the development of strategies for supporting social, cultural and other initiatives in both urban and rural contexts. This text is a record of a conversation between Public Works' members and artist/architectural researcher Angharad Davies, reflecting on the practice's collaborative and non-hierarchical way of working, which challenges both the typical organisation of the architectural office and the architect's role in the design process.

On 6 November 2019 Public Works met for their monthly meeting. It was the first time that all eight members of the practice had been in the same room in many months; an indication of the agile and decentralised manner in which they operate.

Agenda items that day included: a period of 'hanging out';[1] a conversation about how to communicate the workings of Public Works; a discussion of the term 'situated drawing';[2] and updates on current projects.

I, Angharad Davies, was invited to host a portion of the meeting, titled 'the workings of Public Works', the outcome of which would inform this text. This collaboration was a testament to their 'networked approach'[3] – one based on trust, knowledge exchange and the dissolution of hierarchies, and one which allowed me to momentarily inhabit the multiple *we*'s at play within the relational and disobedient workings of Public Works.

WE, PUBLIC WORKS   We are a design practice situated between art and architecture, between academia and activism. Our aim is to aid community-led development through the reclaiming and safeguarding of public resources and assets; such as land, the environment and civic space.

We began in 1999 as two parallel collaborations between five interdisciplinary practitioners: an architect with two artists and two architects respectively.[4] We formalised as one group in 2004, finally setting up as a not-for-profit in 2009. Since then membership has fluctuated from a minimum of two to a maximum of eight people.

We operate simultaneously as individual practitioners and as members of the group. The group supports the ambitions of the individual practitioner in engaging with their chosen research interests and allows constellations of members to work together as projects emerge and develop, while interests overlap.

Our projects are often self-generated; being sought out through individual or shared research, emerging through involvement from within a community and, more recently, as one of a number of architectural practices recognised on the design framework for the Greater London Authority.

We are a non-hierarchical organisation that practices dynamic governance, relying on consent rather than majority rule. This means that project-specific decisions are usually made between individual members, with organisational decisions about the practice being discussed together once a month.

We tread lightly by keeping our overheads – insurance, rent, studio sundries – to a minimum. 20 percent of income derived from each project goes towards sustaining the practice.

We each choose how different forms of labour function (be it waged, reciprocal or gift) within our individual projects. Non-monetised forms of exchange contribute towards creating sustained relationships with communities, collaborators and stakeholders, as well as building a commonality and trust that enables co-authorship and strengthens community projects.

Our interests lie in the process of practicing architecture and we are not pre-occupied by the form that this could take – leading us to outputs that range from events to publications, campaigns to 'discursive dinners',[5] and, on occasion, buildings. These outcomes are rarely static and their aesthetic inconsistency demonstrates the process of reacting to the context and collaborations specific to each project. By relinquishing our hold, these projects aren't ours and instead become part of a *commons*, something made together.

WE, TOGETHER   Since its inception Public Works has sought out opportunities for hosting. Our studios in the past have included an extra space allocated for a practitioner-in-residence; seeking to establish symbiotic, economical relationships based on collaboration, care and shared working practices. Hosting is a way to disrupt the monoculture of the traditional studio.

The format of the 'Friday sessions' extended this logic of hosting from a lone practitioner to the many.

The concept – borrowed from 26'10 south Architects who invited Public Works to participate in a session at their office in Johannesburg back in 2005 – creates shared pools of knowledge that expand opportunities for exchange through access to other practitioners and their networks.

The sessions operate as public events in which colleagues and collaborators from the fields of art, architecture, design, activism, planning, etc. present their work. Topics at times coincide with current Public Works projects and, at others, inform them in the future. This emphasis on exchange permeates throughout the work of the practice to create a feedback loop between projects and learning, live and academic research, prototyping and implementation.

This loop has evolved into the School for Civic Action (SCA): an initiative that operates as a platform for collective teaching and learning within the city to challenge traditional institutional and discipline-led studies. Teachers and students range from activists, local residents, educators, artists and subject experts. The curriculum is developed from the bottom-up through events in localities. These activities make visible the local and 'household knowledges'[6] present within a community and draw out what might be missing – be it spatial, legal or infrastructural.

SCA employs a range of learning models from the incidental (as a side effect of other activities) to the episodic (as an after effect of an event), from the informal (non-classroom based) to instructional (formal classroom learning that would not be sanctioned in the institution). SCA's curriculum is sited within live projects, such as the Lore of Blackfriars project,[7] allowing for engagement that is informal and intimate and, at times, political and academic.

SCA contributes to and sustains a knowledge commons for the practice and its network. A commons that in turn contributes to the institutional and academic research (and a subsequent desire to subvert it) of the members of Public Works.

All eight current members teach.[8] Six out of the eight are former students of two of the founding members. All oscillate between roles while practicing; from teacher to student, gardener to cook, contractor to manager, citizen to architect.

As part of the R-Urban project, Wick on Wheel
(WOW) was a mobile unit that sought to engage
local inhabitants and artisans in the production,
reuse and repurposing of materials, resources
and knowledge.

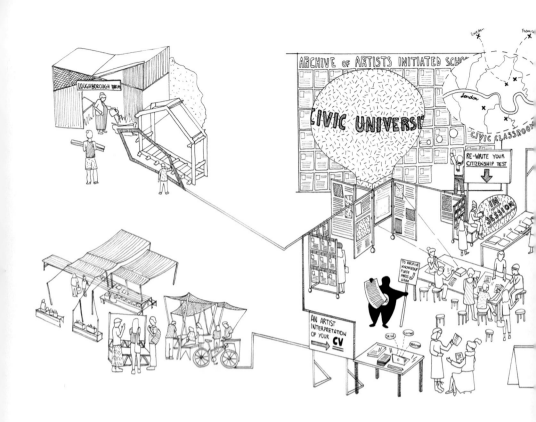

WE SHIFT   from student to teacher, cook to gardener, manager to contractor, architect to citizen and back. Public Works had been working on projects in Hackney Wick since 2008, relocating their studio there in 2012. The location at that time offered a unique social and material situation to the members of the practice; all of whom were living in neighbourhoods abutting the Olympic site. The site's designation for development in 2008 coincided with the financial crisis thereby creating a temporary urbanism in this part of east London. Over several years the area became a testing ground for numerous practitioners to embody and develop new and critical ways of producing and sharing knowledge through alternative economies of gift, reuse, borrowing and lending. This was enacted by Public Works primarily through the implementation of the R-Urban

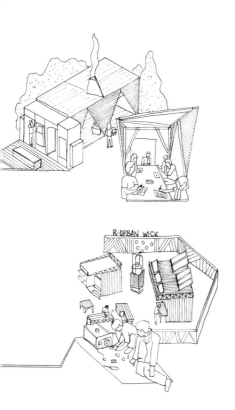

R-URBAN WICK

The School for Civic Action is a bottom-up initiative that facilitates teaching and learning between activists, local residents, artists and subject experts.

project: a series of bottom-up strategies developed in collaboration with atelier d'architecture autogérée in both London and Paris which sought to enhance urban resilience by introducing a network of user-run facilities.

The R-Urban project in London initially started as a mobile extension of Public Works' nearby studio in Hackney Wick. At first it existed as an itinerant programme of events and workshops hosted in part from a milk float, but also occupying many other local venues and collaborating with the people that ran them. In 2015 it came to ground in Mobile Garden City in the Olympic Park where a build project between local stakeholders (including Public Works) prototyped a small scale waste to energy unit (anaerobic digester), a kitchen, a materials reuse centre, a tool lending library and a production space.

Architects After Architecture

Its current iteration, located in Poplar, is the primary base from which Public Works tests, develops and prototypes off-grid technologies. In Hackney Wick an anaerobic digester runs off food waste from local residents producing biogas for the community kitchen. A moss wall is being developed for air purification while a tool lending library and compost toilet are being prototyped alongside a soon-to-be purpose-built studio to host larger workshops and events.

Site becomes studio.

WE RECEDE   and studio becomes site.

This proximity is key. It gives members an understanding of existing infrastructures, architecture and communities, moreover it enables embedded engagement, strategic involvement and knowledge exchange. Over time these relations have been developed into tactics to circumnavigate existing ways of practicing architecture and test alternative models that tip the balance of power away from architect/developer/local authority/central government and back to the citizen.

LJ Works in Loughborough Junction is one such project. Public Works have been involved in this area of south London since 2014, both as residents and practitioners. They initially helped to bring dispersed community groups together to form a steering group[9] in order to resist the planned redevelopment of Loughborough Farm – a community food growing project that had occupied an empty, council-owned site since 2013. The steering group, drawing from their years of experience as community members, proposed an alternative scheme that included retaining the land for use by the farm as well as creating a series of low cost workspaces on the site for local businesses. Funding was eventually achieved for the full scheme, known as LJ Works, through the London Regeneration Fund with Public Works and Architecture 00 working in close collaboration as the project architects.

LJ Works exemplifies Public Works' strategy of protecting public land and community assets through the creation of a neighbourhood commons. It uses mechanisms like Public(s) Land Grab[10] to find alternatives to unequal, capital-led urban development. Beginning at the scale of dialogue (amongst existing community groups and residents) and supported by legislation like the Localism Act 2011,[11] a neighbourhood commons seeks to grow and formalise social, financial, spatial and political relationships within a community.

Since its inception LJ Works has doubled in size. The capacity and empowerment of local organisations has grown, which has led to the safeguarding of the nearby Grove Adventure Playground; a site previously identified for redevelopment by the local authority. In this way LJ Works aims to be a pilot for self-sustaining community economies, the protection of public assets, as well as for the support of local small businesses and an exploration of community driven governance. As with previous projects the intention is that the steering group (with the support of Public Works) will eventually take full control of the site on behalf of the local community.

At which point the *we* of Public Works recedes.

WE, AS IN I   It is a *we* of eight *I's* that constitute the current workings of Public Works. *I's* that shift and recede in order to adapt to the needs of the environments and communities within which they work.

They are the *I's* of Public Works that exist simultaneously as a *commons*, a *collective* or *compost*.

A lot of people try to distill things down, whereas we are quite comfortable with layering, allowing that heat to develop out of it. Compost is *also about maintaining nutrition.*

ONE PROJECT MIGHT BE A COMPOST OF LEARNINGS FROM FIVE OTHER PROJECTS.   I'm not comfortable with it.
    I love it.
Disobedient and in disagreement. Discussions that end with a contradiction and answer with a question.

PERSISTENTLY, POLITELY ASKING.[12]

1 Indebted to the work of anthropologist Clifford Geertz, 'hanging out' describes the research methodology of immersing oneself in cultural, group or spatial experience on an informal level, which is a common approach for all of Public Works' projects and a tool to further collaboration through conversation.

2 'Situated drawing' is a design tool developed by Public Works that involves community members, props associated with a project, and the site itself to create a collage, often, although not always, documented through photography. It is used to communicate the project to both the local community and external stakeholders.

3 With reference to the work of John Seely Brown and Paul Duguid, the term 'network' refers to a set of individuals or groups connected through social relationships, while 'practice' implies the actions of these individuals and groups while conducting their work.

4 Andreas Lang, Kathrin Böhm, Stefan Saffer, Torange Khonsari and Sandra Denicke Polcher.

5 'Discursive dinners' are a format designed by Raumlabor. Understanding the kitchen as a site of dialogue and reciprocity, attendees cook and eat together. During the dinner, invited speakers do a short presentation followed by an informal discussion.

6 'Household knowledge' is used within the practice to describe unique, DIY or self-taught skills that exist within the everyday (often within a household), but operate outside sanctioned knowledge. Collected household knowledge has included making cladding material out of burnt timber, building a self-regulated plant growing system using discarded bathtubs and extracting human-friendly juice out of market waste.

7 Between November and December 2019, residents of London's Blackfriars participated in a series of events devised through workshops in the months prior. These included High Tea Roots, in which public works and residents of Peabody's Blackfriars Estate from Ghana, Ethiopia and Turkey reimagined the very British tradition, and a Complaints Choir devised in collaboration with Eduardo Padilha of Balin House Projects and performed by Camberwell Community Choir. The event used a format developed by artist Tellervo Kalleinen and Oliver Kochta-Kalleinen to set to song the grievances of local residents.

8 Members of Public Works teach or have taught at: Central Saint Martins, London Metropolitan University, Architectural Association, Royal College of Art, University of East London, University of Creative Arts, Umeå School of Architecture and Sheffield University of Architecture.

9 The steering group included Lough-borough Estate Management Board, Loughborough Estate Tenants and Residents Association, Marcus Lipton Community Enterprise, Loughborough Junction Action Group, Loughborough Farm, Greenman Skills Zone and Tree Shepherd.

10 Public(s) Land Grab is a live research project, which is currently being implemented in collaboration with Loughborough Junction Action Group, The Loughborough Farm, the LJ Neighbourhood Planning Forum and other local groups in Loughborough Junction.

11 The Parliament's Localism Act 2011 has sought to change the powers of local government in England to facilitate the devolution of decision-making powers from central government control to individuals and communities.

12 Quotes taken from members of Public Works during their practice meeting on 6 November 2019.

AN ALTERNATIVE PRACTICE IN TIMES OF CRISIS

DOINA PETRESCU,
ATELIER D'ARCHITECTURE AUTOGÉRÉE

In order to address new challenges, the old
model of the private architectural practice
must be questioned. How does it shape the
way architecture is made? Who is it made
with? In what ways does it constrain agency?
Doina Petrescu, co-founder of Paris-based
Atelier d'Architecture Autogérée (AAA)
has been confronting these questions
through her work for almost 20 years. AAA
employs tactics of community organisation
and activism, to create 'commons', sites
of genuine participation and democracy
amongst the crumbling social structures
of the welfare state. _____

Having faced the multiple unpredictable effects of climate change our society, our political and economic regimes, our social models and systems of governance are seriously challenged. Architecture is also part of the problem. The traditional modes of practice focused on building rather than reusing, and on financial profit rather than social and ecological justice, cannot continue on the same path. In response to this, we have sought to develop an 'alternative' way of doing architecture, realised in the form of our practice AAA.[1]

AAA is a research-based practice initiated by Constantin Petcou and myself in 2001 in Paris to conduct actions and research on participative architecture. We consider architecture to encompass both 'the community and the space for it'.[2] As such, our work is directed to creating 'commons', organisational forms in which a community manages space in the city and a common pool of resources. The team is made up of architects, artists, urban planners, researchers, activists, students, institutional partners and residents working in a network with a variable geometry.

We consider AAA to be alternative in a number of key ways: in the way our practice is structured, in the types of projects we undertake, in the working culture we promote, and in the issues we pursue. Together, these factors allow us to operate in a way that is radically different from that of a traditional architectural practice, opening up a new set of tools with which to address the climate crisis today.

SOCIAL VALUE   Inspired by the work of Henri Lefebvre, we view space as a social product. We believe in the social value of architecture, focused on occupancy rather than building, on users rather than clients, and on social wellbeing rather than financial gain. We often represent our architecture in terms of the social connections it creates. The sociality hosted by a building is as important as the building itself for us. To this, we have added what we called a 'resilience value': the invisible value of architecture which by its structure, materials and programme contributes important savings for the state, for the planet, and for society.[3]

This is realised in our work through what we term the R-Urban strategy. R-Urban comprises a series of interconnected, self-managed, collective hubs, which can boost the resilience value of a neighbourhood by providing shared spaces for skills, knowledge, labour and creativity around urban agriculture, recycling, eco-construction and cooperative housing.[4]

This work forms part of a wider movement in architecture today, identified as a return to the 'social idealism, freedom to experiment and scale of ambition of an earlier era, which rejects the 1980s' architecture school of built form fetishisation, yet this time with a new set of tools to play with; no longer subscribing to less is more, but closer aligned with mess is the law.'[5]

AAA engages with this 'mess' by developing transgressive approaches and tools for architecture and urban design. Informed by Michel de Certeau's ways of doing of the 'weak',[6] *Read* our tactics show how to do things with very little money, but with the contributions from as many people as possible: citizens, dwellers, users, stakeholders. According to de Certeau, tactics work with time and are opportunistic in their method; they do not 'plan', but use their own deviousness and the element of surprise to get things done.

In this way, our tactical approach is perhaps in conflict with conventional urban planning, dependent as it is on careful staging and structure. We do not 'plan' but 'act', sometimes without permission and against the rules that we deem to be inappropriate or unfair, but always with inventiveness, time and passion. Tactics survive through their mobility, writes de Certeau, leading us to a formal approach defined by temporality and mobility: momentary occupations, reversible uses, demountable constructions, mobile designs. These tactics are also ecological, enabling agile transformations and resilient land use.

PARTICIPATION   Since the 1970s, participation has been the main tool for democratising architecture and challenging many of its normative values. Our work continues this legacy by providing the space and tools to enable people to find answers to their own (ecological) problems. We propose hubs for participative practices where people can meet, debate, learn and test new ways of doing things together, working towards more resilient futures.

IF WE WANT A DIFFERENT FUTURE IN THESE TROUBLED TIMES, EVERYONE NEEDS TO BECOME AN ACTIVIST.

Unlike other practices that are part of the recent 'participative turn' in architecture, we are concerned with 'real participation'.[7] This involves a long-term commitment and care, with a continual democratic awakening throughout the process. By contrast, participation fails when it is not embedded in a larger process, but is only trying to fulfil the short-term objectives of a public institution in an election year. In the end, not all participatory processes are successful and this is perhaps a good thing; these processes remain risky and open to continual negotiation.

This way of working can leave us open to defeat, as happened recently with the Civic Line project in Paris. We were commissioned to transform an abandoned space under the aerial metro line in northern Paris, by creating a new public space to be managed by citizens. The project was blocked by a group of local residents (white, educated, retired) who had the time to attend all the meetings and to learn the 'official language'.

As we strived to give a voice to migrants, local ethnic organisations, and other groups of citizens, whose needs were not being taken into account, this group successfully drowned out anyone who was less visible, less vocal, and less organised. This eventually led to the suspension of the project, despite having been nominated for the European Innovation in Politics Award. However frustrating, such defeats provide important test beds for the future, and an example of the limitations of participatory processes in the context of a weakened democracy.

RESISTANCE   Community strength can come from conflict too. One of the defining moments of our practice was the campaign to 'save' the Agrocite R-Urban hub in Colombes from demolition by the local mayor, who had another plan for the site.[8] On this occasion, we learned that the social value of architecture can be attacked, even by those supposedly elected to protect it. In this situation, the role of the architect is not only to design, but also to sustain and defend existing and emerging commons together with all those who are involved. In these conditions, activism is not a choice but a duty of care. If we want a different future in these troubled times, everyone needs to become an activist.

Much of our work is in deprived neighbourhoods around Paris, the decaying remnants of the welfare state, with residents now facing high unemployment, poverty, and exclusion. It is there, in their neighbourhood, that the citizen becomes accountable for their actions, and 'learn to be affected'[9] by the world. These estates have seen heavy top-down regeneration schemes, proceeding by either demolition or eviction and gentrification, our work invites citizens to participate in bottom-up repair and regeneration processes, circular economies, and ecological practices, enabling them to reclaim some agency over their space and their lives.

It is through these networks of urban commons that communities can develop other relationships to the state, nature, and the planet. It is in these neighbourhoods that we forge *a sense of belonging*, something that in metropolitan contexts has been eroded and replaced by alienation, atomisation and individualism.[10] It is only by acquiring this sense of belonging that a community is able to face the challenges of our complicated present and uncertain futures. If architects do indeed have a role to play in this process, it should involve demonstrating how an alternative model of practice and production can serve others.

1   Doina Petrescu, Constantin Petcou, 'Tactics for a Transgressive Practice' in Rachel Sara and Jonathan Mosley (eds.), *Architectural Design: Transgression,* October 2013

2   For details see Doina Petrescu, 'How to make a community as well as the space for it' in *The Rururban Plot,* CGAC, 2009, p.107-112

3   For more details see Doina Petrescu, Constantin Petcou, 'Architecture's Resilience Value Against Climate Change' in, *Architectural Design: The Social Value of Architecture,* forthcoming

4   See project website: r-urban.net

5   Chris Bryant, Caspar Rodgers and Tristan Wigfall, 'The Changing Forms and Values of Architectural Practice' (editorial) in *Architectural Design: New Modes: Redefining Practice,* September 2018, p.15

6   See Michel de Certeau, *The Practice of Everyday Life,* University of California, 1984

7   For more details see Doina Petrescu, 'Losing Control, Keeping Desire' in Peter Blundell Jones, Doina Petrescu, Jeremy Till, (eds.), *Architecture and Participation,* Routledge, 2005, p.43-64

8   Justinien Tribillon, 'Why is a Paris Suburb Scrapping an Urban Farm to Build a Car Park?', *The Guardian,* 11 September 2015

9   Bruno Latour, 'How To Talk About The Body? The Normative Dimension of Science Studies', in *Body & Society 10,* no.2/3, 2004, p.209

10 See Matt Dawson, 'Reviewing the Critique of Individualization: The Disembedded and Embedded Theses', *Acta Sociologica 55,* no.4, 2012: 305-319; and Anthony Giddens, *Modernity and Self-Identity: Self and Society in the Late Modern Age,* Polity Press, 1991

PRIDE IN MAKING

Interview with TAKESHI HAYATSU

The increasing professionalisation of architecture and construction acts as a barrier between the general public and the ideas and tools to shape the places they live. In a small village in England's Lake District, Hayatsu Architects have shown how this barrier can be overcome, by creating a series of pavilions in collaboration with students and local residents, who are invited to contribute their skills and ideas. In this interview, Takeshi Hayatsu explores the themes that drive his practice, from the use of traditional Japanese techniques, to John Ruskin and the Arts and Crafts movement, and how these ideas are returning in today's practice of co-design.

EDITORS   Could you start by telling us what you studied and where, and when you came over here to London?

TAKESHI HAYATSU   I first studied architecture in an arts school in Tokyo, and then I came to London in 1993 to do my masters at the Architectural Association, which was a pretty cool place at the time. I really liked Archigram's stuff – David Greene and Ron Heron were teaching – which is the reason I came here initially. For me it was a liberation.

EDITORS   How was the Architectural Association different from your education in Japan?

TAKESHI HAYATSU   The biggest difference was the workshop. I loved it, especially grinding, welding, working with metal, working with wood. You would never have that kind of facility in an architecture school in Japan. That was a really important, and a pretty profound influence on my work today. My diploma tutor was Peter Salter, he was the only one focusing on construction, on material, on tactility, in a very logical and poetic way. Smells, dampness, darkness, all this essential stuff. I don't know how to explain it, but he taught how to make a clear design strategy out of materials, which you would never get in a Japanese education, which is largely about concept. Japanese architects think too much in their brains.

EDITORS   And when did you set up your practice?

TAKESHI HAYATSU   I wasn't planning on being here for that long, I had no plan further after school. Japan was in a recession, and here the Labour party had just got in, and the economy started picking up. When I graduated I found a job with David Chipperfield, the opportunity was there so I stayed. I also worked for Haworth Tompkins, and then for 6a for 11 years, before I started my own practice in 2017.

EDITORS   Your first project was a collaboration with Terunobu Fujimori, to build a tea house at the Barbican, how did that come about?

TAKESHI HAYATSU   Yes, that was an interesting one.
The Barbican were putting on the Japanese House exhibition,
which had come from the MAXXI in Rome, and one of the conditions was to build a one-to-one house. They asked me what
they should build, and I suggested Fujimori.

There's this interesting concept in Japan: 'white
school' and 'red school'. Fujimori, who is also an art critic,
made this term in the 1980s. So the 'white school' represents
the conceptual architects like SANAA and Sou Fujimoto,
their buildings are white, but it's also about the brain, when
you open up the brain, it is white. And then the 'red school'
is the opposite, it's blood, it's emotion, it's tactile, and these
are the strange ones, the outsiders. Fujimori is really dark
red, really far out. And in between them you have pink ones,
like Tadao Ando for example. So Jane Alison, head of the
Barbican Art Gallery, picked Ryue Nishizawa's (half of SANAA)
extremely white Moriyama House on the one side, and then
Fujimori's tea house on the other. The two extremes, which
was quite funny.

And then Fujimori asked the Barbican to collaborate
with me because we had collaborated before, for a project
with my students at Kingston University. He saw that we were
capable of building small pavilions. It was a nice first project.
We went to East Sussex on a frosty morning in January to chop
the Chestnut tree for the legs for the tea house.

> EDITORS   It sounds like a symbolic moment, and a big
> change from sitting behind a computer. It seems like
> this return to materials and making has been a sort of
> guiding approach for your practice.

TAKESHI HAYATSU   Exactly. 6a work like that too. It's almost
'anti-concept', everything comes from construction, from the
way things are put together.

> EDITORS   I was up in Coniston in the Lake District a few
> months ago, and saw two of your pavilions for Grizedale
> Arts, can you talk about what it means to be working
> in that context so far removed from London?

Architects After Architecture

TAKESHI HAYATSU   We've done a number of projects with Grizedale Arts, the director, Adam Sutherland, invited us to run a summer school as part of his Valley Project, where he wants to make a network of what he calls 'idiosyncratic structures' to bring attention and focus to the area around Coniston. With the students of the construction course at Central Saint Martins, the last three years we've built the first few of these pavilions. The students make some proposals, then we pick two ideas. One was the community bread oven, the other was the information kiosk. We got a small budget from the Heritage Lottery Fund as part of a larger copper mine regeneration and interpretation funding to help with materials and logistics. Then we went up there with the students to build them in partnership with people from the community over a couple of weeks in the summer.

THESE ARE SMALL THINGS, MADE BY MANY PEOPLE, BUT WHEN YOU GATHER THEM TOGETHER YOU CAN MAKE SOMETHING AT AN ARCHITECTURAL SCALE.

EDITORS   How does having the community make it change the project?

TAKESHI HAYATSU   Always the idea is to involve members of the community in the making. So for the kiosk, we made a template tool so that local people could decorate their own copper tiles, which were then used as the cladding. The Central Saint Martins students made it, and then Grizedale organised a workshop with the local school. So this is a simple thing that anyone can make. But the idea is about the accumulation of this labour. These are small things, made by many people, but when you gather them together you can make something at an architectural scale.

> EDITORS   It's really interesting as a process, one that can take multiple years, with various different groups of people feeding in at different times, building toward something that is not yet completely defined. You can kind of control it, but you also need to leave things open for others to contribute. Do you see projects like these as processes or systems?

TAKESHI HAYATSU   In this instance, the idea came from Grizedale, where they want to develop the area in a slow way. They are very interested in the idea of co-design, where design should be done collectively, not just by a single author. The challenge is to facilitate the different elements of a project, which things are fixed, and which things are open for interpretation.

We are now looking at how we can tap into the construction industry as part of these processes. So we have run a number of workshops to make 30,000 bricks for the path in front of the Coniston Institute. We are trying to make a partnership with a brick manufacturer, where they can send the raw bricks up to us in Coniston, so we can add a printed design, and then put them back into the industrial kiln. So it's about manoeuvring that kind of a process, and also interfering in it in an economical and creative way, so we don't compromise the integrity of the bricks, but also somehow change the nature of the thing.

> EDITORS   So much of this work is about re-animating the Arts and Crafts, of re-connecting people with making, and the idea that self-improvement can come out of that. Is that an explicit source for the way you approach these projects?

TAKESHI HAYATSU   History is the key to everything we do. We are always looking for a clue in the local history.

In Coniston this goes much deeper, right back to John Ruskin's legacy – who lived in Coniston, and set up the Mechanics Institute there – and his idea of labour and pride. It's kind of simplistic, but it's a useful way to engage with people, especially if you design a way for them to become part of the structure. With the kiosk, the residents were really proud to see their tiles up there.

> EDITORS   People so rarely have that relationship to architecture. Architecture is something that is done by experts, and that sense of continuity between what you can build and what a builder can build has been broken.

TAKESHI HAYATSU   Building is complex, but it's also quite simple to some extent. I mean, it's not a computer, with a building you can touch the parts and understand them.

> EDITORS   Looking ahead, you mentioned when I arrived that your ambition is to do bigger projects. Can this approach of working with people, which is so dependent on collaboration and volunteers, scale up? Or do you need to reconceive of how you practice?

TAKESHI HAYATSU   Where we are just kind of happened, it wasn't intended. All of these community-based co-design projects, it's just what we can do with what we have, with what we have access to. It's kind of great, but also at the same time, we have diverged from the normal architect's job. I'm wondering, when can I design a proper building? So that's the kind of 'dilemma' that I have. More and more we are involved in these community-led design processes, which is great, and I'm not complaining, but at the same time, it's not that I've consciously rejected commercial practice either.

The ideal condition for us would be to be able to work with both lay-people and experts in trade, people with an amazing body of knowledge and skills, who take pride in and enjoy making things. It is about working with people in the most appropriate and effective way for the project, either big or small.

The Road project in Coniston, the Lake District, designed in collaboration with students of Central Saint Martins, Grizedale Arts and local community groups.

REVIVING THE ALMS HOUSE

PETER BARBER

CASE STUDY

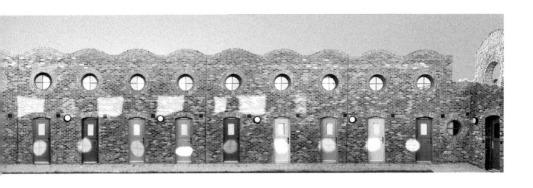

The new studio houses for homeless people in London reinterpret traditional dwellings of the past.

In recent decades, architecture has become so rarefied, that simply designing for those who need it most can seem like a radical gesture. While the rest of London is busy throwing up high-end apartments as speculative investments, Peter Barber has quietly built an impressive set of social housing blocks. This case study presents one of Barber's recent projects, a cluster of cottages for homeless people, built around a garden. Reviving the neglected typology of the alms house, updated with a wavy parapet, coloured doors and round windows, the project shows that who you design for can be as important as what you design. 119

Holmes Road Studios is a beautiful new homeless facility providing high quality residential accommodation together with training and counselling facilities all laid out around a delightful new courtyard garden.

Most of the accommodation is arranged in little studio houses forming terraces fronting the garden, in an alms house typology. These cottages have a double height brick vault with an en-suite bathroom at the back of the plan, and a mezzanine bed space raised above. The rooms are lit via a partially glazed door, pretty looking circular windows and a roof light. The buildings are constructed in a rustic looking brick with a crinkle crankle parapet which gives the project a relaxed domestic scale. All of the rooms look out over the garden.

We imagine a group of residents working with a gardener to create and maintain an intensely planted and beautiful garden. There would be an apple tree or two, potatoes, green veg, soft fruit, herbs, a greenhouse, a potting shed and a sunny spot to sit and rest. We think there ought to be a little room/shed in the garden for private chats and counselling.

The garden creates a homely, domestic atmosphere in the hostel. It will give participating residents an interest and outlet for their energy. It will help to foster a sense of belonging, self worth and empowerment amongst residents. It will provide people with an opportunity to develop gardening skills and encourage them to think about nutrition.

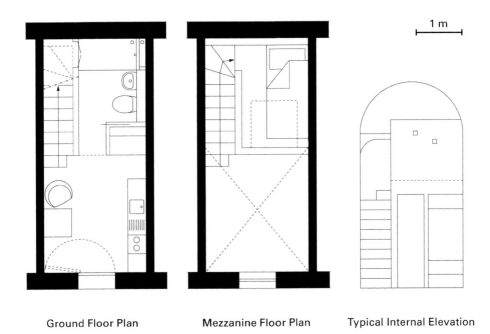

1 m

Ground Floor Plan   Mezzanine Floor Plan   Typical Internal Elevation

TOP   The scheme is built around a garden/
orchard which hopes to stimulate a homely,
domestic and convivial atmosphere.
BOTTOM   Layout of a typical studio apartment.

121

THE ARCHITECT-ORGANISER

SIB TRIGG, THE PEOPLE'S EMPOWERMENT
ALLIANCE FOR CUSTOM HOUSE

Behind the promise of new homes and new jobs, the word 'regeneration' has come to be seen as a byword for the destruction of social housing tenants, to be replaced by private development. How might this process be shaped in a way that respects the rights of local residents? Sib Trigg explains her work as part of a community organisation to create an alternative regeneration plan for a neighbourhood in east London, that rather than being imposed from above, grew out of the wishes of the people who live there, and how through this process Trigg developed the role of the 'architect as organiser'.

The People's Empowerment Alliance for Custom House (PEACH) is a community organisation based in Custom House, a primarily residential area within the former dockyards of east London. The area has been earmarked for a major urban regeneration programme, with proposals dating back to 2003. Since then, residents have been living with the looming uncertainty of demolition, moving and disruption. I started working with PEACH in 2015, when after years of stasis, the residents decided to create their own alternative regeneration plan for Custom House.

After a series of informal conversations with the PEACH steering group (comprised of local residents) and community organisers, we drew up the proposal for the Alternative Regeneration Team who would work on the Plan. This team brought together experience in participatory design processes and community organising, comprising four architects, five local residents, an experienced union organiser and two full-time community organisers who would supervise the process.

It was important for us to have no hierarchy of skills or knowledge within the group, to ensure that all contributions to the project were equally valued. All team members were paid equally, and we deliberately selected architects as independent individuals, rather than appointing a practice. In this way, the team would build relationships with each other, share professional and local knowledge and exchange skills. Through combining community organising methods with participatory design practice, we could work out our own approach to specific local issues.

THE EMERGENCE OF THE ARCHITECT-ORGANISER
From October 2016 the team worked one day a week for a year

to produce four aims and six principles for regeneration, which were then spatially represented in the Alternative Regeneration Masterplan. This plan was supported by an evidence base, including mapping of the area and documentation of the design workshops. Through this process the idea of the architect-organiser emerged as a new form of relational design practice, encompassing participatory design and knowledge production, expanding the traditional understanding of what it is that architects do.

The architect-organiser builds relationships with local residents and businesses as well as bringing specialist architectural and planning knowledge to a project. Working with community organisers, they may be talking to people on their doorsteps, attending or organising community events, mapping the area, planning and running design workshops, and evaluating the results. All these activities are key to building strong community relationships, which, in turn, enable the contribution of specialised local knowledge from residents and businesses to the process. A key skill of the architect-organiser is to translate technical, planning or construction jargon into plain language, and work out interactive ways to share information in order to increase awareness as well as enable analysis and dialogue. The architect-organiser encourages social and political critique of information and processes, which is what enables the development of specific approaches to local problems. This process of translation needs to resonate outside of the community too, establishing dialogue with other architects, designers and professions from other fields, such as economists or lawyers.

POWER STRUCTURES   Power analyses are an important part of the architect-organiser role, requiring them to work out strategies for mitigating against established structural power imbalances. For example, how power over language or access to information structures relationships with peers, the local authority, other stakeholders and the wider community. Addressing these imbalances means going further than just allowing space for others to speak and modifying their language. Interactive dialogue and questioning of the status quo empowers residents and organisers to ask questions and to form their own analyses of political and spatial situations.

Mapping the dynamics between stakeholders and how they intersect with the programme for the Alternative Regeneration Plan, allowed us to decipher pivotal moments to enable residents to situate themselves geographically and temporally within a complex and evolving combination of politics, policy, finance, design and planning. By working with residents to understand how these forces were impacting upon the regeneration process, we could enable genuine participation in decision-making and devise more responsive approaches to the regeneration.

The focus on activities which build power and knowledge for residents and fosters relationships from the ground up is what makes the role of the architect-organiser distinct from that of the traditional architect, who is likely to have a more conventional client-architect relationship alongside a predefined brief and clear project outcomes.

A ROADMAP FOR REGENERATION   According to artist, designer, teacher and activist Shana Agid, this type of relational design practice is one defined by 'working together over time and through acts and instances of proposing and thinking together through our work to produce meaning and objects or representations (or action) significant for the aims and vision of the organization in large and small ways.'[1] This way of working is precisely the one adopted by PEACH to draw their roadmap for regeneration.

Through a series of internal workshops, the interweaving strands of the regeneration process were drawn out and developed into a diagram – our Roadmap – to visualise each stage of the process and the various routes across design, delivery and management, as well as the unknown areas, yet to be defined. This graphical tool was developed by the community organizers while the architect-organizers worked to make visible the relationships between the different steps and actors involved in the regeneration process, for example by breaking down the Royal Institute of British Architects work stages.

The Roadmap was used during specific training sessions as well as during PEACH's regular meetings with residents and community organisers, allowing each party to place themselves in the processes which were happening around them and work out courses of action to enable genuine participation. The engagement with and development of the Roadmap involved not only knowledge of the process but also interactions with new pieces of data and information which the community had never encountered before. For example, detailed planning policy, feasibility studies, capacity studies and the parts of the process which typically happen behind the scenes.

The work PEACH has done in Custom House has started to build trust and belief in the possibility of a regeneration which will be beneficial to existing residents and newcomers. By bridging design, strategy and collaboration, the architect-organiser operates at a critical intersection between the community, and the larger forces governing the city. In prioritising the design of processes over the design product, they are able to build relationships, exchange and develop knowledge as well as spatial propositions, enabling residents to exercise authentic decision-making power in the regeneration process.

1   Shana Agid, *Making Contested Futures: A Politics Of Designing With People*, PhD thesis, RMIT University, 2016

'WE WANTED TO DO THINGS OURSELVES'

Interview with JANE HALL, ASSEMBLE

Few practices so exemplify the idea of redefining architecture as do Assemble. Founded by 20 friends (the precise number is unclear) in 2010 with the modest aim of converting a petrol station into a cinema, the collective has since been awarded the Turner Prize in 2015, and has built an impressive portfolio of projects, encompassing products, exhibitions, public spaces, masterplans, and buildings. In this interview, co-founder Jane Hall offers a view inside the workings of the practice, exploring their collaborations with communities and craftspeople, their attitude to control, and how their structure has evolved as they increasingly seek to attract larger and more formal commissions.

EDITORS   Assemble has taken on a kind of mythical status, as an example of what can be achieved straight out of university. How did it all begin?

JANE HALL   The myth is that Assemble formed as an alternative model to conventional practice, but at the time I don't think we had that much direction or foresight. It really began around realising one project. We have always been focused on the work, and our organisational structure and way of working has adapted over the years to suit this. After studying together at Cambridge, we all moved to London. Back then we had no reputation or responsibilities. Some of us weren't sure if we even wanted to continue in architecture. We were interested in taking more responsibility for professional education as we found it frustrating to see how far removed architects were from knowing how their designs were made. In this sense, our first project, the Cineroleum, a temporary cinema we built ourselves in 2010, was a hobby, something fun to do together, of the kind you wouldn't get in conventional practice.
      What still amazes me when I think about that project is the way we learned from and got excited by each other rather than being guided by a mentor. In conventional practice you always have to report to the person at the top, which can be really paralysing, especially when you are quite young. Building the Cineroleum, we had this sense of urgency, which wasn't born from anger or frustration or some sorts of resistance to the socio/political conditions – although these sentiments were definitely in the background – but rather from being really enthused by each other's interests and passionate about our work.

EDITORS   So this wasn't an explicit attack on conventional practice but rather a way of proposing an alternative way of doing things?

JANE HALL   We wanted to find out how things were made for ourselves. None of us really understood how much it costs to do something or really appreciated labour's financial value in producing architecture. We have now become very good at identifying this value and defending it, especially when we subcontract. But I think what we really learned from the Cineroleum and the Folly for a Flyover, another early project, is that architects are not going to become highly skilled crafts-people, but with a first-hand experience of making, you can form better connections with the people who master that knowledge, which results in a better design process. This is why we created Sugarhouse Studios and made space for skilled makers who are dedicating their careers to craft. We tend not to do the bulk of the building ourselves, as it doesn't represent good value to anybody although we do try to introduce some form of hand making or experimentation during the process.

> EDITORS   This kind of collaborative relationship can be difficult in conventional architecture, where all sorts of rigid systems are in place to regulate modes of exchange, creating artificial barriers between you and the contractor, for instance.

JANE HALL   Precisely. A good friend from Brazil recently came to work for a big European practice and was surprised at how short the meetings are, and focused solely on the project. In Brazil meetings are also about trust-building, the first half an hour you talk about football, or each other's families, so you create friendships through work. Whereas here, especially if you are a junior architect, you are not allowed to talk directly to the client, even though you are probably doing the bulk of the work. This is the culture that we were trying to challenge by making sure that what we do is reliant on friendships, personal connections and shared interests.

> EDITORS   In a widely-shared presentation from a few years ago,[1] your colleague Joe Halligan describes the members of Assemble as having a 'flat hierarchy', where everybody is welcome to have their own thing in tandem with being part of the team. How does this shape the dynamics within the practice?

JANE HALL   The idea that everybody could have their own activity outside of the group, essentially working as freelancers,

A carpentry workshop in Sugarhouse Studios,
Assemble's studio complex designed to bring
together different forms of expertise in making
and design.

Model of a refurbished terrace house as part
of the Granby Four Streets project, Liverpool

was certainly relevant at the time when we made that presentation. We haven't been like that for a while now, as we have sought more financial security. As a freelancer, if your job goes on hold or falls through, you take on the financial risks. We wanted to change that, so now we have equal pay and a monthly salary, but we had to sacrifice a bit of our individual freedom in terms of deciding which projects to pursue and how to manage our own time. Despite this, the idea remains that if someone is not able to do something within the structure we have set up, rather than just saying 'no', we look for ways to change the structure.

At the moment many of us are working on parallel projects – across teaching, furniture making and research, like myself for instance – and, if we do so within normal working hours, our income goes to Assemble. One of the results is that we take more of an interest in what each other is doing externally because it impacts everyone.

As for the 'flat hierarchy', that idea emerged out of the necessity of describing how we were working at the time, it then stuck. In reality we are a closed collective, with a set number of members who operate within a 'flat hierarchy' and five employees who could potentially become part of the collective. In practice though we produce all sorts of unspoken and nuanced hierarchies, which become manifest in our work. In this sense the idea of a 'flat hierarchy' and of being a collective are attitudes we constantly aspire to, and an element of resistance perhaps, but not something which has ever crystallised in a radical and alternative business model. We have simply organised ourselves to make space for things we care about, but we are still forced to operate and survive within a model of architectural services predicated on financial capitalism.

EDITORS   We set out to make this book for people finishing their degree and entering the so-called 'real world', who might be thinking 'this is not for me', by providing a sort of menu of alternatives to conventional practice. Ironically, though, everybody we speak to seems to say that what they do is not really replicable.

Making

JANE HALL   That might be true for us too. What I see though is that, because of the way we set up our practice, the language we use to communicate and the way we have positioned ourselves, we get offered a lot of really interesting work.

> EDITORS   This idea of the image you project is quite interesting. Looking at your website or press coverage it doesn't seem that specific individuals within the practice are associated with particular projects.
> So, maybe, rather than a 'flat hierarchy' within the organisation, would it be more accurate to talk of a 'flat authorship'?

JANE HALL   It is certainly accurate in relation to the way we communicate our work externally. Internally though we are very much organised so that projects are assigned to specific people who take them forward and are responsible for their execution. Which is why we describe Assemble as a platform, a mechanism for individuals to do what they want with collective support. So, for instance, if you see a presentation by me or by someone else, you might see a different selection of projects as we don't have a common slide deck we draw from and, although we know what happens across the board, we choose which projects represent us best and try not to make people work on anything that they don't want to.

> EDITORS   You have often used the word 'multidisciplinarity' to describe the practice's way of working, with different expertise drawn together within Sugarhouse Studios: from ceramics, to furniture making, drawing, etc. How do these skills from both the partners and the broader coalition of people in your studio shape the way you work and approach a project?

JANE HALL   I think multidisciplinarity brings out a strong sense of confidence to each project, allowing us to take more risks and really innovate, especially when it comes to materiality as we are drawing on lots of different people and associated skills. This was the case for instance with the facade

WE HAVE ORGANISED OURSELVES TO MAKE SPA BUT WE ARE STILL FORCED TO OPERATE WITHIN SERVICES PREDICATED ON FINANCIAL CAPITALIS

for the Goldsmiths Centre for Contemporary Art, where we were able to take a cheap industrial building material like corrugated cement board and give it a particular treatment. Because we had the space, the time and the knowledge to work with different types of dyes, we could build a one-to-one mock-up in our studio, work out all of the details and be confident that we could deliver the site package for our first ever 'real' building project. This would have been unaffordable without such infrastructure.

Having this type of in-house expertise also means we can subcontract the work we can't do, while still being involved in it. In a recent project for a workspace in Brixton, rather than picking tables from a catalogue, we commissioned some carpenters in Sugarhouse. The tables turned out to be much more affordable and much better. We could see them being built and follow their installation. Which probably makes us sound like some sort of control freaks!

EDITORS   Your way of working seems almost the opposite of control. You talk about inviting external collaborators, giving up parts of projects or leaving things to chance, with projects you set up, like some of your playgrounds which have taken a life of their own after you delivered them or other community projects where you have continued being involved under a different role. These are all instances where the boundaries within which to exercise control might be a bit fuzzy.

JANE HALL   What we really control is the process rather than the outcome, which can be unsettling for some clients. We really try and set up a strong infrastructure within which different things can happen. Which perhaps is unlike conventional practice, where everything is about the signature, about retaining control over the project at every stage.

EDITORS   I want to ask about Granby Four Streets in Liverpool, where you have brought empty buildings back into use as affordable housing, for which you were awarded the Turner Prize in 2015. It's now up and running and people have moved in, could you speak about what that project meant for you as a practice and how it has evolved?

JANE HALL   Granby was a quiet and humble project when it began. The local residents had entered into an innovative form of community land ownership – the Granby Four Streets Community Land Trust (CLT) – and invited us to renovate the existing buildings. When we started the process, we felt like there was a big trick missing because, due to the lack of funding, the final outcome, which was quite stripped back was not going to reflect the amazing conversations we were having with these incredible people who had the determination and self-initiative to set this in motion. We started the so-called 'enrichment program', where we made products such as mantle pieces and door handles together to enrich these buildings, and make the new homes special rather than just subscribing to the agenda of large scale construction companies.

When we won the Turner Prize we saw it as an opportunity for both ourselves and the CLT. Rather than exhibiting the houses – which wasn't possible as they didn't even exist at that point, but also felt inappropriate – we used the money to launch Granby Workshop: an entirely new business in Liverpool making ceramics, and to develop the products which we then exhibited in the gallery. That was a quite nice operation and in the meantime the housing projects continued within the remit of the CLT and the local community who have now become expert fundraisers. They have pioneered new funding models, which we tendered for and have just won a portfolio of eight new buildings, meaning that the original project has now turned into an incremental master plan.

EDITORS   Finally, what's next for Assemble? Where do you want to take it?

JANE HALL   Several people are interested in spatial design and materiality. Some in construction and delivery and others, like me, live in this installation and research world. But we realised that getting large scale built projects is much harder to do within a self-initiated alternative model. You have to take part in the tendering process, there are overheads, there is insurance, etc. As a result three people are getting registered as architects now and one of us has already qualified. This is all necessary to get bigger projects, especially cultural buildings, like the one we have recently been shortlisted for in Brussels.

Competitions are labour intensive though, and can be quite disheartening because you don't expect to win that many. On the other hand we are aware that, perhaps, if we put that same amount of effort into self-initiating things, which we know we're really good at, maybe we could get the same types of projects. This is why we are exploring many different avenues.

> EDITORS   Are the requirements of tendering and competition processes, such as insurance and qualifications, likely to push you into a more conventional mode in terms of how you are structured?

JANE HALL   It is a bit like being a chameleon, in that the way you present yourself to someone doesn't need to reflect reality, which I'm sure is true for other practices too. We want to be able to appeal to different people who don't know us yet. Most of our work comes out of repeat clients, many of which had initially considered us for one particular job, then, after getting to know us, realised we weren't quite the right fit, but then offered us another project. This is why being able to communicate with different clients is crucial, but this doesn't necessarily mean our core process and values mutate. We are always very open about our values, which is perhaps why we are allowed a lot of agency in terms of challenging the brief, structuring the projects to support the way we want to work and negotiating our fees.

This said, as a business, we do need to scale up in order to sustain 20 people in their mid thirties into the future. Some people now have children, and have moved out of London, which is not a coincidence and, in a way, one of the biggest threats to our practice. It is really hard not to compare yourself to other people working in more conventional settings. While we might enjoy much more flexibility, agency and independence, they often work on big projects, they earn more money and have a mortgage. So these are all aspects to consider when we think about how we can grow as a practice so that it remains not just a great place to design architecture but a financial and social infrastructure that supports us all.

1   See Joe Halligan, presentation at Here London conference, 10 June 2016, www.youtube.com/watch?v=2_yyAys58AY

SAY IT LOUD

PASCALE SABLAN

Until the architecture profession is more diverse, it can never represent the public it claims to work for. It is this which motivates Pascale Sablan, the 315th living African-American female registered architect in the US. Sablan is the founder of Beyond the Built Environment, an agency which provides a platform to support and encourage wider participation and representation within architecture, and curator of the Say it Loud exhibitions, which champions women and diverse designers. By holding up new role models, Sablan's work as an activist and architect seeks to redefine who we consider to be 'great'.

The role of architects in community life today is largely irrelevant, as the profession has historically been, and continues to be, an exclusive resource serving primarily wealthy patrons. Such exclusivity fosters and perpetuates great inequity in the built environment – inequities that more adversely affect communities of colour. In 1968, activist Whitney Young sharply rebuked the profession by stating 'You are not a profession that has distinguished itself by your social and civic contributions to the cause of civil rights... You are most distinguished by your thunderous silence and your complete irrelevance'. The belief is that strong and healthy communities, rich in diversity make strong nations. As architects, we have the power to represent more than ourselves and representation is essential to achieving equitable diversity.

Beyond the Built Environment, the organisation I founded, uniquely addresses these inequalities in architecture by providing a platform aimed at supporting the various stages of a career in architecture. We promote agency among diverse audiences and advocate for equity in the built environment with a method I termed 'the triple E, C'. The triple E, C method is a strategy to: Engage, Elevate, Educate, and Collaborate. We engage diverse audiences through promoting intellectual discourse and exchange to better achieve a just and equitable built environment. We elevate the identities and contributions of minority architects and designers through exhibitions, curated lectures, and documentaries that testify to the provided value of their built work and its spatial impact. We educate the masses through formal and informal learning opportunities that introduce architecture as a bridge to fill the gaps of inequity. We collaborate with community stakeholders and organisations to crowdsource information and amplify opportunities to advocate for equitable and reflectively diverse environments.

The Say it Loud initiative is an international exhibition that features projects by women and diverse design professionals, as well as quotes and video interviews on their experiences in the architecture and design professions. The concept of this exhibit is 'To see our faces, hear our voices, and feel our impact within the colourful tapestry of our heritage.' Say it Loud is the activation of a national movement of sharing, protecting and celebrating the journey of the underrepresented to inspire the next generation. Say it Loud engages diverse audiences through programming organised at the time of exhibition to elevate the identities and contributions of women and diverse designers with curated lectures, and documentaries that testify to the provided value of their built work and its spatial impact. To date, our Say it Loud exhibitions have been viewed by an estimated total of 35,000 visitors since January 2017 and have elevated over 220 designers.

Say it Loud was presented at various venues across the US, including the American Institute of Architects (AIA) National Convention, and in London at the Royal Institute of British Architects. In each case, the exhibition highlighted local women and diverse designers, transforming it into an international movement of sharing, protecting and celebrating the journey of the underrepresented to inspire the next generation.

We are typically invited by local community organisations or stakeholders to host an exhibition and supporting programming to help raise the visibility of the women and diverse designers of their community. We then launch a Say it Loud webpage that is distributed to their local design community. This web portal gathers all necessary documents, ensures quality and complete submissions for review.

The submissions include headshots, bios, a featured project and supporting images, as well as testimonials that all speak to the designers' personal experience in the profession. The submissions are then evaluated and the exhibition is curated. To communicate their experience as a diverse designer, we also capture video testimonials of their experience and journey in the profession. Once the exhibition is designed and installed the venue and collaborating organisation work on various related programming to engage the community frequently and creatively engaging with all age groups.

My personal experience, and that of others I have encountered throughout my career, showed me that the contributions of women and diverse designers are rarely taught in our education system. By raising their value to our world and profession we can create a beacon for future designers to be encouraged to join the profession and be demographically reflective of the community we serve.

The invisibility of women and diverse designers in architecture is further reinforced by the most common sources of information. An online search for 'great architects' returns a long list of men going back to Michelangelo, reinforcing the misconception that women and diverse designers have not made a significant contribution to this profession. On asking a search engine why this was, Beyond the Built Environment were told that not enough content is created that describes women and diverse designers as 'great'. In an attempt to address this issue, we created the Great Diverse Designers Library.

The Great Diverse Designers Library serves as a database to continue to elevate the contributions of those featured in the Say it Loud exhibitions. By calling them 'great', it addresses the challenges the search engine identified. The featured designers from each exhibition are added to the library, which now has over 225 profiles, making it a powerful resource for education and publication. We have the ultimate goal of publishing a Great Diverse Designers textbook, to diversify the heroic figures we are taught and celebrate.

In 2018, we were invited to exhibit at the United Nations (UN) in New York, a tremendous opportunity for exposure, spreading the call to action to the leaders of our world. The UN generously offered to transform this exhibition into a series of posters, translated into eight languages (English, French, Spanish, Portuguese, Chinese, Russian, Arabic, and Kiswahili), and distributed to their information centres worldwide. 25 March 2019 was Say it Loud Day at the UN Information Centres, where schools were invited to visit and experience the exhibition.

BUILDING DIVERSITY

ELSIE OWUSU on BARONESS LAWRENCE

The city is shared by all of us, and yet those who design it are overwhelmingly white and male, not representative of the public at large. The Stephen Lawrence Charitable Trust was established to support young people from disadvantaged backgrounds to succeed in their careers. It was founded by Baroness Lawrence in memory of her son, Stephen, a promising young architecture student who was murdered in 1993. Here, Elsie Owusu OBE, a Ghanaian-born British architect and activist, discusses Baroness Lawrence's impact on her own work, and on that of the wider architectural profession in the UK.

Baroness Doreen Lawrence of Clarendon OBE is one of 44 Black, Asian and Minority Ethnic (BAME) members of the British House of Lords. The remaining 756 are white and predominantly male. She is the founder of the Stephen Lawrence Charitable Trust (SLCT) and the Chancellor of De Montfort University Leicester, where the Stephen Lawrence Research Centre (SLRC) was launched in 2019. Both the Trust and the Centre were named after her son, who was murdered in an unprovoked racist attack while waiting for a bus on the evening of 22 April 1993.

Stephen was an aspiring architect, showing exceptional talent in early sketches and detailed architectural designs. After his murder five white male suspects were arrested, but not convicted. With the support of her husband Neville and their family, Baroness Lawrence challenged structural racism within the UK and made the British police, courts and legal systems more accountable towards members of minority communities.[1] Although Stephen's architectural potential was never realised, in standing up for her son against the British establishment, Baroness Lawrence also created a legacy which challenged the lack of diversity within the architectural profession. Her charities have supported many BAME and minority students through their studies, providing the means through which many young people from diverse family backgrounds entered architectural education and practice.

Through her persistent and dignified campaign and her work setting up both the SLCT and the SLRC, Baroness Lawrence has had more influence over architecture in the UK than many architects. From an iconic building in Lewisham designed by architect Sir David Adjaye, the SLCT has focused on training since its foundation in 2008. With 120 alumni and 300 partners in the construction industry, it has aided over 300 young people and awarded more than 130 bursaries, many of which have supported aspiring BAME architects. The SLRC on the other hand, aims to drive forward conversations about ethnicity and social justice: by asking new questions, debating critical issues around institutionalised racism, denials of justice and the psychology of racial violence, raising awareness to bring about positive change.

BARONESS LAWRENCE PROVIDED THE MEANS THROUGH WHICH YOUNG PEOPLE FROM DIVERSE BACKGROUNDS COULD ENTER ARCHITECTURE.

When Stephen was murdered I was acting as the first chair of the Society of Black Architects and I was hugely inspired by Baroness Lawrence's work. In 2017, she supported the RIBA+25 campaign[2] that resulted in nine, new BAME members elected as trustees of the Royal Institute of British Architects (RIBA) and which has made an enormous difference to the institution and the profession.

In 2018, Baroness Lawrence also backed Architecture: Incubator Project. An initiative aimed at boosting the number of successful BAME practices in the UK, focusing on the business and practice of architecture. This complements the work carried out by the SLCT and the SLRC in the field of education and public discourse respectively. The Architecture: Incubator is a self help group networking and campaigning to offer practical support and business advice. One of our main campaigns is for change in procurement policy. The current procurement system follows a purely commercial model that appears to favour quantity over quality. In the face of the current housing crisis, a few selected practices with a substantial track record of delivering 'housing units' – rather than homes – are being assigned millions of pounds worth of design work. Scant consideration is given to awareness of the differing cultural needs of those who will occupy those 'units'. Over half of the occupants are female and many are from a very diverse range of cultural backgrounds. Yet the people who will be designing their homes, without community consultation, are mostly men, of a certain age, class and ethnic origin.

If we look at the current professional landscape in the UK, we will see that fewer than one in five architects is a woman; only six percent come from a BAME background, though the BAME population in the UK is estimated to be over 13 percent. The current professional landscape of architecture is unrepresentative of the population and the procurement system, with its lack of attention to the needs of the ultimate resident, only perpetuates the status quo.

The homes we live in, the buildings we make and the public spaces we plan are used by all, so everyone should have a say in how we design them. We need a major shift in architectural practice and procurement of a similar scale to that which the Lawrence campaign pioneered within architectural education. With Baroness Lawrence's support Architecture: Incubator aims to achieve this cultural change, advocating for the primacy of the person, family and community in the lived experience and design of architecture.

1   The Lawrence family campaign for justice led to an independent enquiry and subsequent Macpherson report, which has been described by the BBC as 'one of the most important moments in the modern history of criminal justice in Britain'. Subsequently, fresh forensic analysis secured the arrest and conviction of two white men for Stephen's murder. The police leveled serious criticism for professional incompetence while other actions were considered indicative of underlying racism within the police force.

2   Baroness Lawrence was one of the most significant figures, but the RIBA+25 campaign was also supported by many leading British architects, including Richard Rogers, David Adjaye and Alison Brooks amongst the others.

DECONSTRUCTION

ROTOR

CASE STUDY

After conducting a thorough survey, Rotor carefully dismantled the ceramic floor tiles of the Institut de Génie Civil in Liège, in an effort to preserve and reuse the building's original art-deco features ahead of its refurbishment.

Architects like to pretend they are building legacies, monuments that will outlast them, standing as a testament to their ideas. In reality, architecture is but waste in transit,[1] existing in its intended form for only a brief time, before being demolished and disposed of. Rotor, a cooperative design practice based in Brussels, realised that in order to address the climate crisis, they needed to confront architecture's troubling relationship to waste. To do so they created a new kind of architectural practice, one focused on deconstructing and repurposing materials, with outputs ranging from design, research, exhibitions, books, pedagogy, economic models and policy proposals. Here, we look at how their approach is realised across these different fields.

Today, in north west Europe, only one percent of building elements are reused following their first application. Although a large number of elements are technically reusable, they end up being recycled by crushing or melting, or disposed of. The result is a high environmental impact and a net loss of economic value.

The reasons for this are many: the cost of the work-force – you need ten people to dismantle a building and only one person and a truck to demolish it; the time it takes – costing building owners in lost rent while work takes place; a lack of tools or skills for deconstruction; the architect's specification, which determines building products years in advance, unable to incorporate materials salvaged in the interim; and, finally, the question of product certification of used products – who assesses the product's suitability, and who takes the risk?

Rotor has sought to address these issues in a number of ways. We have expressed our views through publications, exhibitions and conferences; we have been involved in the drafting of political plans and strategies; and we have sought to apply salvaged materials ourselves in our design projects, many of which are interventions in existing architectures. We also oversee the dismantling of building components in buildings slated for demolition or thorough revamp. These dismantlings and the associated conditioning and reselling activities of reclaimed elements are conducted under the heading of our associated company, Rotor Deconstruction.

We are also seeking to embed this way of thinking about material flows in the minds of emerging practitioners. Since 2017 we have been teaching studios at TU Delft, Columbia University, the Architectural Association and the Royal College of Art, in an effort to make the reuse of material a more efficient and transparent practice and, ultimately, the preferred option for the architecture and building industry.

Finally, over the past ten years, we have worked to give greater visibility to the thousands of small enterprises specialised in the reclamation and supply of recovered building elements, to integrate them into the building sector. To this end, we have created the online directory opalis.eu, as a way to bridge the gap between these existing traders and the commissioners, building contractors and architects who can specify these materials. To bring these efforts even further, we recently started a new project – titled FCRBE – which, relying on an international network of organisations, trade associations, research centres and architecture schools, aims to double the amount of reclaimed building elements being circulated across north west Europe by 2032.

1   Peter Guthrie, cited by Jeremy Till
    in *Architecture Depends* (2009), p.67

With students from the Architectural Association, Rotor surveyed reclamation specialists in the UK and collected samples in an effort to give these operators greater visibility within the construction industry.

UNDERGROUND ARCHITECTURE

CHIP LORD and CURTIS SCHREIER of ANT FARM
in conversation with AMALE ANDRAOS and
DAN WOOD of WORKAC

With inflatable domes, floating structures,
land art and explosive media performances,
the countercultural art and architecture group
Ant Farm, pioneered a new form of experimental practice. In this conversation between
generations, Amale Andraos and Dan Wood
of WORKac speak with founding members
Chip Lord and Curtis Schreier about Ant
Farm's origins, influences, and how their
radical environmentalism could offer paths
forward out of today's climate crisis.

AMALE ANDRAOS   When you started Ant Farm
in the late 1960s, who did you consider to be your
peers, your influences, or the people who you were
reacting against?

CHIP LORD   We were trained as architects. Curtis graduated
in 1967, and I graduated in 1968. The cultural and political
world that we graduated into, beginning with the civil rights
movement, and then the anti-war movement, and then the
student movement, created a sense that there was revolution
in the air. For that reason, and the rise of the counterculture
alongside these political movements, nobody in my graduating
class wanted to go to work in a large corporate architecture
firm. We formed an alternative.
      We described to a friend what we were doing as an
'underground architectural practice'. And she immediately said,
'like the Ant Farm toy that I had as a kid.' So we instantly had a
name. The context was this countercultural community. In San
Francisco at that time, the city was pulling in people because
of Haight-Ashbury and the Summer of Love. There was a sense
of a utopian idea of a new, unique community being formed.

AMALE ANDRAOS   It seemed like a moment where
you could imagine dropping out of society, grouping
around new things and completely starting afresh.
And yet I think you also spoke about the influence of
Robert Venturi, who was already breaking away from
dogma, Modernism, and Brutalism, and bringing a
dimension to architecture that situated it closer to art.

CHIP LORD   Yes, I'd say Venturi and Buckminster Fuller were
two of our main influences. I'll let Curtis talk about Bucky,
but I had read Venturi's book *Complexity and Contradiction
in Architecture* in 1966. When we graduated we wanted to
renounce the dogma of Modernism and in a sense Venturi had
written a guide to that, or a map of how to do that. It really
seemed like a radical polemic. At the same time, he was a kind
of artist – a stylist or a designer. He would probably hate that
term, 'stylist', but there was a sense of 'the artist at work,'

as well as this elaborate theoretical basis for it. Taking on the monolith of Modernism required having that theoretical argument, probably. It's kind of odd to think that Ant Farm comes out of Venturi, but Doug Michels did study with him at Yale, and really respected him a lot.

NOBODY IN MY GRADUATING CLASS WANTED TO GO TO WORK IN A LARGE CORPORATE ARCHITECTURE FIRM.

DAN WOOD   What was Buckminster Fuller's influence?

CURTIS SCHREIER   Fuller would breeze through the Generalists HQ in San Francisco a, well, highly generalised architecture and planning office. Dr Gerald M Feigen, a principal of the firm and a founder of *Ramparts Magazine* invited me to attend a discussion with him and Fuller following their tour of the South Pafacific Islands. I remember the subject of dolphins came up, about extra-human intelligence, and his idea was to essentially start the dialogue by playing back the sounds of human infants to the dolphins. Unfortunately it didn't go much further than that. But Fuller is interesting because you can't really fit him into any of the movements, because he tends to squirrel out of them. We didn't know whether he was an architect or an engineer, and suddenly his foundation said he was dropping out of the design world and looking for a way to categorise the world's resources. I saw this and got on to this – I was looking to categorise the nation's resources and did a model of the US Federal Government for Washington DC as a thesis project in my senior year and almost didn't graduate because half the teachers said that wasn't architecture. It was outside the realm of architecture.

> DAN WOOD   There is that theme of 'not art, not architecture' that resonates with Fuller and with Venturi at the beginning, where there were books, there was research, there were projects that were more theoretical or projects that didn't look like other projects. I think that later they became more conventional architects, but there was a moment when I think it wasn't clear.

> AMALE ANDRAOS   With Ant Farm it is very clear that you're coming from these two extremes. There is the environmental dimension with Fuller, and then there is the representational dimension that Venturi was really into. The projects are communicating an idea about a new relationship to the environment rather than just performing on the technological level. So these two things get really hybridised, right?

CURTIS SCHREIER   Before Venturi, no one actually laid out on the architectural table the fact that the sign that was holding the giant cupcake was as important as the building behind it. Venturi was essentially one of the first ones who systematised thinking about that.

> AMALE ANDRAOS   I think both thinkers and architects have a sort of populist dimension. With Venturi, and then with Denise Scott Brown, if you think of their book *Learning from Las Vegas*, it's really questioning the canon. They look at the non-architecture, the non-art, and see something to learn from it. Ant Farm's work also has this immediate communication to a large audience, rejecting ideas of what is canonical, by looking for ideas from outside of architecture.

> DAN WOOD   This idea that not everything can be done through architecture is something that resonates

with us as well. At WORKac, we have taken that to mean collaboration with a wider set of professions and experiences of the world, rather than, the art world, for instance.

CURTIS SCHREIER   Yes, this is evaluated off and on and in cycles. Lloyd Kahn, following Fuller's example, systematised the idea of building geodesic domes for the masses. There's an entire world of people that have made shelters for centuries and some of the principles are as valid as anything that we could come up with in the technological world, we just haven't been able to look at them. So we go back to architecture from non-architects, bring them into the limelight. Everything else that we see, everything that we know about architecture is re-cast in that light.

DAN WOOD   Yes, I think that geodesic domes represent the only time that the avant-garde of architecture, the crazier ideas, really caught on with the general public. Nobody knows what an axonometric is, but probably everybody knows what a geodesic is.

CHIP LORD   Another key influence for us is Pop Art. Andy Warhol was an influence simply because he crossed disciplines and became a filmmaker. That also was a model of how easily you could cross into another discipline, as well as the idea of the performance. The press conference is a kind of performance, a presentation, but we wanted to highlight it as performance art on some occasions. The final output, you could say, of Convention City was a press conference and it was published in the local paper as if it was a real development project, which it was far from. There was no developer involved.

DAN WOOD   It's such a typical thing we do as architects in the professional world, but one that no one had ever made conceptual before. There are a lot of constraints that we have to work with to create exciting architecture, but no architect would think of extending that to press conferences.

CHIP LORD   Doug Michels would always put his suit and tie on for the press conference.

> AMALE ANDRAOS   If you look at every action that constitutes architectural or art practice, and at every moment you try to turn that action on its head, it really becomes interesting. These performances create a context for the work, a kind of discourse around the work. Your ultimate goal was to get something published, and you were very concerned about the audience. What I love is that with very few acts of architecture – whether they were press conferences, a drawing, or a building – you maximised broadcast. It was very powerful.

CHIP LORD   And it begins with the titles: House of the Century, Convention City. Titles are so important because it is the first idea through which the viewer, the audience, enters the project. That was inherent to the process. It has to have a good title. House of the Century, that title was given in a very sarcastic way. It was grandiose but also ironic, because it was a modest project really, at the beginning in 1972.

> AMALE ANDRAOS   It's about scale at different levels; the scale of things then and the scale of things now. The House of the Century has this sense of compression and intelligence in terms of the program, removing walls wherever necessary. And it has a verticality in terms of the site: it's very compressed and the footprint is minimal. Ant Farm's Convention City in our book *49 Cities* is the smallest of the cities. It boils the city down to its essence, to the political arena of the Greek democracy.

CURTIS SCHREIER   10,000 people, right, that was the Greek ideal?

> AMALE ANDRAOS   Thinking about scale across time, it is really interesting how bloated everything has

become now, in the age of the iPhone. Architecture is so bloated when everything else is miniaturised.

CURTIS SCHREIER   Your iPhone replaces secretaries, butlers, all kinds of people. Imagine how big your house would be if you had to house all your servants on your property. You'd end up with a monastery of slaves.

AMALE ANDRAOS   But now people are ending up with monasteries whether they have butlers or not. It's just a scaling up of everything.

CHIP LORD   Another interesting link back to the 1970s is EF Schumacher's book *Small is Beautiful*, which I first saw in the *Whole Earth Catalogue*. That idea that small is beautiful was a radical idea. And now, again, it's obviously a prime example of a radical idea for the age of climate change.

AMALE ANDRAOS   The common language that you enlisted was not only inspired by certain references but was also anti-Brutalist and anti-Modernist, right? Do you want to talk a little about that?

CHIP LORD   Yeah, the first architectural experiments we did in actuality – not on paper – used a parachute as a simple form of architecture. Just tie it down and all it was good for was shade, but as a symbolic opposite of Brutalism, it couldn't have been a better choice. We never talked theoretically about opposing Brutalism, per se, but going from a parachute to an inflatable, which is also lightweight, malleable, transportable – all these qualities were opposites of Brutalism. Even the ant farm toy itself, of course – the ants are building these organic underground spaces that are more beautiful than the rural barnyard scene and the nineteenth century image of the farm included at the top of the toy. So the ants are in opposition to what was above ground. And then, of course, the automobile – growing up in the 1950s, it was all about the fantasy of the dream car. Dream cars were designed objects, sculpture. All of these things, then, went into the House of the Century,

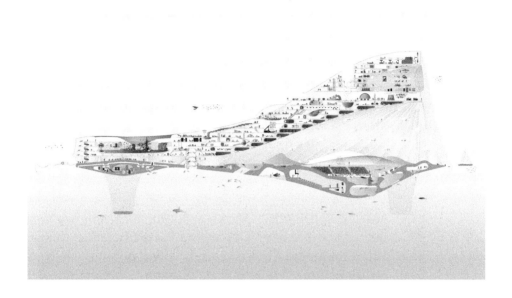

Section and detail of 3-C City, a collaboration between Ant Farm and WORKac for a floating city which aims to 'facilitate inter-species dialogue'.

in a way: taking the inflatable and hardening it, the shape of the fender and the front of the 1939 Cord, or any of the dream cars from the 1950s.

CURTIS SCHREIER   Here's the nasty thing about Brutalism, though: the thing that makes Brutalism and all of those chunky concrete buildings work is the joint that's filled with that butyl membrane, a plastic thing that is close to the film that we used in the inflatables. In other words, if you pull all of the joints out of Paul Rudolph's Art and Architecture building at Yale and spread it all out, you could make a decent-sized bubble and have your art classes inside the membrane.

> AMALE ANDRAOS   That's beautiful, a completely radical compression and an economy of means; thinking of the behind-the-scenes, unloved goo that keeps buildings together, and turning that into architecture.

CURTIS SCHREIER   Actually in the page for the *Inflatocookbook* book, it described the inflatables as the vapor barrier, the paint membrane, the roof membrane, held up by the air conditioning system. Just get rid of all of the other construction elements, you know?

THE SELF AS A DESIGN SUBJECT

JACK SELF

A career path tends to acquire a logic and purpose only in hindsight, as the accumulation of a series of chances and opportunities, taken or passed. But how might one set out to deliberately shape their career? In this personal and honest narrative, emerging architect and writer Jack Self offers an explicitly self-conscious approach to making an impact in the architectural field, by looking beyond the private practice, to embrace publishing, curating, consulting and housing development.

All autobiographical accounts are necessarily works of fiction. Any attempt to explain a life in coherent, narrative terms involves such incredible selective editing that it will at best only partially resemble reality. When we make decisions in life the outcomes and consequences are impossible to predict. Often, even the importance of the decision itself is obscure. If our lives have any meaning at all it is only constructed after the fact. This is what makes autobiographies fantasies. They are also unrepeatable and at best can only speak to themselves.

I was keen to get that disclaimer out of the way early on, otherwise I fear we might be speaking at cross purposes. I reserve the right to alter the following myth, as future needs may require.

I was born in London in 1987 and lived in the UK and Ireland until I was seven. My family then moved to rural Australia, where I remained for more than ten years. I did not integrate with Australian society. As a teenager, I was reclusive and distant. I spent a lot of time watching foreign films and reading alone; some fiction, but mostly classical works (my preference was for Greek philosophers and Roman poets). I was driven by an almost Victorian compulsion to progress and self-improvement. In another age, this could easily have become zealous faith; however after a brief attempt to find God, I knew by 17 that I would be forever godless.

I chose architecture because it was a profession (I don't come from a wealthy family so earning potential was important), and I didn't get the marks for law. I studied three years at the University of New South Wales, where I was an average, unremarkable student. I finished my last semester with the architect Glenn Murcutt. I felt claustrophobic in Sydney. Glenn referred me to Jean Nouvel in Paris. I worked there for almost two years, from 2007 to early 2009. I learnt French fluently, grew my hair long and abandoned the Anglo-Saxon worldview. I came to London to work on Nouvel's One New Change project, but the Irish developer went bust shortly after I arrived, and I lost my job.

At that time, I was living in social housing in Battersea with my elder brother. I was unemployed and surviving on £75 per week. The bus was a luxury. Our flat was on the eighth floor, with paper thin slabs (the neighbours above frequently fought and then watched loud porn) and paper thin external walls (in winter it could get to -1°C indoors). I couldn't afford a bed or a mattress, so I slept on a thin 'overnight guest' futon from Habitat. Unemployment amongst architects in London was high. I eventually managed to find work with a publishing house on Fleet Street, mostly editing and typesetting university textbooks and ebooks. This required me to learn HTML and Java. I was sliding into depression. To combat this, I started a blog called Millennium People. I already owned a laptop so it was the one thing I could do for free. I set myself the goal of writing 500 words per day. Through the blog I met Liam Young, who was teaching at the Architectural Association. He encouraged me to return to university.

I applied to the Architectural Association, because it was the cheapest school for an international student. I was ignorant of its reputation or history. Although I am a British citizen, I was not resident in the UK for three years before my studies, so received no state loans or support. My mother didn't have any money, and my father didn't want to lend me any; so my uncle and aunt kindly fronted my tuition for a year. The precise conditions of this debt subsequently became the source of a deep and ongoing family feud. My uncle and father haven't spoken since the sub-prime lending crisis. The Architectural Association was unimpressed with my work. They could not offer me a place for fourth year. At best, they could offer me a place in second year (thus repeating two years). I accepted the downgrade gratefully and went back to school. This takes us to the end of 2010.

Then I got serious about my future. I took out a pad of paper and started designing myself. The year 2011 marks the beginning of my first ten year plan (as well as my proper arrival in adulthood, I was 24). If I am lucky, I will get four or five plan periods in total. The reason for dividing my life into decades in this way, each focussed on particular outcomes, was a recognition that the individual life is insignificant and brief. It can thus be thought of as a project in itself. To fully embrace such a concept requires extreme abstraction of the self and relinquishment of the ego. In other words, I understand Jack Self as a kind of fictional construct, a persona that can be deployed in service of my agenda. My actual being, a deeply private natural person, is untouched by the fate of Jack Self: in my core, I am neither affected by his professional successes nor his failures.

I UNDERSTAND JACK SELF AS A KIND OF FICTIONAL CONSTRUCT, A PERSONA THAT CAN BE DEPLOYED IN SERVICE OF MY AGENDA.

So what did I decide to do with Jack Self? The first plan was based on two sub-sets: first, spend five years finding out what the scope of the life project is, catalogue your resources and abilities, and develop a strategic brief. Second, spend five years making at least one material example of what you have in mind. So I started a weekly sheet at the Architectural Association called Fulcrum. I used it to engage with architects I admired, in order to learn from their biographies and expose myself to their ideas. It became a popular student publication and ran for 100 issues.

Having lost my bursary at the Architectural Association, after third year, I had to take a year out to earn money. I got involved with the Occupy LSX movement. I did a masters in philosophy and macroeconomics, writing my thesis on the morality of neoliberal economic theory.

I became a feminist and a socialist, then just as quickly backed away from all labels (I have a deep dislike of groups). I started writing for the *Architectural Review*, parlaying my blog experience into the architectural press. I started pitching my various services to mid-size legal firms in regional capitals (Exeter, Bath, Reading, Liverpool) offering to redesign their logos, business cards, websites, and write all the text for their promotional material. As long as I got twelve of these gigs a year, and wrote at least 30,000 words of journalism, I could make enough money to stay at the Architectural Association. I became addicted to pseudoephedrine as I struggled to work 16-hours a day, seven days a week. To quit, I took up smoking.

When I returned to fourth year, I was intensely angry at society for forcing me into such a precarious state of being. This is when I decided that my life should be dedicated to the design and construction of the home. I believe that executing large volumes of low-cost, high-quality housing that promotes freedom and equality within the family is the greatest social good possible as an architect. The outcome of this realisation was a project called 'The Ingot', which proposed a new financial mechanism to deliver a new type of dwelling. I immediately planned to do a series of ten annual projects, each intended to teach me how to get closer to my ultimate goal.

I graduated from the Architectural Association. I spent one year lecturing widely and writing frenetically, realising that my future success would be built on establishing a public reputation. I understood the power of print to shortcut traditional practice. In the years 2011-2019 I wrote half a million words, with a quarter million published. With Shumi Bose and Finn Williams, I applied to curate the British Pavilion at the 15th Venice Architecture Biennale, knowing that the democratic selection process would give us a one in 12 chance of winning – if the idea was good. I honestly believe that we won because of the conviction with which we answered the jury's final question. The power of confidence is its ability to leverage action. This was the first moment I stopped feeling angry about my position and started to reflect on the essence of my privilege.

Certainly, as a middle-class, white, well-educated, heterosexual, cis male (amongst other things), I have a lot of

OPPOSITE   Pairing bold statements with oblique imagery, Self asks how architecture may address larger questions of climate and society.

underserved advantages. Privilege is never justified. Rather than deny this condition, for me there is an ongoing question of how to address it, assume its responsibilities, and ultimately deconstruct it. There is, however, one unique type of privilege that I have purposefully cultivated myself, and that is being able to speak well and explain myself clearly. I worked at this skill very hard. The result is what I would call 'the violence of eloquence'. It is an interpersonal and political act of dominance by obscure means. Control of language and its rules allows an individual to rise in society disproportionately quickly, while subjugation to the language of others puts an individual at a structural disadvantage. This power dynamic is often overlooked in architectural education.

I researched practice models (legal and conceptual, as with partnerships, limited companies, sole traders, as well as offices, ateliers, bureaus, studios, etc). When I decided to launch my own architectural firm, I already knew that no existing model of practice would accommodate my ambitions. I wanted to do three things: redesign the social role of the architect along more ethical lines; shift the discourse in architecture towards materialist analyses of everyday life; and design new models of housing based on power equality and alternative economic realities than late capitalism. I therefore pursued this by doing three things. First, I created an architectural firm with the governance structure of a foundation. This obliges us to only take on projects that promote democracy, inclusivity and equalities of many kinds (amongst them, but not limited to, race, wealth, class, gender and space). It is called the Real Estate Architecture Laboratory (Foundation), or the REAL foundation or just REAL for short. As soon as I could, I registered as an architect. Second, I pursued cultural projects, like book publishing and exhibition design. I only wanted to do

There is very little time remaining
for architecture or revolution.

Take a moment to reconsider
your role in the world.

projects where I would be substantially or totally in control, otherwise the compromise would blunt their efficacy. I also launched *Real Review*, our contemporary culture magazine dedicated to 'what it means to live today'. I realised that my own media platform would better serve my ideological agenda. Thirdly, I started researching how to execute housing in the UK, designing and refining my business model and typology.

The first five years was thus 2011-2016. By then, I had already defined what I wanted to do with my life, and began to put the structures in place needed to realise examples: I had published *Real Estates: Life Without Debt* and curated the British Pavilion at the Venice Architecture Biennale. I still feel these projects accurately define my agenda. I had also successfully kickstarted *Real Review*, and was working on bringing it to financial stability. I had effectively founded my own publishing house, and other book projects like *Symbolic Exchange* (2016), *Mies in London* (2018) and *Utopian Communes in the New World* (2019) would follow. Finally, I was exploring a partnership with a developer to realise the low-cost housing I described.

In the five years 2016-2020, which will mark the end of my first decade-long plan, I have tried as best I can to push each of these three aspects along equally. REAL has continued to publish, exhibit, curate, and (crucially) consult (that's how we pay our bills). The studio has expanded and contracted in size, largely because we pay people well and don't ask them to do overtime and that puts us fundamentally at odds with the world of architecture.

I did eventually find a developer prepared to work with me on the housing aspect, but after negotiating to purchase land from Transport for London and/or the Greater London Authority, they pulled out and the deal fell through. This was June 2019. I was extremely disappointed, because it seemed to me that finally I would realise housing of the kind I have dreamed, as well as have a built work to point to as an example. Consequently, I am now in the process of starting my own housing company. It would give me a lot of satisfaction to found it before the end of 2020.

The career itself is a project that can be designed; the self is a subject of design.

THE ARCHITECT-DEVELOPER

ROGER ZOGOLOVITCH

Architects have long considered the business side of the profession to be a contamination of the goals of design, even taking 'befuddled pride in our business ignorance', as Peggy Deamer writes in this volume. But architect-turned-developer Roger Zogolovitch shows that business and design are not at odds, indeed together they can act as powerful tools for making great buildings. Here, Zogolovitch discusses his journey through architecture, and reflects on where the real agency lies in shaping the city, describing a new model of practice he terms the 'architect-developer'.

169

STARTING OUT   In my early twenties, while still a student at the Architectural Association, I was working on a couple of shops in South Molton Street, Mayfair. It was the late 1960s and fashion boutiques were all the rage. All of the street's properties were owned by the City Corporation, and as part of our remodelling, we needed consent from their surveyor. I nervously made my way to the Guildhall in a vintage shirt, tieless, and without a stiff collar, while the surveyor sat behind his desk dressed in a black jacket, striped grey trousers and a plain tie. A surprisingly positive meeting later, and he'd agreed to the alterations.

With a common ground having now been established, I made the unsolicited suggestion that it might be financially beneficial to the City Corporation as landlords if South Molton Street were to become pedestrianised. The room went cold and the City Surveyor looked as if he was about to choke before terminating our meeting. As he sent me on my way it wasn't without firm admonishment, 'young man, you are an architectural student intent on a career in architecture, what do you or will you ever know about property values?' His expression, which I recall to this day, was one of utter disdain for the thought that someone such as I should have an opinion on value let alone a strategy for its enhancement.

Of course South Molton Street went on to become pedestrianised and later rose in value. While I found that when being right requires disruption of the status quo, it doesn't necessarily bring you friends. It did however give me an appetite for using my imagination as a path to value. This approach has proved to be my raison d'être.

On graduating in 1971, Nick Campbell, Rex Wilkinson, Piers Gough and myself set up in practice as CZWG.

Our big break came in 1976 with a chance commission; the refurbishment and remaking of an industrial warehouse into what were to be auction rooms, offices and houses in Bayswater, London. With this commission we mistakenly thought we had made it, but the phone stayed strangely silent. To survive we became dealmakers or, rather, I became the dealmaker. To win work I discovered the art of making work.

During the decade spanning 1976 to 1986, I endlessly sought new clients and commissions. This wasn't easy. As young London lads, we didn't belong to any golf clubs and, although early memberships to the Zanzibar and later Groucho clubs were always pleasurable, they were yet to provide a suitable alternative to the traditional circuits for winning work. I recall the days spent on the phone to estate agents. I had discovered the *Estates Gazette*; a weekly trade magazine and veritable cornucopia of opportunity. It appeared on newsstands on Saturday mornings and the process of devouring it cover to cover and assiduously marking all those plum opportunities quickly became ritual.

At that time London was still rich with lovely old warehouse buildings; solidly built with their appealing cast iron columns and industrial steel windows. What excited me was the challenge that transforming these structures into apartments and studios posed. To find work for the practice, I had taught myself the development appraisal methodology known colloquially as the 'stack-up'. I searched for buildings then prepared speculative designs for their remodelling and presented them to potential clients. I demonstrated the money to be made from the project rather than the architecture. Our reward was the architectural commission.

I remember we gave a Young Lions lecture at the Royal Institute of British Architects (RIBA) in the late 1970s. My contribution was a slide presentation based solely on numbers where I tried to convey to the audience the excitement and possibilities of working creatively with figures to persuade clients to proceed with projects. To put this into context, architecture and numbers were not customary bed-fellows at the time.

In 1987, Margaret Thatcher revised the planning use classes order, suddenly creating B1 that would permit light

OPPOSITE   Eight new homes and an office space in Bermondsey, London. Commissioned by Solidspace, designed by AHMM.

industrial, office and research uses all within the same class. This was a godsend for those of us struggling away, trying to defend or create studio use as part of the light industrial use category. We had stretched the function of studio offices to the very limits of the use class interpretation of 'making' activities. It was these wonderful old warehouses that had been the focus of our practice, and these new freedoms to change their use created a viability and an acceleration towards their wider revitalisation that would become standard in the decades that followed.

I was often asked in the early days of CZWG how we were so lucky to have clients that permitted us to make such exciting architecture. I would reply truthfully that our clients were not great patrons or particularly philanthropically minded but, simply, that they were motivated by financial returns. This was the language we understood, it was what we offered and delivered.

Looking back over my career, I can see that I had to hone the skills to understand the property market. It is clear now that, although we weren't able to charge a fee for the service, I was, in effect, acting as the development manager. It was a tipping point for me when I was able to move from taking briefs, to giving them. This was my pathway to becoming the client.

I have always reacted, sometimes a little hastily, when a negotiation or presentation denies added value. I try to make sure that every situation is exploited to its full. I have long been surprised that the profession of architecture doesn't teach these skills. As a young man, there may have been an element of arrogance involved, however, what I had discovered in myself was a natural aptitude and excitement for the entrepreneurial challenge. This was a creative response directly influenced by an education in architecture.

SOLIDSPACE I believe it was these earlier experiences that led me to change careers and move from architect to 'architect-developer' (an 'architect-developer' is a qualified architect first and a developer second and is therefore required to abide by the professional code). My development advice to clients proved to be sound and made them substantial profits which they didn't pay for. I decided that the time had come for me to take the plunge.

I DEMONSTRATED THE MONEY TO BE MADE FROM THE PROJECT RATHER THAN THE ARCHITECTURE. OUR REWARD WAS THE ARCHITECTURAL COMMISSION.

In 2003, I established Solidspace; an architect-developer focused on making high-quality homes on so-called 'gap sites', those small and awkward left-over plots of London. As I would stand on the pavement, looking and observing a site and its surroundings, I found myself instantly imagining the development's form in my head. That vision became an architectural proposition.

I recall a conversation with Ron Herron, my then tutor at the Architectural Association, where – in his inimitable gravelly drawl, while chewing gum and chain smoking his favourite 'Disque Bleu' French cigarettes – he offered a simple two word message: 'no compromise'. These words reverberated in me and I made a commitment. I decided I needed to make architecture where I could control every aspect.

I started with the practice of CZWG but realised after a decade that the role of the client was the key one. It seemed that only by being the client I could avoid unnecessary areas of compromise. The promise of development seemed so tantalising, and so exciting, that it had to be grabbed. Recently re-watching The Fountainhead movie with Gary Cooper as Howard Roark, that architectural rigour and that fight for independent thinking all came flooding back.

Being the client rather than the architect is like moving from centre to backstage. Your name isn't in lights, developers aren't credited with authorship. As the architect you are the creative, the architecture is yours. As developer you are responsible for a very wide role; the scrutiny and decision making for every piece of the project, the land, planning consent, ensuring the building meets market demand, leading your team of experts and driving the project forward despite all of its hurdles.

I thoroughly enjoy commissioning other architects, I enjoy this creative exchange. As a qualified architect myself, I can and do exchange drawings, sketches, act as muse, mentor and critic. It's all a collaborative practice that works to make the architecture better. I am of an age where Modernism still exerts a restraint and demands finesse. We remember that Mies Van der Rohe quote 'God is in the details'. The collaboration between myself and the selected architect helps both of us to check the other and generates in us discussion and a form of critique that I have found always improves the end result. We impose on each other a rigour that reinforces the design quality of the finished project.

Development for me is a work of architecture. I have used the expression 'development as art' to describe this as striving for perfection, or, in reality, the best we can achieve. That I chose to exploit this practice of architecture through the position of a developer was odd back in the 1980s, but has since become mainstream. My intention in all our projects is to use them as the means to experiment with typologies to test their future possibility as both a form and a manufacturing process.

Let's consider for a moment some simple truths: when an architect is commissioned to make a building it is expected that it will not leak. When a developer makes a project it is expected that it will make a profit. While both of these are truths, neither represent the ambitions of the architect or developer. For the architect they want to make a great building and for the developer to make a great development. We differ from other developers by treating this as a creative endeavour. This is not commonplace.

I would like to see the architectural profession establish a new field: 'architect-developer'. The advantage for their customers is that this would establish a new type of developer where bringing the combination of a professional code of conduct and skills would set a new level of competence and enable the public to build trust in development.

Our development at Weston Street was undertaken on a gap site in Southwark, London. We worked in collaboration with Simon Allford of AHMM for the development of eight units sitting over an office building. It was a long project, five years in the making, and a beautiful example of the end result to our approach. I would place this alongside our single house project called the Houseboat on a site as part of the garden of our house in Poole which was undertaken with Meredith Bowles of Mole Architects. Weston Street won a RIBA national award in 2019 and the Houseboat won both a RIBA national award and the Stephen Lawrence award in 2018. There is a consistency in the use of materials and finish that make the architecture and the experience both intriguing and uplifting.

They are a good demonstration of Solidspace's dedication to make housing using a particular section arranged around three interconnected spaces, each separated by a half level. This connects the social spaces of the home together. We call this eat, live and work. This arrangement creates a large double internal volume. It defines the distinctive architecture made from each apartment we build.

We build on gap sites left over from redundant buildings. They are the recycling of valuable land which we husband to intensify the opportunity for the creation of new homes. We appoint architects to act as collaborators with us as developers. We invite them to explore design responses to the site using our Solidspace 'design DNA'. All our developments are recognisable. The interior space and volume with double height windows all contribute to the feeling of wellbeing and generosity. We use materials that are simple and functional reminding us of those old warehouses that were so inspirational. I consider Solidspace homes as a portfolio of work, they are our contribution to a constant endeavour towards remaking the city. I demand that they should be a creative approach to the process of development and that they need to challenge the ordinary and demand reinvention of the status quo. We believe that we need to lead, experiment and drive forward a brand that delivers housing made for the way we live now.

As we question the intensity of development needed to provide new housing we also witness a breakdown in public trust for developers. As architects carry a wider level of public acceptance, our initiative of the 'architect-developer' could help improve this position. If we are to intensify our cities with new housing they need to be more acceptable, but also more beautiful. I believe that building the Solidspace typology on gap sites and abiding by the principles of brand and design could be the right approach.

CONCLUSION   When I was an architect, I wasn't in control of the development process or the projects I had authored. What is intriguing in nearly 40 years of continuous development activity is that my training as an architect has allowed me to adapt and apply an architectural thinking process to all the stages and elements of making a development. When you make this creative approach your guiding star, you inevitably make good projects.

My projects develop collaboratively with both the professional teams and execution teams alike. They all need leadership. This means allowing your teams to make their contributions, never forgetting that the project is conceived by you and the integrity of the project is policed by you, the project is driven forward by you and the enterprise, when complete, is your reward. As an 'architect-developer', there is no one to blame but yourself if things go wrong. For some this is too scary, but for others it is a liberation not to be missed. For me it is an enduring passion.

WHEN IS AN ARCHITECT NOT AN ARCHITECT?

HOLLY LEWIS, WE MADE THAT

The training of an architect is broad and deep, taking in research, strategy, communication, design, and much else. And yet the potential of these skills is limited, rarely applied beyond the task of making buildings. We Made That, co-founded by Holly Lewis and Oliver Goodhall, are one of the few practices to escape this limitation. By not focusing on buildings, they realised they were better able to serve the public good, by working with local authorities, charities and community groups, to help them achieve their varied aims. Here, Lewis reflects on the perception of her practice, asking, 'when is an architect not an architect?'

First things first, a current headcount of We Made That team members tells me that roughly 40 percent of us are qualified architects, and 80 percent have had some level of architectural training. To my mind, that makes us an architecture practice. However, we have a diverse portfolio that includes research, strategy and design, so I have – on occasion – had to justify that position. By way of example, a quote that has been levelled at us online:

> 'Very disappointing... This "firm" is a planning firm not an architecture firm.'

I have to admit that those quotation marks sting a little bit.

As a practice, We Made That is grounded in our interest in how our projects can serve the public good. Over the years we've built up a portfolio that focuses on working with local authorities across the country, as well as charities and community groups. If you're interested in the social and public impacts of your work as an architect – as we are – it seems essential to look beyond the bounds of any individual site. It is just this inclination – seeking to maximise positive social impact – that has led us to explore strategic and policy-level thinking and research through our work. The 'lack' of conventional built projects in our portfolio isn't because we *can't* build, or aren't mature enough yet, but because our curiosity sometimes leads us in other directions.

In recent years I've attended panel discussions with artists and graphic designers, brand consultants and tech innovators, academics and civil servants, all of whom happened to have started out as architects. What a fantastically diverse and interesting bunch, I hear you say! And yet for some reason, these are not celebratory events. Audience questions generally start with lamenting the retraction of the architects' role from the all-powerful master builder to the current state of loss of ground to project managers and Design and Build contracts, and descend from there. Amongst this wider sense of impending doom amongst the profession, the implication seems to be that to move away from 'pure' architectural practice is somehow to have failed, to have conceded defeat. Sometimes it feels that people think we're just waiting until the 'real' work of building stuff can start.

Developing We Made That's expanded portfolio of projects hasn't been an accident, we've been strategic in how we've built the practice. To have a successful business with lots of interesting work seeking to make a positive impact in the built environment certainly doesn't feel like defeat, but I do recognise the existential identity crisis that seems to wash over architects when confronted with such work.

It seems to me that at least part of this phenomenon of *career shame* is self-made; between and amongst architects only. Non-architects that I speak to are generally at first a little confused that we don't have any projects that would feature on Grand Designs, then, once I've explained a bit more about what we do they're interested, or indifferent. They don't say, 'You're not really an architect then, are you?' That line of questioning – whether explicit or implied – only comes from other architects.

I can see that having trained for seven-plus years to reach the hallowed status of capital 'A' Architect, diverting from the designated path could seem like that effort was wasted. Far from it, I say. The dexterous, multi-faceted skills that architectural training bestows can be a great asset in so many fields, and there is so much work to be done. Rather than stand in judgement of our fellow professionals, let's celebrate the diversity that our eclectic and wide-ranging (not to mention expensive) educations have successfully prepared us for. By way of illustration, here are a few of We Made That's projects, across a spectrum of architectural and urban design. Don't judge us.

THE UNLIMITED EDITION – A NEWSPAPER   *The Unlimited Edition* is a super-local newspaper exploring, celebrating and speculating about the future of particular places. Each issue is place-based, delving into key themes, which shape our cities including places of work, cultural spaces, food networks and development legacies. The paper invites guest writers, policy-makers, artists, architects and community members to contribute creative snapshots of each place. The series began as a result of a commission from the London Borough of Tower Hamlets about High Street 2012. The papers were distributed, for free, from dedicated newsstands. We Made That continued *The Unlimited Edition* series in 2016 and 2017 with issues in Bermondsey, Liverpool and Aarhus in Denmark.

HIGH STREETS FOR ALL – AN IN-DEPTH STUDY   We Made That were commissioned by the Greater London Authority to carry out an extensive study of the social value of London's high streets. High Streets for All examines the value of London's high streets across economic, social and spatial dimensions. The research works to better understand how these different strands of value can best be identified and expanded.

Social value – how it's experienced, who it's offered by, how it's measured – is the key concern informing this high street research and as such different modes of provision and evaluation are considered throughout the study. This is one of the most extensive high street studies of its kind, with a key aim to capture the views of Londoners through surveying over 300 users, businesses and stakeholders.

LONDON MADE – A FILM   London Made is a film – commissioned specially for the Seoul Biennale of Architecture and Urbanism 2017 – that celebrates the people, processes and places that make London a productive city.

Looking behind the stage, the exhibition explores the 'back of house' supply threads of one of London's most distinctive cultural venues: the Barbican. Set makers, food and drink manufacturers, lighting specialists and logistics companies are just a sample of the activity that makes London thrive.

Recent strategic thinking and research has revealed that London's spaces of production and industry are under threat. As the city strives to achieve good growth that benefits its citizens, the film interrogates how architects, urban designers, developers, planners and policy-makers can sustain and support London's strengths as a productive city.

THE DEXTEROUS, MULTI-FACETED SKILLS THAT ARCHITECTURAL TRAINING BESTOWS CAN BE A GREAT ASSET IN SO MANY FIELDS, AND THERE IS SO MUCH WORK TO BE DONE.

WHAT WALWORTH WANTS – AN INCREMENTAL STRATEGY
We Made That worked with local stakeholdersin this South London district, to develop a catalogue of projects that aims to celebrate Walworth's unique character, help build resilience in the area in the face of widespread surrounding development. In the context of regeneration in the Old Kent Road Opportunity Area and the Heygate Estate redevelopment, the project seeks to deliver value to the local community. A particular feature of the project has been to work together with traders on East Street Market, the Walworth Society and local community groups to generate ideas to ensure that the area has a vibrant future.

Proposals include precursors to future functions that will be introduced to Old Kent Road, including opportunities for physical enhancement and activation of new open spaces on the high street. A range of projects from the strategy have also been delivered by the London Borough of Southwark and local partners, including improvements to East Street Market and the East Street Exchange.

EAST STREET EXCHANGE – A LITTLE LIBRARY   Following the What Walworth Wants strategy for the area between Walworth Road and Old Kent Road in Southwark, We Made That were appointed to deliver one of the key projects from the strategy. East Street Library was identified as a catalyst project; a well-used public library that could enhance its current offer, test new ideas for what libraries offer and build momentum for the move to the Aylesbury Estate. The proposal – East Street Exchange – allows the library to host a flexible range of new uses, as well as better provision for its current users. A modest extension with a distinctive form and colourful cladding bring a new lease of life to this vital community asset.

At their heart, each of these projects is concerned with improving the relationship between local communities and their built environment through robust understanding, better decision-making and excellent design. That ambition seems fundamentally architectural to me, or at least what architecture can and should be. That's why our portfolio will remain diverse, and we will continue to be architects who aren't always architects.

DEPROFESSIONALISATION

PEGGY DEAMER

A key limit to the applicability of architectural training beyond the field of architecture is its status as a profession. This status is strictly codified in education, in registration, and therefore, in practice. Peggy Deamer, professor of architecture at Yale, principal of the firm Deamer Architects, and founder of advocacy group The Architecture Lobby, weighs up this professional status, asking, What benefits does it bring us? And in what ways does it hold us back? In advocating for deprofessionalisation, Deamer sees a pathway to better pay, better respect, and a renewed public relevance for architecture.

What does architecture get from being a 'profession'? This essay argues, not much, if anything.

First, what is a profession? A profession is an activity/industry that is regulated by state licensure. In the US, what is determined to be a 'profession' is governed state by state, but it includes, variously, locksmiths, ballroom dance instructors, hair braiders, manicurists, interior designers, massage therapists, and upholsterers. What is called a 'profession' is really nothing more than 'occupational licensing' and in the US, at least, it has been one of the fastest growing labour markets, due to free-market, anti-labour neoliberal policies. Studies have found that licensing has hindered job creation, especially at the lower level of the workforce, while not resulting in better services. The growth of occupational licensing, as one might assume, is in reverse proportion to declining union membership.[1]

But still, there are professions and 'professions' (not all professions assume the same privileges), and the 'learned professions' such as law, medicine, engineering, and architecture are recognised by the government and antitrust laws as a distinct category, defined by the length of study and their responsibility to society (usually defined by a code of ethics).

The professionalisation of these 'learned' industries was the result, as Magali Sarfatti Larson has pointed out, of liberal capitalism. The three simultaneous goals of professionalism, she says, have been: to ensure a guiding, elite knowledge sector; to (ironically, at the same time) hark back to pre-capitalist ideals of craftsmanship, universal protection of the social fabric, and *noblesse oblige*; and to offer conventions of standardisation, scientific and cognitive rationality, and a functional division of labour.[2] While the nineteenth century might have been enhanced both socially and economically from these imaginaries, they surely are not relevant or effective today.

If the fear is that without monitoring competency through licensure, unqualified architects would be unleashed on society, there are other ways to ensure competency. For example, certification is used in other industries to guarantee sufficient training, a system which is managed by the industry itself, unlike licensing that is administered by the state. The state's job is to ensure the safety and fair access to an industry for the public; industry certification ensures that those operating in the field comply with what it determines is essential to function competently in the field. Ironically, while the state is meant to look out for the public interest, its main function in administering licensure is making sure that prices remain competitive and as low as possible. In architecture, this guarantees not better or more ethical practices but, rather, a race to the bottom as firms figure out how to cut costs to compete, a situation that in no way assures our delivery of the best product to our clients.

Beyond overcoming unhelpful myths of the need for licensure, there are many advantages to specifically not being one, to deprofessionalising. The following list of these advantages are not in any particular order and they range from psychological to practical, but they are ideologically linked, characterised by the general plus of not indulging our exceptionalism.

OVERCOMING THE NEGATIVE PUBLIC IMAGE OF THE ARCHITECT   The public holds a schizophrenic view of architects. On the one hand, people think it is really cool when we each say we are an architect: they always wanted to be one, they think it is pretty fabulous that you can be both professional (read: financially stable and super well educated) and artistic (read: culturally sophisticated, a little wacky, liberal, and wearing cool clothes). On the other hand, if they have been in a position to hire an architect, they think expensive, unnecessary, interested in our own vision, won't listen, and will cause their building to leak anyway. They also have a weird sense of what we do. Many sophisticated people don't realise that we are not developers and no, we didn't bring those pencil-thin super-tall residential towers into being; while others think, as my sister put it, our time is spent deciding between square or round windows. The point is: the word 'architect' conjures up nothing real and nothing helpful, to the public or to us. If, as is the case in Sweden, anyone can call themselves an architect, people would ask more questions. What scale of work? Where trained and how? Environmental work? Private work? etc., etc. People would want to know if we're the plumber type of architect or the 'fancy' type or the civically-minded type. In other words, the word, in meaning many possible things, would invite a more engaged set of questions that no longer rest on myth.

OVERCOMING THE UNHELPFUL IMAGE ARCHITECTS HAVE OF THEMSELVES   As Sarfatti Larson suggests, a (learned) professional comes with aristocratic class identification. It was true in the nineteenth century that the gentleman architect was identified with the class he served; indeed, the late arrival of the first owner-architect contract in 1921 – and coming nearly 30 years after the first owner-contractor contract – indicates that for a long time, there was virtually no divide between the owner and the architect: same social standing, same friends, same education. The architect was, until the owners got economically savvy, the right-hand of owners who relied completely on the architect's expertise. For many years, only the contractor was the worrisome actor (ah, a different class) warranting a contract. This false identification of us with the owner nevertheless makes us feel good (or at least more important than we are) and allows us to indulge other, secondary, unhelpful traits. We take befuddled pride in our business ignorance, so we stay oblivious. We secretly think that our aesthetic gifts to society come from *noblesse oblige*, so we don't need to experience on-the-ground engagement with complex and diverse social forces. In thinking that our special access to formal virtuosity is what determines our 'learnedness,' we perpetuate a narrative of autonomy (from society, economy, and politics) that only gives credence to the public's view that we don't care about their problems. Let's instead say that our expertise is architecture, not that we ARE ('licensed') architects.

HORIZONTAL ALLIANCES   One of the main functions of a license is keeping others who do not have our training out of our jurisdiction. But that same fence that keeps other disciplines out – contractors, interior designers, engineers, landscape architects, designers and draftsmen – keeps us caged in, unable to make easy partnerships and alliances. In New York, architects cannot be contractors if one is a design-build firm; each of these activities must be in different companies. If you are a developer-architect, these, too, must operate as separate legal entities. Likewise, if you are licensed in one state, you can't practice in another state that doesn't have reciprocity.

The shift away from laws that put us in defined confines is as much psychological as it is legal. There are territories that we currently think are beneath us that actually give us more oversight, more credibility, and more income if we didn't self-restrict. For example, if we were to hold on to the Building Information Model (BIM) and know more about the completed project, architects would be well-placed as post-occupancy maintenance managers. This would not only be a source of income, but a sign to the developers and occupants that we architects care about the long-term functioning of the buildings we design.

BETTER VALUE; BETTER PAY   Whatever advantages that might exist for being a 'learned profession,' labour and business laws are not among them. The rules that enforce minimum wage and overtime pay come with exemptions for 'learned' professionals, meaning that licensed architects don't have access to this worker right. Labour law says that salaried workers whose yearly income is under $47,476 yearly ($913 per week) need to be paid time-and-a-half for hours that exceed 40 hours a week. In other words, architectural workers whose salaries are under this threshold (many) should get paid overtime if it weren't for the 'learned profession' exemption. Those for whom overtime pay is excluded are directed by the following: 'The employee's primary duty must be the performance of work requiring advanced knowledge, defined as work which is predominantly intellectual in character and which includes work requiring the consistent exercise of discretion and judgement; the advanced knowledge must be in a field of science or learning; and the advanced knowledge must be customarily acquired by a pro-longed course of specialised intellectual instruction.'[3] Lucky us for being 'learned'.

Likewise, because the states fear the mixture of licensed individuals with unlicensed individuals in an organisation, professionals are not allowed to form a cooperative, a business model that is worker owned and worker run.[4] The advantages of being a legal coop is, for many of us architectural firm owners, an ethical goal: profits in a co-op go directly to the workers, and decisions of governance are made according to one worker, one vote. In an effort to lift architectural practices out of the standard hierarchical pay structure that milks employees of a voice in salary, work distribution, and the direction of the practice (what work it takes and why; how that work is distributed), cooperatives are a natural choice. And yet, professionals cannot legally cooperativise.

And, perhaps most significantly, deprofessionalisation would mean the cost (and hours) of getting a license is done away with! The exams, the marginalised pay during the internship period, the tutorials – all these economic and psychological burdens are thrown out the window and in their stead, more time for the work we want to do, the community we want to support, and the family with which we want to spend time.

CONCLUSION: THE STORY OF SWEDEN   All of these arguments can be backed up by Sweden's approach to architectural organising. As indicated, architects are not licensed in Sweden; a plumber can call himself an architect. Interestingly, in a cross-European survey, it was determined that Swedish architects make the most money; there is, in other words, no link between licensure and pay. But there is more. The Swedish Architectural Association (SAA), their equivalent to our American Institute of Architects (AIA) or Royal Institute of British Architects, is a union, not a fraternal organisation. This leads to cooperation between the architects that are in the union so that they don't compete on fees and agree on what the industry needs to be sustainable, relevant, and respected. And because unions are integrated into the political system, the SAA has power in the parliament. The head of the SAA, indeed, is a member of parliament and recently initiated and helped pass a strong environmental bill.

Perhaps because there is no licensure, architectural education matters more in Sweden than one might expect. Education (and its accreditation) and not licensure is the proof of competency, the indication that one indeed knows more than the plumber. And because the government has a vested interest in the competency – both because their economy is based on innovation technology and because they will be the clients of most architects – it gives large sums of money to the universities for forward-looking approaches to architecture and to architectural offices for research grants. And finally, the union that is the SAA consists of employees, not employers. This means that those on-the-ground architectural workers are the ones shaping the direction of the discipline.[5] The result is an openness to innovative procurement techniques.

One day, other countries might become as enlightened as Sweden. As a country organised by unions, it sets an example that goes well beyond architectural licensing. But in the meanwhile, we can begin with the one controllable act we architects have – deprofessionalisation.

1   By 2008 occupational licensing in the US grew to 30 percent of the workforce, up from below five percent in the 1950s. In contrast, in the same period, unions represented, at its peak in 1950, over 30 percent of the US workforce, but declined to less than 12 percent by 2008.

2   Magali Sarfatti Larson, *The Rise of Professionalism: Monopolies of Competence and Sheltered Markets*, Transaction Publishers, 2013, p.xiii

3   See US Department of Labor, *Fact Sheet #17D: Exemption for Professional Employees Under the Fair Labor Standards Act (FLSA)*, www.dol.gov/whd/overtime/fs17d_professional.html

4   The spirit of a cooperative can be approximated within other business models such as a Limited Liability Corporation, a. partnership, or an S Corp by creating cooperative-like bylaws. However, the one person one vote cannot be part of those bylaws. For additional articles on architectural cooperatives see Aaron Cayer, Peggy Deamer, Shawhin Roudbari, and Manuel Shvartzberg, 'Socializing Practice: From Small Firms to Cooperative Models of Organization,' in Melanie Dodd (ed.), *Spatial Practices: Modes of Action and Engagement with the City*, Routledge, 2019; and Peggy Deamer, 'Cooperativizing Small Architectural Firms' in Bryony Roberts (ed.), *Log* 48, forthcoming.

5   Employers are part of another union made up of professional firm owners from various industries.

'ONLY A CRIMINAL CAN SOLVE THE CRIME'

Interview with EYAL WEIZMAN and CHRISTINA VARVIA,
FORENSIC ARCHITECTURE

Architecture would seem to have little to say on the subjects of border disputes, humanitarian crises, or political violence. But in the hands of Forensic Architecture, the architectural techniques are redeployed as powerful tools to advocate for human rights in conflict zones around the world. Using open-source investigation, digital and physical models, 3D animations, cartographic platforms, and witness testimonies, Forensic Architecture makes evidence public in different forums such as the media, courts, truth commissions, and cultural venues. In this interview, founder Eyal Weizman and deputy director Christina Varvia discuss the origins of the group, and the challenges of operating at the intersection of aesthetics and violence. 195

EDITORS   Through this book, our aim is to explore how architectural thinking can be applied in other domains. Forensic Architecture is one of the most significant examples of this today. To start with you Eyal, can you begin by telling us what you studied, and how that experience shaped your understanding of architecture?

EYAL WEIZMAN   I studied at the Architectural Association. I was a student there for about 12 years. What I liked is that they used to leave me alone, and the more they left me alone, the better I did. In my fourth year I got into media and film, before starting my PhD with the London Consortium, under the supervision of Peter Thomas and Catherine du Toit. With them I went to South Africa, where I had my first brush with colonialism.

This experience pushed me to volunteer at the Palestinian Ministry of Planning during my year out, which is when I started to articulate the differences and similarities between Palestine and South Africa, realising that these were not isolated instances of conflict or responses to concerns around national security. They were contemporary forms of colonialism, where architecture was an instrument of violence and a vehicle of political power. I felt the need to devise a toolbox for anticolonial struggle, one where architectural analysis could be deployed to understand and dissect the colonial project and expose its weaknesses.

Of course at the time Post-Zionism had already been a decade in the making, led by people like Ilan Pappe and Oren Yiftachel, but I felt there was a need to dissect the structure of power, to look at its workings through the lens of architecture. In the same way you might take a clock apart to understand its mechanism and know what are your chances, even as remote as they may be, to jam it.

EDITORS   What happens when architecture, which typically exists in a completely different context, is applied in this way?

EYAL WEIZMAN   There are two aspects to architectural analysis. One is that architecture could be the object of investigation and you don't need to be an architect to do that. Historians, artists, geographers, anyone can look at a set of buildings, their design, surrounding environment and have an opinion about them. But the architectural analysis of politics is something different, it implies looking at structures and patterns to know how things stand, how they move and operate. It interrogates the material form to determine how to break apart the logic of governance, which was the subject of my first book, *Hollow Land: Israel's Architecture of Occupation* (2007).

read

In architecture, to understand the structure of a building we typically use the section – an abstract notation that exposes relations which the naked eye couldn't see in reality. By applying this representational tool to a huge bit of territory I could reveal its stratification: from deep water to minerals, archeological sites, valleys, hills, magnetic space, airspace, outer space. I could see how those layers were organised as a system of domination of the territory. I also looked at the spatial logic of military manoeuvres, analysing how they produced space through both construction and destruction, which are not separate ontologies and they both involve the movement of matter across the territory.

So what emerged is a new category of elastic space, where political actions define and redefine space, whether on the level of soldiers moving through the city, reworking its syntax through the movement of bodies in space, or through bulldozers, bombs or through setting up temporary frontiers.

> EDITORS   There appears to be a straight line from *Hollow Land* to the work you do now as Forensic Architecture. Both are using architectural research as a tool of revealing what is concealed. At what point did you conceive of this idea of Forensic Architecture as a practice?

EYAL WEIZMAN   The idea for Forensic Architecture developed gradually from different trajectories and patterns of thought which at some point started colliding. Mapping was one of those trajectories. Google Earth was launched, and cartography turned into photography. We started posing questions about resolution, framing, asking when a particular image was taken, in which season, with what exposure, under which sunlight conditions, etc. Photographic analysis replaced cartographic analysis and counter cartography became counter forensics. At that point you could start operating cartographically, from the inside out, rather than from the outside in. When mapping an incident for instance you could start in space and time from a moment of intensity, which I think is very much in line with the way we as architects approach the analysis of urban situations. This is when I felt the necessity to develop a new kind of practice to integrate models, videos, testimonies, etc.

Another trajectory was my second book – *The Least of All Possible Evils: Humanitarian Violence from Arendt to Gaza* (2011) – which sought to fill a big gap in *Hollow Land*, where I had described a force field occupied by military people, architects, politicians, the resistance, but I had not registered my own position within that landscape, I had overlooked the role of the humanitarians. I as the author – the person who writes, brings evidence and describes a situation – am also an active player rather than a passive observer. This introduces paradoxes and difficulties, as very often this practice can, whether consciously or not, contribute to the system of domination. The book deals with this ethical issue, but it also describes the material practice of activism through different notions – the camp in the first chapter, the wall in the second and urban destruction in the third. There are different characters – Muhammad Dahla, Ronnie Brown in Ethiopia and Marc Garlasco in Gaza. Each embodies my own predicaments.

While working on the Garlasco chapter, I realised he was conducting forensics on architectural destruction. Then I looked again at the sentence and rewrote his practice as 'architectural forensics', and then finally I came up with 'forensic architecture'. When those two words combined for the first time in my head they sounded familiar, I realised later that there were surveyors who already used that phrase to describe their work. But the person I was writing about, Mark Garlasco, was an assassin working for the CIA, designing bombing. So Forensic Architecture was born on the pages of a chapter titled 'Only the Criminal Can Solve the Crime', where I describe the problems of this practice. It is worth pointing out that none of the critiques we have received so far has been harsher than my own critique in the book, having compared our practice to that of a criminal.

I was already fully aware of the privilege of tools – of the kind of militaristic gaze associated with them, and of the skirting close to evil that is necessary in order to do good. I remain convinced that doing good in the world doesn't come out of the safety of moral certitude, but out of deep engagement and getting very close to problematic conditions. This is where agency lies. If you want to describe a situation in a supposedly objective or neutral manner then you can hold on to a certain moral purity, of the kind that engaged political practice will never allow you to.

The third trajectory was practice. Already at the turn of the century there was an established intellectual field of practice associated with post-structuralism which was predicated on the critique of reality and on the suspicion that things are not what they appear. This resulted in an obsession with representation, calling for the need to pierce layers of appearance to unveil some kind of essence buried underneath, be it a Nietzschean quest for power or Freud's subconscious. The practices which did that, although very effective in terms of raising suspicion about the so-called 'reality', were not actively trying to assemble alternative truth claims and finding lines of escape. I believe that if we destroy we also need to reconstruct.

I am absolutely committed to the current post-truth impetus of the many anti-institutional organisations which attack institutions of power or knowledge. I am with them as long as they replace what they destroy with alternative models, which I believe should be less hierarchical, relying upon the creation of communities of practice in which the production of knowledge and evidence is socialised, rather than imposed from top down. Meaning that it relies on a set of relations between people who experience violence, activists who take their side, a diffused network of open-source investigators, scientists and other experts who explore what happened and disseminates the findings. This is something I call 'open verification'.

There are several other trajectories besides these, such as the people I encountered and learned from, like Christina, whose sensibility was always formative in the development of ideas. Nothing emerges out of a single trajectory, it is always an encounter.

EDITORS   Thank you Eyal. Christina, can you tell us about your studies, and how you came to be working with Forensic Architecture?

CHRISTINA VARVIA   I studied architecture at both the Architectural Association and the University of Westminster, where I developed an interest in different imaging and scanning techniques and their technological limitations. When I graduated, Eyal needed help with a project which presented different pieces of evidence generated by smartphones, cameras, remote sensing, satellites, allowing me to apply my theoretical understanding of these different tools. I have been working at Forensic Architecture for five years now.

EDITORS   One of the fascinating aspects of Forensic Architecture is the way you deploy architectural research with such a clear and powerful purpose, often in a legal context, for instance. At what point did you realise that your work could become more interventionist?

CHRISTINA VARVIA   We do not distinguish between analysis and presentation. These moments often overlap, particularly because our way of understanding the forces at play within a territory – the way they interact in space and time – is very much dependent on the tools we use, which vary depending on the nature of the project. We typically start with existing tools or methodologies, we deconstruct them to understand what they are good for, what are their limitations, and then reassemble to create something different which fits our needs.
    Both the visual analysis and the structure of our narratives proceed hand-in-hand from the start until the 'final product' is disseminated in the media, or it becomes an exhibition,

The Bombing of Rafah analysed an attack
on the city in the Occupied Palestinan
Territories by Israeli forces, proving that they
were responsible for the killing of civilians.
The research led Amnesty International
to label this use of munition as a war crime.

or a court case. Questions regarding the output are always present throughout the process. We constantly ask ourselves: what are we trying to prove? To whom? Where do we need to create pressure to advocate successfully for this?

DOING GOOD IN THE WORLD DOESN'T COME OUT OF THE SAFETY OF MORAL CERTITUDE, BUT OUT OF DEEP ENGAGEMENT.

EDITORS   I remember a story you told in a recent talk, about presenting your work to a human rights lawyer, who recoiled when you used the word 'aesthetics', as though it was somehow offensive to even use that word in that context. Can you expand on the role the visual plays in your practice?

CHRISTINA VARVIA   Aesthetics is often associated a bit too simplistically with beauty. But we see it in a different way: we work with materials and the evidence they bring is either visual, sonic or haptic. These are dimensions that can be perceived through our senses or through sensors, which is why aesthetics is our starting point for any investigations. For instance we often have to consider things like resolution, framing blur, shadows, etc., to determine how a piece of evidence has been aestheticised by a particular medium and unpack the relationship between the two.

EDITORS   In the recent Chicago Architecture Biennial, you presented the work The Killing of Harith Augustus, which investigates the police killing of a barber in Chicago's South Shore. You made the decision not to show the films, to withdraw the aesthetic component of the project from the gallery. Does this show the limits of the use of aesthetics, in that violence is 'aestheticised', turning the audience into voyeurs?

CHRISTINA VARVIA   In Chicago we were confronted with the difficulty of having to speak about a black body that had been represented over and over again in the media. On the one hand we didn't want to glorify that violence, while on the other we felt the need to frame the issue and do it justice. These two opposing views were being brought forward by our two collaborators. An activist on the one hand, advocating for the necessity to show the graphic reality of police violence in Chicago, and a poet who was living in the neighbourhood and felt that being exposed to that type of visual violence was an act of terror itself.

To take both of those views onboard, our approach was to introduce the idea of *consent* and acknowledge that this kind of content would require a different kind of viewing, one that might have not been possible in the context of the Biennial, where one is overwhelmed by so many other things. We thus decided to install that work in another gallery, at the Invisible Institute, our partner organisation. As a visitor, you had to take a trip there specifically to see that work.

One of the dangers of overexposure to violence is a certain type of fatigue. There is only so much one can take on a daily basis. This is why it is important to understand how our attention works. That piece in Chicago used different time frames – from years, hours, days, minutes, milliseconds – to introduce that idea that there can be different scales of engagement and modes of interactions in each of them. We are interested in how, through the act of viewing, by moving outside the fast cycle of information, we can stimulate civil society to play an active role within reality.

ARCHITECTURE AFTER CONFLICT

MALKIT SHOSHAN, FOUNDATION
FOR ACHIEVING SEAMLESS TERRITORY

The realm of military design, architecture, and planning sits beyond the reach of the architectural profession, and yet it has a profound effect on the lives of millions of people around the world. Architect and researcher Malkit Shoshan discusses her ongoing work with the Dutch military and the United Nations (UN) to apply new ways of thinking to the compounds, camps, logistics hubs, headquarters, and checkpoints which comprise this oft-overlooked architecture of peacekeeping. The result is a new mode of practice, sitting at the intersection of architecture, international relations, policy, and activism.

The Foundation for Achieving Seamless Territory (FAST) applies the tools and knowledge of architecture to advocate for social and environmental justice. Less interested in giving our services to wealthy clients or powerful institutions, instead we seek to create space for the powerless. For us, architecture occupies the complex intersection of social, political, cultural, financial and ecological terrains, and holds the potential to transform these relationships.

Our work employs drawings, maps, diagrams, models, competitions, exhibitions, and publications. We use them to make visible the hidden realities of segregation and violence; to challenge institutions and power structures; and to engage with various publics to create counter-narratives of relations between people, the places they inhabit, and power. Through this work, we ask, Can design instruments better communicate people's wishes, stories and histories to policymakers who may determine their fate?

BORDERLANDS   FAST was established in 2005 with a focus on Israel-Palestine, a place where ideology, politics, oppression and resistance are played out in the built environment, and are contingent upon the territorial organisation of the country. A key device in the Israel-Palestine conflict is the border, a physical apparatus used to divide communities and people. In our 2010 book, *Atlas of the Conflict*, we presented more than 500 drawings of the border of Israel and its constant encroachment over the years. Walls, border controls, checkpoints, buffer zones, ceasefire lines, demilitarised areas, occupied territories, sterilised strips, cleared land, settlements, refugee camps, blue line, green line, red line, and withdraws. These are only a few of the words used to describe the edges of Israel and its interface with Palestine and other neighbouring countries. Each shift of this border deeply affects the configuration of the built environment and the communities that inhabit it.

Israel functions as an exemplary case, a laboratory, for the study of borders, border regions, and migration. Whether on a micro or macro scale – national, regional, municipal – borders are used as a physical construct to impose socio-economic segregation, exclusion, or even a sense of belonging, depending on which side of the line you stand. Israel's frontier is where new spatial typologies emerge, continuously, as a response to a crisis, and as an embodiment of spatial politics.

Borders are central to FAST's practice. We use design to identify hidden realities, and reveal them to the public sphere. With our maps, we trace policies of segregation and dispossession on various scales. The information we put forward, we hope, can empower and prepare the ground for future interventions by us, or by others. It is in Israel-Palestine where we learned that architecture and spatial expertise could play an important role in activism.

BLUE   This is the approach we have adopted in our ongoing research project BLUE: The Architecture of UN Peace Missions, which investigates the impacts and legacies of UN peace missions on cities, rural communities, and the environment. BLUE was not commissioned, it emerged after an encounter in Kosovo that led us to question the presence of UN peace missions. When we visited in 2007, the material footprint of the UN and the international community appeared massive and disproportionate to the local scale. UN compounds, camps, logistics hubs, headquarters, and all manner of checkpoints were spread throughout the country. The iconic blue logo, of a globe surrounded by a wreath, seemed ever-present. We were left with many questions. How does this foreign presence impact the local population? Who designs all of this space and infrastructure? For whom? How are they maintained? And, most critically, what will be left behind after the mission has gone?

Today, the UN Peace Operation is the largest agency of the UN in terms of the number of personnel, budget, material, and environmental footprint.

Camp Castor, in Mali, where FAST has
explored the potential to transform UN
bases into catalysts for local development.

It deploys troops provided by 123 countries to make, keep and sustain peace in conflict-affected regions. From the early days of lightly armed soldiers monitoring ceasefires, its mandate has been transformed by the changing nature of conflict. Wars have evolved spatially, financially, technologically and logistically, and occur more frequently within nations than between them. UN peacekeepers are now called upon not only to maintain security (there is often 'no peace to keep') but also to protect civilians, strengthen institutions and local governance, monitor human rights, provide electoral assistance, support the reform of national security sectors, and contribute to the disarmament, demobilisation, and reintegration of former combatants. Michael Kenkel has described this expansion of mission mandates as advancing 'from the thin blue line to painting a country blue.'[1] As of 2018, peacekeeping operations covered an area of over one million square kilometres, with over 100,000 personnel in the field, at an annual cost of roughly $6.8 billion.

At FAST, in wondering how to interrogate this highly complex terrain, we found ourselves in a new cross-disciplinary realm. The questions we encountered in Kosovo and of the UN missions more broadly, took us into the world where international relations intersects with architecture, policy, and the built environment. If one can actually intervene in such a tangled global system, where to even begin?

RESEARCH IN PUBLIC   In 2016, FAST was invited for a research fellowship at Het Nieuwe Instituut in Rotterdam, where we initiated the project Drones and Honeycombs. We used this platform to engage directly and publicly with governmental institutions, policymakers, peacekeepers, and other relevant actors to contribute to the research.

Via the Dutch Ministry of Defense and Foreign Affairs, we invited colonels, military generals, military engineers, diplomats, human rights activists, designers and a reporter to contribute to a workshop. In an event that was overwhelmingly open and sincere in spirit, each participant prepared a detailed presentation of their experience. We discussed the design processes, challenges and footprints of the mission bases, a collaboration which led to the reports *The Future of Compounds* (March 2014), and *Reimagining the Peacekeeping Mission: Legacy Scenarios for Camp Castor* (January 2015).

This work led to the invitation to curate the Dutch pavilion for the 2016 Venice Architecture Biennale, where we presented the exhibition BLUE: Architecture of UN Missions. This high-profile public platform, set within the gardens of the elite in Venice, enabled us to further elevate the ranks of those engaged in the conversation. The first official guest was the Dutch Chief of Defense, General Tom Middendorp, who joined the opening of the exhibition with a delegation of soldiers wearing colourful traditional celebratory uniforms with pom-poms and bells. Their march through the Venice Biennale resembled an art performance.

The exhibition featured a large wall of more than 170 lights, each representing a town in Africa with a UN base, directly affecting the lives of more than 30 million people across the continent. General Middendorp was surprised by the magnitude, and considered the policy recommendations we put forward, leading to his advocacy for the need for a paradigm shift within the ministry. Our questions resonated deeply with the civil servants, politicians, and journalists who covered the projects. The Dutch Ministry of Defense posed our questions to its defense partners from across the world, inviting them to participate in a two day conference titled 'Ecosystems and Future Force' in The Hague. This was supported by parallel research conducted by knowledge and policy institutes.

As the process above unfolded in the Netherlands, the Dutch mission to the UN was campaigning for a seat at the UN Security Council. Looking to promote a new approach for UN missions, they invited us to join Bert Koenders, then the Minister of Foreign Affairs, to present our project at the UN headquarters in New York. The presentation included an address to the African Union and an exhibition next to the Security Council chamber titled 'Blue: Islands in Cities.' New partnerships, amongst others, with the international policy institutes such as the Center on International Cooperation at NYU and the International Peace Institute, helped us translate the project into policy papers that are now used by various nation states and UN agencies.

A WORLD ON THE MARGINS OF ARCHITECTURE   Slowly we formed a new practice somewhere on the margins of architecture, international relations, policy and activism. On these margins, we found a world. We nurture multiple partnerships and relationships with people who care. We draw maps, analyse spaces and publicly share our observations. We surface stories of multiple complex realities: life in conflict-affected regions, from Israel and Palestine, to Kosovo, Mali, or Liberia. We record the stories of people we meet along the way, document sites, and collect materials to place on the table of policymakers. Although these stories can never be complete or comprehensive of real-life complexity, they can shift a conversation.

These evolving tactics – incidents, events, and interventions – on multiple scales help us to shift the discourse, grow our allies within and outside the power regime of the nation-state, intergovernmental institutions, cultural institutes, and on the ground. When we engage with remote realities in places and disciplines that are invisible to us as architects and planners, we get to know the world. These are the spaces that form the majority of the built environments in the world. They are not part of the powers we know, not part of wealth or privilege. They often exist on the forgotten side of history.

While we look away from conventional architecture, critical theory, crisis/poverty/disaster porn, or aid, we discover avenues for the subversion of power and change. Rather than designing physical spaces, we now recommend policies, words that help to create spaces for the empowerment of local communities and shift the power from foreign to local hands, such that they can build their homes, towns, and countries by themselves.

1   See Kai Michael Kenkel, 'Five Generations of Peace Operations: From the "Thin Blue Line" to "Painting a Country Blue", in *The Revista Brasileira de Política Internacional* 56, no.1, 2013, p.122-143

Shoshan guides the Dutch Chief of Defense,
General Tom Middendorp, through her
exhibition of the architecture of peacekeeping
at the 2016 Venice Biennale.

TO PROGRAM A SITE

KIMBERLI MEYER

How can art and culture play a role in addressing wider social issues of race, gender, privilege, and power? As director of the University
Art Museum (UAM) at California State Long
Beach, architect-turned-curator Kimberli
Meyer sought to address these issues, both
through her programming, and through
hosting a process of institutional change at
the museum. But days before launching a
show about police violence against Black
victims, Meyer was removed from her position, with no reason given. In this piece,
Meyer discusses the resistance faced in her
efforts to bring about institutional change,
asking 'What would an anti-racist museum
practice look like?'

Architecture's appeal was that it presented a direct way of impacting the public-private continuum while operating in an artistic modality. Its scale range – from intimate personal space design to megastructure and urban planning – touches the human and other natural bodies in fundamental ways. Yet, architecture is often overwhelmingly governed by the flow of capital. It is real-estate based, ultimately beholden to land owners in a system with a history of genocidal conquest, racial segregation, and profit-driven urban displacement. As radical as an architect aspires to be, it's hard to get around that fact. A few years after I graduated from architecture school, working in Chicago, I began to feel discomfort with this position and considered expanding my practice into other disciplines. Art presented itself as more open and idea-based; art can be an act, or a drawing, or sound, or words, or many other things, none of which require a piece of land for full realisation. So I found my way to California Institute of the Arts (CALArts) for an MFA.

OPENING UP THE BRIEF   My mentor as a graduate student was the conceptual artist Michael Asher (1943-2012). His response to institutional invitations was to research the organisation in depth, ideate, propose, if rejected repeat as necessary, and ultimately present an artwork in direct relation to the host. Asher's forms vary widely because they're always a function of the subsite within the institution and the ideological role that subsite plays in the overall context. His work made sense to me, because site is a primary starting point for architecture. Indeed, the two key components of an architecture brief are typically site and program. Site is the physical location; program is the commissioning entity's list of needs. The architect responds to the brief to produce a design solution for the client.

In art, the brief is more open. Site can be discursive, spatial, cultural, institutional. Program is a way to read the site and explore its corners, vistas, connections, logic systems. Program draws a new map and follows it wherever it may lead.

PROGRAM AS A VERB   When I was offered the opportunity to lead the MAK Center for Art and Architecture at the Schindler House in 2002, it was the chance to program an auspicious site. The 1922 landmark building is both a generative work of architecture, and an intentional disruption of patriarchal nuclear family structure in favour of a salon culture of avant-garde art, leftist political action, and communal living. Architect RM Schindler called for a new form of modern architecture. Co-client Pauline Schindler called for a democratic artistic social space within the boundaries of her home. Pauline's programming of the site began at the architectural brief, continued for decades in the day-to-day cultural life of the house, and persists in the present-day philosophy of the MAK Center. I approached the site from various angles: architectural, artistic, institutional, cultural, and political. My curatorial method and artistic direction was not dissimilar from tackling an architectural problem: conduct site research, analyse questions posed by the site, propose a programmatic overlay that addresses one or more questions, produce the resulting event in whatever form it calls for, reflect, archive, repeat. For example, because the traffic-snarled site of the Los Angeles basin is filled with corporate speech in the form of billboards, the urge to replace commercials with artistic speech resulted in How Many Billboards? Art In Stead, an exhibition co-curated by Lisa Henry, Nizan Shaked, and Gloria Sutton and I, in which we commissioned twenty-one Los Angeles billboards by contemporary artists. Or because Esther McCoy, architecture critic and historian that defined California architecture and Modernism, was employed as a draftsperson by RM Schindler when she published her first essay on architecture, Susan Morgan and I co-curated an exhibition about her work.

SITE AND CRITIQUE   Over the years, I became more interested in the idea of institutional critique from within. Since we all inhabit and are subject to multiple institutions – how can our

Installation of American Monument by artist
lauren woods, an exhibition which examined
the cultural conditions under which African
Americans lose their lives to police brutality.

participation become a critical act? How could institutional workers, dwellers, voters, etc. make space for self-reflection and analysis? Surely cultural work has a role to play? In 2013, the Supreme Court struck down the Defense of Marriage Act. I experienced the news, coming in over the car radio, as titillating. The ruling meant that now I, too, could 'take' a wife. But that week of decisions turned out to be bittersweet, because in addition to the good news for queers, there was terrible news for citizens of colour in the south. The Civil Rights Act of 1964 was gutted by the Voting Rights Act of 2013. Jim Crow southern states were released from federal monitoring of election processes, which unleashed an onslaught of voter disenfranchisement efforts. That week, with my newly acquired phallus of marriage rights, I vowed to divert my activist energy from queer and women's rights toward racial justice. As a White woman,[1] I understood that I benefit from the racist structure, and if I don't actively resist it, I enable it.

RACISM WAS PART OF THE BRIEF THAT SETTLER COLONISTS BROUGHT TO THE NATIONAL PROJECT. OUR TASK IS TO REPROGRAM THE BRIEF.

In 2016, after nearly fourteen years at the MAK Center, I left to helm the UAM at California State Long Beach (CSULB). I was excited to think about a new kind of site, an art museum allied with a critically-minded museum studies program, on the flagship campus of the Cal State System.

Culture

The university enrolls over 37,000 students, 82 percent of whom are non-White, and many are the first in their family to participate in higher education. The campus is the location of Puvungna, a historic Tongva village, sacred space and active archeological site. The day I started my new job, Alton Sterling, an unarmed black man was killed by two police officers in Baton Rouge, Louisiana. The next day, Philando Castile was shot dead by a Minnesota police officer, an incident that was Facebook live-streamed by his girlfriend Diamond Reynolds. These murders hit hard, collectively. My first weekend working at the UAM was spent reckoning anew with my role and position in the perpetuation of White supremacy. A quote from the conclusion of James Baldwin's essay 'Stranger in the Village' kept coming back to me:

> People who shut their eyes to the reality simply invite their own destruction, and anyone who insists on remaining in a state of innocence long after that innocence is dead turns himself into a monster.[2]

The choice was clear, and the platform I had been offered via my appointment beckoned. The question presented itself: what would an anti-racist museum practice look like? This became a guiding enquiry. It showed up in meetings, workshops, program planning, and the UAM reading group I co-organised with museum studies. My engagement of artist lauren woods brought the first public opportunity to address it. I loved working with woods in the past; she was the first artist I called after I got the job at the UAM. She was excited to partner on developing an anti-racist museum practice and accepted my invitation to do a solo project at the museum. After deep discussion, she proposed to transform the UAM into a monument that prompts consideration of the cultural conditions under which African Americans lose their lives to police brutality. I immediately agreed.

POWER AND RACE   Research and development for the monument commenced, aided by a team of students who submitted over 120 Freedom of Information Act requests on cases of police brutality. The legal documents we retrieved, such as dispatch transcripts, police and prosecutor reports, witness testimonies, and dash cam and body cam footage, formed the basis of the work. Shortly after I presented to staff and campus stakeholders the full concept of American Monument, push-back came from the university administration and the employee union. Allegedly, there were concerns that a monument challenging police brutality against Black citizens would encourage violence against the museum. I was getting pulled into increasingly tense high-level meetings with (White) officials, in which conditions were demanded. These included the installation of a panic button at the front door, advance-reserved ticketed entry (to a free campus museum) and releasing the transcripts of all sound files to the administration in advance of the opening. I was also told that the staff union was threatening to call in the California division of Occupational Safety and Health because of safety concerns. The fact that the entirely non-Black staff and their union representatives were voicing fear for their 'safety' in the context of a focus on state violence against actual Black victims, was striking.

On another front, people in the administration were concerned that I was using the term 'anti-racism' too often – it was pulled out of a job description I wrote, and I was asked to find language less 'negative' when presenting the concept. On 11 September 2019, five days before the launch of American Monument, I was abruptly removed from my position with no reason given. Woods went on to launch the work with an artist walk-through that included her playing a recording of Philando Castile's death. Then she announced that she would 'pause' the work until I was reinstated, stating that the museum and university 'have kneecapped a project that is focusing on Black lives and police brutality. They have killed a leadership initiative whose focus was to not only address white supremacy but to disrupt it.'[3] Despite my administrative appeal and our attempts to find common ground with the university, American Monument was never un-paused at the UAM.

Fortunately, the Beall Center for Art and Technology at the University of California, Irvine (UCI) was eager to take the monument on the work's terms, and we moved it there, re-launching it in October of the next year as American Monument 22/2019. Where there was fear and rejection at CSULB, there was interest and collaboration at UCI. Woods and I were set up as researchers in residence, which gave us access to scholars and resources in the School of Law and the departments of Social Ecology, African American Studies, Art, and Art History. The work highlights how law and culture are intertwined, and became a powerful vehicle for interdisciplinary co-creation. It's a triumph and honour to have played a part in seeing it through thus far, where it can live in the world and evolve as a participatory artwork.

Still pending is the ongoing challenge of creating institutional change. CSULB, like many educational and cultural organizations, has adopted language promoting diversity, equity, and inclusive excellence. Yet when change happens, members of the system often respond with anxiety and aggression. The key structural distinction between American Monument at the two universities is this: CSULB was confronted with an internal institutional critic calling for systemic change, and American Monument was the first public project to reflect that directive. UCI hosted a significant work of art that would come and go; nobody was asking for the institution to change. Each site and each program were distinct. At the larger site known as the US, structural racism is present and persistent at all levels. Racism was part of the brief that settler colonists brought to the national project, and it's been well-fed and active ever since. Our task is to reprogram the brief. The hard part is the self-critical work of facing racism on every level that it manifests. It may require building parallel processes, structures, institutions, and pedagogies. Over time, forms of racism have changed in response to anti-racist resistance. Surely, we can muster the imagination and courage to map out a different way.

1   My capitalisation of 'Black' and 'White' when referring to people is in deference to conventions employed by thinkers such as Ibram X Kendi, author of *How to Be an Antiracist* (2019); Rachele Kanigel author of *The Diversity Style Guide* (2016) ; and the *Guidelines for Bias-Free Language* by the American Psychological Association.

2   James Baldwin, 'Stranger in the Village,' in *Collected Essays*, Literary Classics of the United States, Library of America, 1998, p.129

3   For full statement see American Monument blog www.american-monument.blog/lauren-woods-opening-remarks-uam/

EXHIBITION-MAKING

JUDITH CLARK

From formal gestures – folds, pleats, proportions – to the relation to the body, architecture and fashion share many qualities. How might you make the jump from one to the other? Judith Clark takes on the dual role of curator and designer, building on histories and concepts of dress to make them present in space. In many ways this perspective has fostered the understanding of historical dress as a conveyor of information, values and personal stories through time, and a discursive discipline in its own right. In this piece Clark reflects on the many influences in her career, from her architectural training through to the development of her practice.

I work as a fashion exhibition-maker. The subject of my exhibitions for over 20 years has been dress, both historic and contemporary. I always work in the round, building the exhibition's curatorial list around the possibilities of its installation. If given the choice to curate or design an exhibition, my desire is always to design it. The design of it feels like it holds the thesis together. I think that is because I studied architecture first.

My interest in dress history strangely did not mean reading books about dress history, but instead trying to squeeze ideas about dress into and out of an architectural reading list. I think the moment I can remember feeling this was going to work was attending Adrian Forty's Reyner Banham Memorial Lecture at the Victoria and Albert Museum in 1988 whilst I was an undergraduate at The Bartlett. His metaphorical linking of fashion and architecture sent me down a route of the most primitive analogy: cover/shelter.

At the time Elizabeth Wilson had already published her *Adorned in Dreams: Fashion and Modernity* (1985), but Beatriz Colomina's *Sexuality and Space* (1996), and Mark Wigley's White Walls: Designer Dresses (1996) had not come out yet. It was not until Liz Diller and Ricardo Scofidio's Bad Press (Dissident Housework) was made and exhibited in 1993, and Diller came to speak about it at the Architectural Association in 1994 – for a series entitled 'Reconstructing Her Practice' about female architects – that I can say anything acted as a direct precedent to my own practice. By that time I had completed a History and Theory Diploma course at the Architectural Association and started attending the MPhil seminars.

Diller and Scofidio's project, whilst on a small scale (Diller qualified it as 'minuscule' vs urban in her talk), and apparently about ironing, created a powerful thesis in the form of an exhibition of clothing; achieved through the alternative folding of a series of white shirts – the object around which so many post-Taylorist housework manuals were created. It helped me to imagine the staging of dress and space, where the two were inter-animating and politicised. It didn't matter which white shirts were chosen, it was about how they were shown.

I wrote essays on Mario Perniola's account of 'Between Clothing and Nudity' published in Zone's series on the Body. I attended Mark Cousins' Bachelard-ian lectures which prepared me both to read Adam Phillips, and to collaborate with him – to imagine the spaces in his sentences.

I chose to write my thesis whilst in graduate school at the Architectural Association on Vsevolod Meyerhold (1874-1940), the avant-garde theatre director who famously recruited Constructivist architects and designers (including textile designers) to design the sets for his productions. The historic photographic stills recorded the actors dressed in costumes that completed his ideas. Whilst writing I had the time to read Manfredo Tafuri's pairing of Piranesi's interrupted Carceri to Popova's designs (set and costume) for Meyerhold of Crommelynck's The Magnanimous Cuckold and to look repeat-edly at the bodies stuck in dynamic poses and configurations in space. I was not sure how the transformations and interrelations between text (dialogue), direction, set and costume actually worked, but they were what interested me. (I was also inter-ested in what a mis-interpretation of these things might be, were they necessarily causal and connected? And how were each of these aspects mutually explanatory?) I was delighted by the quality of collaboration this suggested. The late, extraordi-nary architectural historian Catherine Cooke was an external examiner at the Architectural Association at the time and cham-pioned my research. For at least two years, the research organ-ised something that was essential about architecture for me and that seemed to be integral to the work that I wanted to do.

The first museum exhibition that I ever staged, enti-tled 'Malign Muses. When Fashion Turns Back', was directly indebted to this research. It was commissioned by Linda Loppa who was the then director of ModeMuseum in Antwerp in 2004. She invited me on the back of a series of small exhibitions that

I had presented at the experimental gallery dedicated to fashion I ran in London's Notting Hill between 1998-2002. This was an opportunity to translate accumulative ideas about fashion's patterns of references, and to use fashion theorist Caroline Evans's book *Fashion at the Edge* as its organising text. Each time she used a spatial analogy in her text, the cycle, the labyrinth, different ways of describing fashion's relays, I drew it. With the help, importantly, of ERCOLA (Experimental Research Center of Liberal Arts) based in Antwerp, my drawings were translated into sets populated by mannequins. Fashion's cycle became interlocking giant cogs, the labyrinth was drawn on the floor of an open platform. The walls were painted on by New York Illustrator Ruben Toledo, human attributes were added to mannequins by jewellery designer Naomi Filmer, and as an imperative nod to the constructivist aesthetic I so loved, Yuri Avvakumov created a 'coda': ladders in a constructivist manner, leading vertically to precarious platforms.

I always researched projects at college for longer than I spent on design. I still do. It was still the era of the 'art historical' double slide projector – I like twos. The comparison, the reference, the provenance of an idea is key, its lineage. I love genealogies, perhaps because of Australian descent I long for certain roots, perhaps because of Roman birth I am certain they exist. As an exhibition maker I get to put object and referent side by side – testing different configurations, interlocking, above and below. Malign Muses, subsequently renamed, Spectres when it travelled to the Victoria and Albert Museum in 2005, was about lopsided readings of fashion. The 'twos' interrupting the progress of fashion and turning it back on itself. Like Diller's shirts, the exhibition was not about the individual objects, but, in this case about the fashion system and its promiscuous uses of history.

BUILDINGS TASTE LONELY TO ME

ALEX SCHWEDER

CASE STUDY

OPPOSITE   My Precise Self learnt to account
for the existence of other selves within it.
TOP   My Rigourous Self unlearnt rigidity.

New York-based architect-turned-artist Alex
Schweder's practice explores architecture
through the senses and emotions that architects typically neglect: smell, taste, sweat,
desire. Describing his work as 'performance
architecture', Schweder's installations act
as 'props for inhabitants to form and perform
their identities'. In this brief idiosyncratic text,
Schweder describes his inflatable piece
Sensefactory, evoking a form of architecture
that is dynamic, unstable and erotic.

TOP   My Detailing Self drew in supple
fluctuations.
BOTTOM   My Collaborative Self learnt to
use its other selves as scaffolding to satisfy
its urge to rise up.

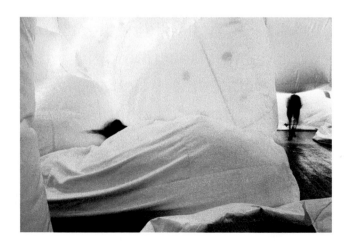

As with most understandings, spatial discoveries arrive through my body. Mediating them are buildings. Embedded in these structures are restrictions to the possibilities my sensing body contains/constrains. Restrictions that were assumed during their design. Stable, binary and hermetic, these idealised foistings are incommensurate with the lived experience of my fraught leaky corpora.

Pursing and pouting, animated by currents, inflatable spaces unlike assumptive buildings have offered a recognition that approximates my sense of flesh... my desire for other peoples'... the foreignness of my own... the meanings stuffed into it... the seduction of its stink. Tossed in the roiling of inflatable space, I press against its occupants, subjectivities previously without permission, without possibility, the suppler of my selves. Drinkers of the milk I yearn to leak. Tiny drops sweating through my shirt... expanding in a stereo broadcast of my longing to nourish... lacteal masculinity leaking out.

Developing each inflatable, in this way, has had the quality of learning a self with whom I have always lived but never met. They've been hairy and luminous, pliably metallic, and transparent to an absence. Yet selves, I've experienced as my own, are anything but discreet. In their latest subjectival iteration, Sensefactory,[1] the choreography of inflatables displacing one another mirrors this understanding. That is of their movement. Of that which insufflates form into them, of their substance, I am less sure. This conglomeration of eleven writhing sacs, constrained by one that never disgorges, suggests that one's perceived containment in a rigidly stable singular self might instead be a subjectival flashing plucked from a fluctuating dynamic between selves that are many. In substance, this conglomeration makes, out of supple buildings, supple selves.[2]

1 Exhibited at Munich's Muffathalle in 2019, Sensefactory was a 25 by 15 by five metre installation.

2 Alex Schweder would like to thank that self that is only possible in combination with Lamis Bayar.

FROM ARCHITECTURE TO VIDEOGAMES

MIRIAM BELLARD, ROCKSTAR NORTH

The parallels between architecture and video-games would appear to be close, but making the leap from one to the other is not necessarily straightforward. From studying architecture in New Zealand, Miriam Bellard worked as a set designer for film, and developed her own indie game before landing her role as art director at Rockstar North, creators of block-busters Grand Theft Auto and Red Dead Redemption. Here, Bellard explores how the various steps on her path have shaped the way she thinks about space, and the particular challenge of designing for games.

FROM ARCHITECTURE TO SET DESIGN   I wanted to study fine art at university, but my father wanted me to follow in his footsteps and become an engineer, so architecture was the compromise. This is a decision I've never regretted. While studying I fell in love with designing spaces and experiences, but I soon realised that I didn't want to be a 'real' architect. Architecture at that time seemed limited to minimalist designs made from concrete, glass and steel, or wood and stone if you were lucky. I didn't want to limit my creative palette, and also wanted to find greater meaning in design. It wasn't enough that something looked pretty, or fashionable, or had an interesting concept, I wanted to find deeply rooted reasons behind design decisions. I was attracted to the film industry, because it felt like it answered both of those needs. In film, there's a lot more variety in designing, and a narrative purpose driving the design decisions. Everything is there to express a story.

The New Zealand film industry is strong and well established, although breaking into it was still a struggle. I contacted local production designers looking for runner work, approached the university's film course offering to work for free on student short films, and quit my job so I'd be available to start on a moment's notice. This eventually led to a mix of badly paid art assistant work on low-budget productions, and unpaid production designer work on no-budget short films and on one no-budget feature-length film. To pay the bills I worked on architectural visualisation commissions, which was only just becoming a thing at the time. My breakthrough moment in film came when I received a phone call from Grant Major, the Oscar-winning production designer behind Lord of the Rings, who offered me a role as a set designer for Peter Jackson's King Kong, which was to be filmed in New Zealand.

The role of a set designer is to design the physical sets, as well as create the architectural plans, sections, elevations and details used to construct them. Sets could be anything from a building interior, a street exterior, to a section of natural terrain. Anything that would be physically built, life-size, was our responsibility. Most of the other set designers came from similar backgrounds to me: architecture, interior design and drafting. But unlike 'real' architects, we were designing for aesthetics and story only, and didn't need to concern ourselves with real-world functions such as drainage or planning constraints. For example, I helped to design facades for our version of downtown 1930s New York, an extremely large outdoor set which included the ground floors of a number of city blocks (the upper storeys would be made digitally). Every single building needed a design for the construction workers to use. We focused purely on how the outside of the building would look, and didn't concern ourselves with how they would be structurally supported. In the final film our designs were not the focus of the narrative, but instead formed the backdrop to the characters and to the action.

FROM SET DESIGN TO VIDEOGAMES   My role on King Kong should have been the start of a solid film career, but I discovered that set design wasn't quite the right work for me after all. It answered my desire for variety, and my need for a meaningful basis to design, but I wanted to challenge my more mathematical and analytical side. I went back to Auckland to work in architectural visualisation when I was offered a role as an art director at a video game start-up. At the time the games industry in New Zealand was minuscule, so they were looking to bring an art director over from film. In addition to the typical skills expected of a good art director (giving aesthetic feedback and direction), they were also looking for someone with experience in 3D modelling. With my background in architecture and experience in film, I was well placed to make the transition into games.

Where in film all of our set designs were – quite literally – the backgrounds to the characters and the story, in video games, players care about the whole environment.

They move through it, and interact with it and exploit it in order to achieve gameplay goals. I soon realised that in order to learn, I needed to work with experienced people. I emailed a hundred-or-so companies around the world asking if there was such a thing as a set designer for video games. Mostly my emails were ignored; a few people replied with a polite but encouraging 'no'. One company said 'yes': Guerrilla Games in Amsterdam. Their concept department was filled with people with strong product design backgrounds, and they liked the idea of having an architect on the team. After passing a visual design test, I was hired as an architectural specialist on the concept team. I learned a lot at Guerrilla but didn't quite manage to settle. I was used to temporary freelance work, not full-time permanent roles.

After a year I decided to try and do it myself, and created an indie game with my partner. It was a disaster. The game's aesthetic standards were strong, but they didn't match the gameplay. Players expected adventure/story gameplay, rather than strategy/tactics, resulting in low reviews. The game only sold a fraction of what we had hoped, leading us to run out of money and almost lose our apartment.

That was the lowest point of my career. I didn't know what to do next since I didn't fit any of the job descriptions that games companies were advertising, and didn't want to face making another indie game. While my partner and I were planning to return to New Zealand, I casually sent out some applications for jobs that were tangentially related to what I could do, and was surprised when I got a few call backs. While our indie game had been a financial failure, the aesthetics were strong, and my portfolio was attractive because of it. I was even more surprised when I got a call from Rockstar North, one of the top triple-A game developers, based in Edinburgh. They gave me a test, liked my work, and created a bespoke role for me in their company working with their lead concept artist, Ian McQue, who was making architectural sketch models and looking for expert assistance. Although I thought I knew what I was doing when I arrived, given I had after all trained as an architect, worked in film, and worked in games before this, I soon realised that I lacked skills in two important aspects of game design: the 'flow' (how it feels to move through a space), and 'making-3D-look-good-in-2D'. This led to a lot of research and reading to try to figure out what else I had missed. It's only in the last couple of years that I've felt like I finally have a handle on it.

THE ARCHITECTURE OF VIDEOGAMES   Like designing for the real world, videogame designers create spaces and environments for people to inhabit. In that way we are still the architects and interior designers that we trained to be. The biggest difference is the criteria by which we judge a good design. The four most important criteria when designing for games are player experience, visual storytelling, cinematics, and creating a functional space.

'Player experience' is the moment-by-moment experience the player has when playing a game. It's the awe when they see a grand and expansive space; it's the frustration when they are lost and can't find their way; it's the curiosity when they want to know what's around the corner; it's the sense of flow as they move through a well-designed space; it's the love they feel over their own properties; and it's the anger when they die because we didn't signpost a hazard. Playing a game is a deeply emotional experience for the player, and the environments are a big part of that.

'Visual storytelling' is all the stories that are implied by the environment. It's the changes to a building that imply time and history; it's the human traces that are left behind by activity and habits; it's the style of elements that reveal taste and cultural context; it's the level of design cohesion which communicates the money/time/care invested by the people who created the space; and it's the construction and structure which communicates the technology of those who made the space. Good visual storytelling brings the game to life and adds a sense of richness and solidity to the game-playing experience.

'Cinematics' is how the design looks on screen. Our 3D environments need to be designed to look good on a 2D screen as the player runs through the space. Everything that film does through the camera, we need to do through the environments.

Working with the team at Rockstar North,
Bellard developed the architectural design for
Grand Theft Auto V Online: The Doomsday Heist.

233

While we can't control the movement of the player camera, we can control the environment the player moves through. This means that in order to control the 2D screen, we need to control the environment.

'Functional Space' refers to spaces that don't crash or look glitchy to the player, and can be made in a reasonable time. Spaces need to work with optimisation and tech budgets (will it run?), other departments limitations (will it work for AI, animation and game design?), and production budgets (how time consuming is this design to make?). The role is surprisingly technical. It is also extremely creative. We get to mix the two extremes.

I have been at Rockstar for six years now, and was recently promoted to art director for visual development – a role and title that I never imagined possible back when I was studying architecture all those years ago. I have found the perfect balance of artistically interesting, technically challenging and constantly evolving work, and I get to work with talented people designing a remarkably diverse array of spaces I can be incredibly proud of. I don't think conventional architecture could offer me anything close to this level of innovation and creativity.

'IT'S WHERE DIFFERENT FORMS OF KNOWLEDGE COLLIDE'

Interview with MATT JONES, GOOGLE

The field of technology has long been described using spatial terms – highway, web, platform, cloud – and as it becomes further embedded in our lives, the distinctions between 'real life' and life online continue to break down. But what might technology learn from architecture, and vice versa? Matt Jones studied architecture in Wales in the 1990s, and now works at the forefront of the tech industry, as principal designer at Google AI. In this interview, Jones reflects on how architecture has shaped his work, and asks how architecture might learn from technology-scale thinking to make a real impact.

EDITORS   To start off, where and when did you study architecture?

MATT JONES   I studied at the Welsh School of Architecture (WSA) in Cardiff in the early 1990s. The WSA was and still is a place with a strong sense of practicality around architecture and building. Afterwards I did a year in the architects department of the National Health Service in Wales, working on hospitals and care centres, which I really enjoyed. And then between 1994 and 1995, during graduate school, something happened which distracted me a little bit: Tim Berners-Lee invented the web.

EDITORS   What was your first encounter with the web?

MATT JONES   I always loved messing about with computers as a kid. I got my first computer when I was eight or nine. That was a big part of growing up for me. Again, at university I was lucky, as the school had internet access in the CAD room. I thought, well I'm crap at making models, I'm good at computers, I'm going to teach myself AutoCAD and 3D Studio. And I basically lived in the CAD room the whole time.

EDITORS   So you're messing about on the early web in 1995, a time when lots of spatial metaphors were thrown around – information superhighway, cyberspace, etc. Looking back, did you see any connection to the architecture you were meant to be doing?

MATT JONES   We had access to this thing called a 'MUSH', a multi-user shared hallucination, which was like a primitive text-based version of Minecraft. You were able to create anything you wanted, as long as you could describe it in words. So it was spatial in the way an old-school text adventure was, you move north, there are entrances, and so on. There was a spatial imagination you had to bring to it, but all rendered in text. I was completely hooked, to the extent that it was probably hurting my studies. But I was good at CAD, so my tutors thought 'oh he's doing fine'. I did my thesis on virtual reality in 1994, in the first wave of hype around it, when people had to wear huge fish bowls on their heads. So I was really swept away with it all, away from physical building and into this imaginary potential of digital space.

> EDITORS   How did you make that leap after gradua-tion? How did you transform this obsession into a job?

MATT JONES   It was just dumb luck I suppose. I had won a travelling scholarship, and I went to Los Angeles to revisit Reyner Banham's *Four Ecologies*, and basically just take lots of photos of buildings. I got back to Cardiff and had to make a report for the scholarship, and I was so broke I couldn't afford the colour printing. So instead I asked the school if I could make this new fangled thing called a website. And they said 'I have no idea what you're talking about, but why not?'
Again, more dumb luck, it turns out it's one of the first websites about architecture, and it gets picked up in the *LA Times* and all sorts of other places. I then got contacted by a guy starting up a web company in London offering me a job. And that was that really.

> EDITORS   Did it feel like a big decision at the time? As in, if I do this, I'm leaving architecture?

MATT JONES   Not really. There was a recession in archi-tecture, and I didn't have parents who could support me, so I would probably have had to get a job outside of archi-tecture anyway. And meanwhile, there's this big shiny thing in front of me.

> EDITORS   Obviously you brought your interest in com-puters and the web with you, but was there anything from your architecture training that was helpful in this new tech world?

MATT JONES   Something which came from working in practice on my year out, was the act of translating between fields of design or fields of knowledge. It was hanging out with clerks of works on building sites that was really useful,

Architects After Architecture

translating between engineers and quantity surveyors and the client, for instance. As the architect you are the translator, sitting at the boundary of all these different specialists. You may not be able to do what these specialists can do, but you are interested in what they're doing, you like talking to them, you can ask the right questions, and you can do something synthetic in the middle to make it all make sense somehow and propel it into something new. That's a key thing, I've come to realise. And it's the same in tech. You need to translate between the computer scientists, the business person, the marketing person, and so on. It's where the different forms of knowledge collide. And it's the quality of an architect or of a designer in how they respond to these collisions. 30 years on, I still think that way.

> EDITORS   I want to jump ahead now to BERG, the design and technology studio you set up with Matt Webb and Jack Schulze in 2005. How did this way of thinking shape that company?

MATT JONES   In a way, BERG was a practice founded to address these collisions, to try and get ahead of them. Our starting philosophy was that everything has a grain, everything has a thing it wants to do. Even these things which seem to be immaterial, like technology. We were very curious about how the material culture of technology becomes broader cultural material as it were. We were fascinated with technologies which were cheap enough to be ubiquitous, rather than perhaps the very latest technology. And we would look for collisions between this cheap technology and new contexts, cultural tropes from gaming, comic books, graphic design, and TV.

Jack Schulze had this idea of 'cultural footprint', something significant that could be in the hands of many many people. A lot of our contemporaries at the time were looking at design as a form of artistic provocation – 'speculative design' for instance – rather than something that could be mass produced. I remember Jack saying, 'I don't want to do that, I want to make things that are in Happy Meals.' The people who make Happy Meals are the people who know how to make joy at scale.

EDITORS   This idea of 'scale' is one that I feel is critical when we compare architecture to technology. One of my criticisms of architecture is that we talk a big game about changing the world, but only ever have a very tiny impact. Architecture is obsessed with the single prototype – the most sustainable building, for instance – which shows what's possible. But it never makes the jump into real transformation at scale, which is what is really needed if we are to tackle the climate emergency. Jumping ahead now to your current job at Google, one of the early projects you worked on was 'Project Sunroof', which seems to apply this technological-scale thinking to architecture.

MATT JONES   The idea for Sunroof came from a Google engineer, and Google engineers are just not interested in small problems. It's like 'come back when you've got a couple more zeros on the end of it and we'll talk.' Carl Elkin, who was one of the original progenitors of Sunroof, was working adjacent to people working on Google Maps, and was personally very interested in energy transition. He had this synthetic moment, where he thought, what happens if we look at every roof?

Project Sunroof uses satellite imagery and computation to model how much sun any roof is going to get, and therefore how much energy it could generate. The idea was to use that information to make it a little bit easier for the roof owner to add solar panels. It really was a genius idea, one where you've got all of the ingredients already, and one of those ingredients is scale.

Last time we met we were talking about Rem Koolhaas's book *S,M,L,XL* (1995). So if you're working at the XL scale, you're thinking about a different set of issues, and you have a different set of possibilities available. Thinking at this planetary scale is something that's semi-native to anyone working on internet systems, because – with some exceptions, of course – you have to expect that anything you make could be used anywhere on the planet. That leads you to a different set of ideas. It leads you to thinking about a sort of 'compound interest' and emergent effects of a design, which is what I find so fascinating about the work I've been doing the past ten years or so, particularly at Google.

> EDITORS   You mentioned Koolhaas's interest in the mega-scale, are there any other architects who you feel are looking in this direction, or who have informed your thinking?

MATT JONES   I think this is something that architects have maybe been good at historically. A lot of the people I fell in with from interaction design or digital design had been informed by cybernetic thinking from the 1970s and 1980s, people like Archigram, Cedric Price, Christopher Alexander, Nicholas Negroponte, etc. These ideas still have a big grasp over my mind. Certainly this period of thought seems much more mappable onto the work I'm doing now, compared to the ideas coming out of architecture in the past twenty years gone by, which seemed to be more about the image rather than systems.

In the past five years or so you do see a new wave of architects who are thinking much more about the public realm, about public housing, political systems, economic systems and so on – that big swathe of problems in the middle: social economics, shelter and the environment. They see the systems that we're embedded in and see them as something they can design or redesign. That's encouraging.

> EDITORS   To try and explore that thought further, what can architecture learn from the internet? Or from this large-scale, Google-scale thinking?

MATT JONES   I should start by saying that while the tech industry as a whole has been very good at thinking at planetary scale technologically, it has been poor at thinking socially or culturally. That's why we're in the moment that we're in. So I don't think the tech industry has all the answers by any means.

But certainly architecture can learn from this approach to working at an enormous scale, and how big impacts can emerge from an accumulation of very small interventions. And you can see some people in architecture are working

Google's Project Sunroof applies technological-scale thinking to architecture, by using satellite images and computation to model how much solar energy each household could generate.

241

in this way already, but they're probably not drawing buildings, they're more likely to be drafting a legal instrument, or proposing a covenant over a bit of land for a particular use. These are ideas which can be more easily reproduced, and could even be open sourced.

WHILE THE TECH INDUSTRY HAS BEEN VERY GOOD AT THINKING AT PLANETARY SCALE TECHNOLOGICALLY, IT HAS BEEN POOR AT THINKING SOCIALLY.

EDITORS   I really like this notion that a small idea through its multiplication can have a systemic effect. Because often in architecture, when we think of making a bigger impact, we draw bigger things, like megastructures. But despite the immense scale of some of these buildings, you're unable to benefit from network effects as long as you're the one holding the pen.

MATT JONES   That's right. Whoever designed the first electric motor that was cheap and efficient enough to make those little e-scooters has done more for cities in the past ten years than any architect or urban planner. Particularly in China.
It's not quite the right analogy, but I certainly think that design decisions which can be copied or reproduced rapidly are what can create real change. And if they are open source, then they can scale even faster, because it takes some of the brakes off the copying.

EDITORS   Open source is one of those wonderful big ideas that comes from software, which has been exploited to some extent in architecture – in projects like Wikihouse, for instance – but it still remains largely untapped. I feel like somewhere deep down in architecture there's an unacknowledged obsession with originality. The designers that we recognise and celebrate are the ones who do singular things which are different, rather than those who design things which can be more easily copied, and therefore get to scale.

MATT JONES   You're right, the originality is what's celebrated. There are exceptions, I walk past a Walter Segal estate most days on my way to the train, here is somebody who was designing open systems that could be picked up by almost anybody.

But the biggest difference between open architecture like Segal, and open source software, is that whatever gets added goes back into the pot. In architecture you don't get that feedback loop. The boats don't all float higher each time as a result of what is learned on site and what gets changed or added. That's what enables the software community to develop and advance so quickly and to metastasise into something huge as a result.

There's a huge potential in architecture for this software-style copying and learning, particularly in the legal, contractual or regulatory space. If one group creates a covenant that allows you to do something smart with the city, and that gets copied and added to and gets fitter and fitter, then you start to get some of those dynamics you see in software.

EDITORS   One final question, what advice would you give to a young person setting out on their career, somebody who might feel more at home in the CAD lab, like you were, and may be thinking of what to do next?

MATT JONES   Architecture is a brilliant education, it's a brilliant nest to bring the shiny things from other fields back to. That foundation allows curiosity and wandering, it's a fantastic base.

FROM ARCHITECTURE TO TECH

BLAKE HUDELSON
and GAVIN JOHNS, ARCHITECHIE

In this digital age, where our lives are increasingly lived online, and the world's most valuable companies are all in tech, the lure of Silicon Valley is a powerful one.
But what can you offer as an architect?
Blake Hudelson and Gavin Johns established the organisation Architechie as an answer to this question. Here, they offer eight ways an architecture degree is relevant in tech – from the similarity of the design process to 'scrappiness' – and urge other designers to follow them by making the leap.

After working as architects for a number of years, we came to realise that the broad range of skills we had cultivated in architecture school were mostly going unused in practice. We knew there had to be more we could offer the world. Living in Silicon Valley, you can't throw a stone without hitting a company that is working on world-changing ideas. As Marc Andreessen, founder of Netscape, famously said, 'Software is eating the world.' And yet architects are largely absent from contributing to this work. We had a hunch that we could apply our skills in emerging roles in the technology industry, including user experience, design technology, design strategy, user research, and software development, and quickly discovered that we were well-positioned to take them on. We went from designing spaces that only a handful of people ever get to experience, to designing products and services that millions of people touch every day. We came to see software as simply a different medium of architecture.

Architects have been trained to shape the world according to millennia of design discourse. Giving form to culture is a skill that calls on all the senses and requires a deep understanding of how people interact with their environment. By understanding the potential of new experiences created through software, architects have the opportunity to shape the world through this new medium.

We've had many architects reach out and ask us when and why we decided to transition into software. This puts us in the dubious position of praising architecture's skill-set, while promoting a departure from it. That said, we have a very abstract definition of architecture and believe if architects have the interest to pursue any other design discipline, they will have a high chance of success.

Having gone through this career transition process ourselves, we decided to put together a list of eight reasons why architects are well positioned to find success when transitioning into the technology industry.

THE DESIGN PROCESS IS NEARLY IDENTICAL   One thing that architecture school instills in you is the ability to approach any design problem with a rigorous approach of research, concept, iteration, and building, while continuously questioning assumptions along the way. Architects know that to design anything properly, whether in the built world or digital world, you must first understand the problem. What is the goal? What does success look like?

This rigorous reflection, developed in phases from schematic design to construction, is nearly identical to software. The main difference between the two fields is the end point. In software, it is critical to continue iterating based on the feedback received from users, not so easy in architecture once the clients have moved in.

WE ARE IN THE DUBIOUS POSITION OF PRAISING ARCHITECTURE'S SKILL-SET, WHILE PROMOTING A DEPARTURE FROM IT.

YOU'RE TECHNICAL   Not just 'I know lots of software' technical, but 'I know how things go together' technical. Architects are used to knowing the fundamentals of every decision in design. You have the rigour to learn how building elements come together, and then work tirelessly to design a solution that's both functional and beautiful.

When designing a technology product, having the ability to create technical specifications for both hardware and software is critical. The ability to go from view at 10,000 feet, and then zoom in to the pixel, is a skill necessary to bring big ideas to life.

YOU DESIGN FOR PEOPLE   Architects are trained to always have their client's and occupant's best interests at heart. As a software designer, you need to have the user's best interests at heart, which requires constantly soliciting feedback as your product is used, sitting face-to-face in order to understand if your work is successful. Since software is so malleable, it makes it easy to iterate constantly, which is much more difficult to do in the built world.

YOU'RE SCRAPPY   In architecture school, learning new techniques and being resourceful is essential. Only eight hours to make a model and the shop is closed? You find materials in the dumpster and create beauty from it. Never created an animated walkthrough of your design before? No worries – you have the internet, a pot of coffee, and you won't move on until you learn. This scrappy mentality of 'just figure it out' is ingrained in the DNA of architects, a mentality that's especially helpful when moving into the technology industry where change is constant.

YOU TAME THE AMBIGUOUS   Since plans change so rapidly in architecture, architects learn to be comfortable with ambiguity. The ability to form structured thinking from unstructured conditions is fundamental to the architect's thinking. Often this comes in the form of actively looking for constraints to help provide guardrails for design decisions.

In technology, many digital products need to scale massively, to be used by anyone, anywhere, divorcing the product from the context, as an architect would typically see it. Context becomes more about when and why someone would use your product, rather than the things that architects pay attention to, such as climate or site. Although that even depends on the product being created – designing a weather app?

YOU'RE NOT AFRAID OF FAILURE Architecture school is notorious for breaking students down and rebuilding them. The combination of honest (sometimes harsh) feedback, high expectations for work output, and the need to continuously iterate, gives you thick skin. These habits become invaluable when working in the fast-paced technology world, where pivoting happens frequently, and failure is a requisite for success.

YOU PUSH INNOVATION Navigating relationships with a diverse team – from engineers to contractors – to build amazing places requires ingenuity and grit. It's the same in software. It's critical to know how to work collaboratively to innovate, defend design decisions, and push into uncomfortable new areas of design. It's exciting!

If you're an ambitious architect fresh out of school and want to try designing a building in a way that challenges existing processes, you'll likely get laughed out of the room. But since the technology industry is so new, people are much more open to experimentation and testing new ways of working. Pushing the boundaries of the profession is a requirement for success.

YOUR IDEAS SCALE Architects are expected to define design systems that can scale, from the door knob to a city block. Architects are also good at employing big picture thinking and expressing their vision in tangible terms. This ability to communicate complex ideas in a simple manner to people who don't have a good understanding of design becomes especially useful when designing technology-based experiences that will potentially impact billions of people.

These are just a few examples of why architects are better positioned to move into roles within the technology industry compared to other professionals.

Realising how much opportunity there now is in technology, in 2016 we created Architechie, an organisation that helps people working in architecture, engineering, and construction fields to transition into new careers. Architechie was founded on the belief that any architect can thrive in the fast-paced, ever-changing environment of the technology industry.

Architechie provides a network of experts, resources, and events to help anyone who is interested in finding a new career.

We started Architechie as a small group of like-minded friends in San Francisco and now have active chapters in New York, Pittsburg, Los Angeles, and Singapore, with more in the works. We have grown into a network of thousands of people working at the intersection of technology and the built environment, a global brain trust of creatives and builders, brought together by a shared excitement for the built world, and the opportunity to improve it using technology.

Our work is founded on four core principles:

- We are first and foremost people;
- Our unconventional backgrounds are our best asset;
- Everyone has a different path, and that's a good thing;
- Together we make up a living wiki: ask us anything.

Many Architechie members have transitioned from roles in traditional architecture practice into new roles at leading companies working on smart cities, AR/VR, autonomous transportation, connected environments, blockchain, and computational design. Some members have also taken the entrepreneurial leap and founded their own companies.[1]

Technology is creating opportunities for design and innovation that have not existed before, and as architects we are well-positioned to be leaders in these emerging industries at the intersection of our digital and physical worlds. Our world is changing more from software than skyscrapers, and as keepers of culture, architects need to be involved.

1   See AECstartups.com for an index
    of these new companies in the
    architecture and technology space.

'CRYPTOCURRENCY HAS ENTERED MAINSTREAM CONSCIOUSNESS'

Interview with MATT STORUS

One of the fizzier waves of technological optimism in recent years has been for cryptocurrency. While fortunes have been made and lost in Bitcoin, the interest in a fully decentralised financial system has only risen. But what of design? Architecture-trained Matt Storus leads the design team at Coinbase, one of the world's largest cryptocurrency exchanges. In this interview, Storus discusses the similarities and differences in working in architecture and technology, cautioning those eager to make the leap that there is a lot to learn.

EDITORS   How did you become a digital
product designer?

MATT STORUS   I studied Architecture at both Waterloo and Harvard, then began working as a user experience designer in 2012.
        When I started at Harvard GSD in 2008 the App Store
had just been launched. I was always keenly interested in technology and it was inspiring to witness the Cambrian explosion
of apps happening in real time. The pace, scale, and impact
of digital design seemed like the polar opposite of architectural
practice. After graduating and practicing architecture I inevitably found myself looking for some way into that world. Luckily
for me, my classmate Greg Tran has similar ambitions and
we both eventually made our way out to California and landed
jobs as user experience designers. At Samsung we worked
on apps, wearables, and internet of things interfaces.
        Around 2014 I started to become interested in Bitcoin.
I was initially quite skeptical but became a believer as I learned
more and got to know people in the community. At the time,
I felt like I was already too late to the next big thing, and I was
trying to find my way in. After seeing a presentation by Balaji
Srinivasan at a Bitcoin meetup, I immediately applied to his
startup 21.co hoping to be their first designer. At 21 our mission
was to drive the mass adoption of Bitcoin. We started by focusing
on the software developer community, and created a product
called the Bitcoin Computer. It was a small developer kit that
included Bitcoin-specific hardware (miner, node) and software,
and it allowed developers to build and host Bitcoin-enabled apps.
        Our next product was called the 21 Inbox. It was an app
that allowed a network of experts (like software developers)
to earn Bitcoin by completing microtasks – like answering
surveys or answering professional questions. To better
communicate our value proposition we changed our name
to Earn.com, and we soon started adding thousands of users.
It was during this period of growth that we attracted the attention of Coinbase, and in 2018 we were acquired by them.

EDITORS   Could you expand on what were the triggers
which made you abandon the architectural profession?

MATT STORUS   Back in 2008, parametric design and digital fabrication dominated the academic discourse at Harvard. From my point of view the discussion was largely focused on exploring ways to generate novel geometries while loosely pointing towards the optimization of 'performance'. While I found the form-making process exciting, I also felt like it was inward-facing conversation. Increasingly, people's experience of the world was being modulated by their interaction with technology, and I felt like the discipline was blind to it. At the same time, particularly in the midst of the financial crisis, career prospects in architecture were slim. Architects could look forward to graduating after six plus years of school with dim financial prospects and intense competition.

MY ARCHITECTURE BACKGROUND CONDITIONED ME TO FIND CREATIVITY WITHIN THE CONSTRAINTS OF MULTIPLE OVERLAPPING SYSTEMS.

EDITORS   What are, if any, the skills you have acquired during architectural training and then translated into your current practice?

MATT STORUS   I think there are many parallels between digital product design and architecture. Both architects and product designers think in systems. Buildings aren't simply abstract formal compositions, they must orchestrate structure, building codes, program, circulation, environmental systems, materials, construction sequencing, etc. The same goes for building an app. Apps aren't simply graphic design. They are assembled while taking into account engineering constraints, platform-specific usability patterns, business logic. At Coinbase we deal with the financial industry and as such the various regulatory and security considerations make an impact on how an app is designed. In this sense, I think that my architecture background conditioned me to think this way by default, and to find creativity within the constraints of multiple overlapping systems.

> EDITORS   Besides this idea of dealing with complex systems, are there any other aspects which were transferable to the field of digital product design? For instance, a way of taking the human experience into account or a certain mindset?

MATT STORUS   I think there is a lot more that architecture can learn from product design. One specific area is the integration of user research and usability testing into the design process. Prior to launching into a project, we typically spend time going out and talking to prospective users to understand how we might build a product to address an unmet need or pain point. When designing the product we build multiple rounds of interactive prototypes and put them in people's hands. This rapid prototyping process is essential to making sure that what we're building is the right thing and that our potential customers can intuitively understand how to use it. More often than not, the usability testing process uncovers all sorts of issues and pushes us to make our designs better and more intuitive.

A parallel to this does not exist in architecture. While a design may be reviewed by other architects and the client, I'm not aware of any widespread process by which a project is reviewed by potential inhabitants during the design process. Furthermore, architectural projects are typically reviewed from a very abstract point of view. Plans, sections, scale models, and even 3D renderings are difficult for the non-expert to really understand. We can contrast this with interactive product prototypes, where there is no layer of abstraction between the user and the potential product. The prototype runs on a mobile device and feels almost exactly like the final product.

Aside from this, I think the rigorous crit culture in architecture is highly transferable to digital product design. There is no doubt crit culture can go too far and become toxic, but I believe it is also an invaluable tool to teach presentation skills, critical reasoning, and an eye towards continuous improvement. In my case, it helped me separate my work from my ego. Once the work gets out of your head and into an external medium (drawings, models, etc.) the criticism was no longer about me, but about the work.

> EDITORS   Who else is in the ecology of digital product design and cryptocurrencies? Other designers, app developers, economists? In other words, are you wishing amongst wolves or is this field full of 'architecture refugees'?

MATT STORUS   The Crypto industry is dominated by technologists and venture capitalists with few designers involved. It was exactly this imbalance that led me to join 21.co back in 2015. At the time I recognised that 'open source finance' was going to have a massive impact on people's lives, but it was comically under-designed. Since then, many designers have entered the space. In fact our design team at Coinbase is planning to roughly double in the next 12 months. I think it's safe to say that cryptocurrency has entered mainstream consciousness, and as a result many designers are taking notice.

Zooming out to the tech world at large I am seeing more and more 'architecture refugees' entering product design. I think many are attracted to the tech industry by promises of better compensation and greater impact. However, many underestimate the effort necessary to switch careers. Becoming a product designer means more than replacing Rhino for Figma. It requires learning an entirely new discipline with new skills, a new peerset, and a new vocabulary. I think architects are perfectly poised to make the leap, but I'd encourage them to seek out mentorship and learn as much as possible first.

SEEING UPSIDE-DOWN AND AROUND CORNERS

SCOTT PATERSON

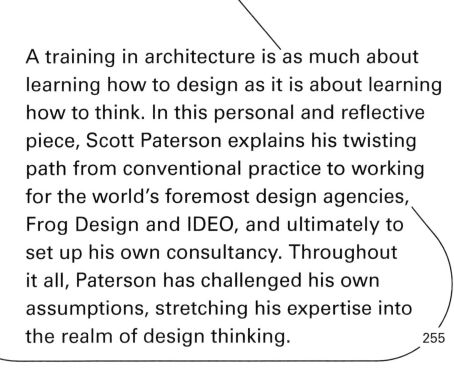

A training in architecture is as much about learning how to design as it is about learning how to think. In this personal and reflective piece, Scott Paterson explains his twisting path from conventional practice to working for the world's foremost design agencies, Frog Design and IDEO, and ultimately to set up his own consultancy. Throughout it all, Paterson has challenged his own assumptions, stretching his expertise into the realm of design thinking.

I was a very inquisitive kid. There was always more to be learned once you got past the surface. I enjoyed taking things apart. Gaining a new perspective was instrumental to assess whether the question I was exploring was going to reveal anything new. Having the right answer to the wrong question didn't teach me anything.

I chose the five-year bachelor of architecture program at the University of Minnesota, my local school. It was 1993, CAD was still in its early days. While working at a firm after graduation, I noticed a difference between the good work we created and the work recognised in magazines. The value system was different. I was really curious about how that work was getting created.

So I then went to Columbia GSAPP in New York for graduate school. Bernard Tschumi was the dean. Students and faculty were engaged in heated discussions about the impact of computer-aided design on the creative process. Many questions emerged about authorship, intent, and method. For example, rather than simply drawing a line by hand, as I might have done before graduate school, at Columbia my focus had shifted towards designing the very process through which that line was drawn.

In parallel, I was working part-time at the slide library that was digitising its collection. Scanning slides was quite a slow process so I had spare time to teach myself HTML and JavaScript. It was 1995 and free tutorials had started to populate the internet. Through them I discovered and got involved in what was characterised as the global new media art community, which was still emergent and therefore devoid of institutional sanctioning. It felt open, transparent, and inclusive. All of which allowed me to shift perspective on many of those questions which I had begun posing within academia.

It was an exciting and prolific time, but it wasn't until years later that I fully appreciated the extent to which those two communities – an established institution and an emergent online network – had shaped my career.

COLLABORATING ACROSS DISCIPLINES   After graduation I worked for six years as an architect in New York, and after a brief stint working as a designer in a data visualisation company, I joined Parsons School of Design as an adjunct professor in their MFA Design and Technology Program, allowing me to make a living while consolidating all the knowledge of digital systems I had gathered since graduation.

My career as a digital artist also officially started at this point. The same year I joined my friend, Marina Zurkow, for an art residency at Eyebeam Atelier. Here we developed PDPalt exploring the impact of mobile devices – in this case personal digital assistants – on our everyday lives. The set of questions and experiments explored through PDPalt paved the way for what I consider one of the highlights of my career: an alternative audio guide for the Whitney Museum which is now in their permanent collection. At one point I started to miss the design of physical objects. I joined Frog Design to help create a portfolio of large-scale interactive installation projects, developed in collaboration with architecture firms. Designing interactive systems, I expanded my perspective on time from linear sequences to non-linear networks. I used the phrase, 'from handrails to scrollbars' to demonstrate the interconnectedness of these two types of environmental cues or guides. New perspectives like these helped me to become a better consultant too.

KNOWLEDGE THRESHOLDS   After Frog Design, I moved to California to join IDEO. They hire staff based on this concept of 'T-shaped' skills, where the vertical of the 'T' represents your disciplinary depth, and the top represents your ability to be conversant across numerous disciplines. This approach helps them form multidisciplinary teams that work collaboratively from start to finish. At IDEO I connected with other designers who had, much like me, gained a self-taught, in-depth knowledge of other disciplines. That was humbling. But it inspired me to consider what role my discipline played in defining the problems I could tackle. Could I define my practice as being post-disciplinary? And what might be the consequences of this reframing?

Most of the time at IDEO we were not designing architecture. For example, we developed a strategy for a Korean home-shopping company, figuring out what products to sell and how to sell them across different channels. Projects such as this, a long way from architecture, allowed me to develop the generalist top of my 'T'. But this trait can be a challenge too: how can you be a generalist, acquiring knowledge of other disciplines, without losing your core? A stint in Singapore revealed a path forward for me. I was working with the Ministry of Manpower on a major innovation project to improve the experience for their customers – all foreign employees.

It was my first time working in the public sector. That experience was impactful, infectious, and changed my life. I decided to move back to the US and experiment with other ways to help clients' strategic planning. A number of exciting prototypes came out of this period including a series called Tomorrow in Progress, which explored the future of life in San Francisco's Bay Area. By leading these experiments I compiled a new set of speculative methods that I call 'Adventuring'.

This became the basis for my new endeavour, Adventuring Ventures, a consultancy that combines design thinking, strategic futures and civic engagement. My path from architecture hasn't been a straight one, but has veered into various adjacent disciplines, collecting ways of seeing the world through time. Seeing upside-down and around corners. All of this experience is brought to bear in this new venture, to help organisations to ask the right questions to tackle complex futures. Throughout it all, I still haven't lost my childhood curiosity.

RECLAIMING ATTENTION

A young user engages with the MP 01 – the first version of Punkt.'s minimalistic phone – to collect insights for the design of the MP 02.

CASE STUDY

The MP 02 seeks to reduce the complexity of a smartphone back to its 'phone-ness'.

The smartphone is the defining object of today. And yet its sophistication and complexity endlessly demand our attention in ways that are disruptive and even addictive. In an effort to resist these distractions, Swiss electronics manufacturer Punkt. set out to create the MP 02, a phone with just the essentials: calls, texts, calendar, and simple navigation. In this case study, Studio Folder presents the process of designing the MP 02's user interface. Established in 2013 by Elisa Pasqual and architecture graduate Marco Ferrari, Studio Folder's work shows how architectural intelligence can be applied to graphic and interaction design, critical fields in today's digital world.

OPPOSITE   The MP 02 was approached as an architectural project, with a number of workshops focusing on the relationship between screen information and context awareness.

The concept behind the Punkt. MP 02 is that of essentialism. It seeks to reduce the complexity of a smartphone back to its 'phone-ness', by distinguishing between the features we really need to remain connected to people and those which are a drag on our attention. Founder of Punkt., Petter Neby, explains that the MP 02 is 'aimed at people who want to be in charge of the technology they buy', it's about 'using technology to help us adopt good habits for less distracted lives.'

The phone has physical buttons, rather than a touch-screen, and a solid body, designed by Jasper Morrison. Studio Folder formed part of a team, alongside Arup Digital Studio (Dan Hill, Anne Frobeen) and software designer Erik Hellman, tasked with developing the concept and realising the MP 02.

Firstly we established ten principles: 'durable, not throwaway; confident, not anxious; self-sufficient, not needy; surplus, not deficit; convivial, not solitary; social, not mediated; robust, not delicate; useful, not clever; seamful, not seamless; human, not machine.' These principles helped us with crucial decisions about the relationship we wanted to create between the user and the phone and, critically, what to exclude from the typical suite of features available on a smartphone.

This striving for simplicity was realised through the interaction design and use. Building on a base of Android, we developed a stripped back palette of black, white and grey, using modern typefaces, and graphic interactions that felt tactile, reinforcing the physical buttons on the handset.

Ultimately, all of this adds up to a phone which is about being in the world, not apart from it. As Dan Hill writes, 'It's all about enhancing sociality and connection with your immediate environment, whether natural, social, urban, etc.' In this way, we see the MP 02 as an architectural project, one which brings simplicity and focus to our digital, social, and urban lives.

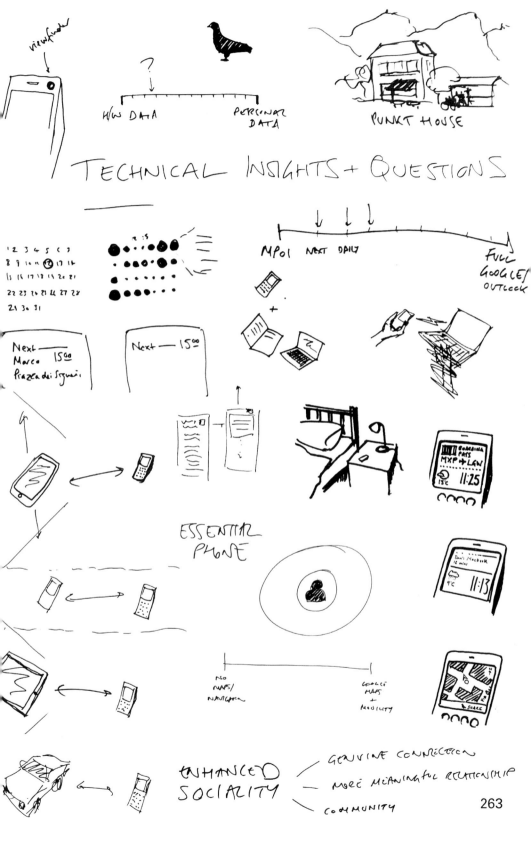

viewfinder

?

H/W DATA — PERSONAL DATA

PUNKT HOUSE

TECHNICAL INSIGHTS + QUESTIONS

1 2 3 4 5 6 7
8 9 10 11 (12) 13 14
15 16 17 18 19 20 21
22 23 24 25 26 27 28
29 30 31

MP01   NEXT DAILY   FULL GOOGLE/ OUTLOOK

Next ——
Marco   15:00
Piazza dei Signori

Next —— 15:00

ESSENTIAL PHONE

ROMAINA PASS
MXP → LAN
15°C   11:25

Don't: Macbook 12 mins
9°C   11:13

SHARE

NO MAPS/ NAVIGATION

GOOGLE MAPS + MOBILITY

ENHANCED SOCIALITY — GENUINE CONNECTION
— MORE MEANINGFUL RELATIONSHIP
— COMMUNITY

263

It will be windy
until 15:00 today

● Weather   ∧ ∨

09:41

Your next meeting
is at 4:30 PM

● Calendar ✕ Dismiss   ∧ ∨

It is likely to rain
in 2 hours from now.

● WEATHER   ⌂ DISMISS

⇄ Dan's MacBook Pro   25 MB

3:52 PM

🗓 Monday, 27 November

● MENU

HRS   MIN   SEC

02:10:32

● PAUSE   0 CANCEL

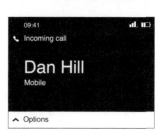

09:41

📞 Incoming call

Dan Hill
Mobile

∧ Options

MESSAGES

● John Tree   1 NEW
   Dan & Petter   3 NEW
   Carl Sagan   3h
   Joseph Grime   1d

Wed
Ehi I just wanted to know if
everything is all right.
                        7:04
        Ok! Keep in touch
14:02
Nice! Thank you and
see you really soOn
                        +9

Calling...

Hiroyuki Okuyama
Mobile

● OPTIONS   📞 SPEAKER ON

↘ Hiroyuki Okuyama
Mute
Divert call

T-Mobile 80%
On a call with   01:36
John Tree

London
10:45 AM

Today   Sun ↑ 07:37 AM
                  ↓ 04:44 PM

● SET

December 2018

MO	TU	WE	TH	FR	SA	SU
47						1
48	2	3	4	5	6	7	8
49	9	10	11	12	13	14	15
50	16	17	18	19	20	21	22
51	23	24	25	26	27	28	29
52	30	31				

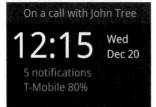

On a call with John Tree

12:15   Wed
           Dec 20

5 notifications
T-Mobile 80%

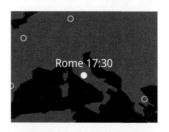

Rome 17:30

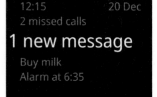

12:15   20 Dec
2 missed calls

1 new message

Buy milk
Alarm at 6:35

New message
John Tree

Dismiss

On a call   01:36
        Ok! Keep in touch
14:02
Nice! Thank you and see you
really soon.
                      ../ Abc
Thank you too! T|

Send to Luca Ferro

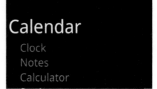

Calendar
Clock
Notes
Calculator

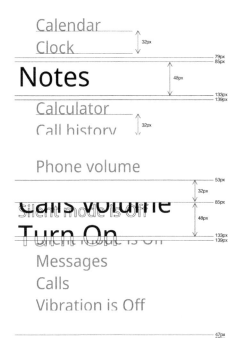

Calendar
Clock
                                              32px
                                              79px
                                              85px
Notes
                                              48px
                                              133px
                                              139px
Calculator
Call history
                                              32px

Phone volume
                                              53px
                                              32px
Calls volume
                                              85px
                                              48px
Silent mode is Off
Turn On
                                              133px
                                              139px
Silent mode is Off
Messages
Calls
Vibration is Off

                                              47px
                                              53px
1 assigned to
                                              85px
Voicemail
                                              133px
                                              139px
New shortcut
                                              48px
2 not assigned
3 not assigned
4 not assigned

Punkt.

12:15   Wed
        20 Dec
5 not fications
Fully charged

OPPOSITE   The MP02's user
interface went through a
series of iterations. Icons and
illustrations were abandoned in
favour of a text-only experience.
LEFT   The UX/UI guidelines.
TOP   1:1 illustration of the MP02.

DESIGN FOR HOMELESSNESS

CHRIS HILDREY

While homelessness may appear to be a challenge squarely within architecture's remit, seeking to find solutions may require going outside of the profession altogether. Galvanised by the ongoing impacts of the financial crisis of 2008, and the austerity which followed, Chris Hildrey looked for ways he could use his architectural training to help those on the streets. He conceived of ProxyAddress, a tool to provide a stable address for people made homeless, allowing them to access key services such as benefits, bank accounts, and medicine. It is a reminder of architecture's duty to serve the public at large, not just those who can afford it.

It all began in 2009, when I left university eager to begin a career in architecture practice only to find out that the profession awaiting me was not the one I had expected. The financial crisis saw the UK's architecture profession incur more job losses than any other industry in the country. As projects of all scales were put on hold, a third of all architects became under-or unemployed, and the number of architects on benefits grew by 760 percent. Against this background, it was with a sense of startled gratitude that I accepted my first job in an architecture studio.

London, where I graduated, was not an inconsiderable factor in this stroke of luck. This is a city which holds around one eighth of the UK's population yet it contains a quarter of all its architectural workplaces. Also, rather conveniently for those designing something as expensive as buildings, it is disproportionately wealthy: the only place in the UK to feature in the top ten richest cities in northern Europe. For context, of the ten poorest, the UK holds nine. In other words, if there was a place to insulate oneself from the prospect of architectural unemployability it was London.

Yet finding a job didn't insulate me from the wider issues that were to affect the country and industry in the decade that followed. During my first year of work, then leader of the opposition, David Cameron, described his intention to usher in an 'age of austerity' in response to the financial crash. Eight months later he became prime minister.

At the time of that election, I was working on a project under the umbrella of the Building Schools for the Future programme – a legacy of the outgoing labour government that sought to rebuild or refurbish dilapidated schools across the country using public-private finance. Soon, however, the programme was disbanded, with the new conservative education secretary, Michael Gove declaring: 'We won't be getting Richard Rogers to design your school. We won't be getting any award-winning architects to design it, because no one in this room is here to make architects richer.' It was a moment of disillusionment. We had been taught at university that the act of building was an inherently political one, but it wasn't until then that I appreciated the politics involved in the act of not building. With growing questions around the nature of contemporary practice, I started a part-time research degree to explore the issue of architects' agency in the face of increasingly ruthless cuts to public spending.[1]

WHEN YOU BECOME HOMELESS YOU LOSE ACCESS TO THE SUPPORT YOU NEED. THIS IS A SPATIAL PROBLEM.

Over the coming years, in full view of architects, yet somehow beyond their influence – these cuts would come to cripple social services and erode the quality of our built environment. By 2017 one in five regional museums had closed; over 500 public libraries and the majority of public toilets had been shut down; vast swathes of public land were being sold off to private buyers. To cope with the lack of funding, some councils took to outsourcing critical services – from child protection to care for vulnerable adults – to the private sector. All of which compounded the fact that over a fifth of the UK population was now living in poverty.

It was at this point, having just been named a designer in residence at the Design Museum, that I started to formulate my own approach to architecture: one where my skills could be put to work for those most marginalised in society, in a manner that did not depend on the allocation of capital by others. And there are few more marginalised in the built environment than the homeless.

Though statistics can never communicate the suffering and hardship of those going through homelessness, they can convey the gravity of the situation. Between 2010 and 2017, the amount of government-built social housing fell by 97 percent, while the number of people sleeping rough in England rose by 169 percent. The average age of death of a rough sleeper was just 47 (now 44) – nearly half the UK life expectancy and three years lower than the world's lowest national life expectancy in Sierra Leone.

In 2013 the Red Cross launched its first national food aid programme in the UK since World War II. At the same time, the scarcity of social and affordable homes across the country meant that those who could be housed found refuge in temporary accommodation. As a result, there are over 80,000 households today, including 120,000 children, under constant risk of being moved on with as little as 24 hours notice. There are also the so-called 'hidden homeless', whose numbers can't be counted: people who, to avoid sleeping rough, move from sofa to sofa, floor to floor. Though out of sight, they still suffer the same debilitating effects of instability.

Today, one in 200 people in the UK faces some type of homelessness and, despite assumptions to the contrary, the number one cause of this condition is not mental health or substance abuse, but rather the end of a private tenancy. The picture is pretty clear: without enough affordable housing, rent prices have increased; yet the housing benefits intended to help meet these rents have been frozen since 2016, as a result of the government's austerity measures. As the gap between required rent and received benefits grows, more and more people are met with eviction and the beginnings of homelessness. Most people who experience this are fully capable of recovery if given access to the right support at an early stage. So why then are so few people recovering?

The problem, I found, was that when someone lost their home, not only did they lose their shelter; they also lost their address. An address today is not merely the description of a location, it is a de facto form of identification. As a result, when you become homeless you automatically lose access to the services and support you need. This, I realised, was in many ways a spatial problem. and I wondered how architects could tackle it.

Traditional responses did not seem enough: reasoning around housing typologies or delivering sufficient units to solve this crisis would take decades and require the mobilisation of forces which are beyond our remit. Motivated to act quickly, I created ProxyAddress: a system which uses the address data of empty or unused properties and links these with those who have no permanent abode. Whether one of the 500,000 empty homes in England already recorded by councils for council tax purposes, or one of 160,000 number 13 properties around the country that are missing due to superstition (some councils have banned the use of this number in all future housing developments), ProxyAddress duplicates these addresses and provides them as stable proxy credentials to those facing the instability of homelessness. In doing so it allows these people to access services, get identification, a job, a doctor, benefits and receive post – all vital services otherwise removed at the time of most need. The original property suffers no effects, either to its post or credit rating.

The system is currently approaching its first pilot in London to establish its compliance with anti-fraud regulations. Working directly with the Financial Conduct Authority as part of its Regulatory Sandbox programme, we will be starting with the hardest possible level of compliance: opening bank accounts with a ProxyAddress in place of a proof of address. With partners including *The Big Issue*, Crisis, Monzo, Ordnance Survey, and Mastercard's Center for Inclusive Growth, this will, I hope, ensure that losing your home no longer means losing support too.

Looking back, stepping out beyond the boundaries of traditional practice was a nerve-wracking experience. The expected outcome of my Design Museum residency was, I'm sure, a model on a plinth; there were more than a few raised eyebrows when I revealed that I would be exhibiting an intangible system. But when that same nervousness resurfaces today,

Homelessness

I think back to a moment when, after a late night of research, I found myself alone in the museum. At that time, I was giving a lot of thought as to what it meant to be an architect. I had been trained to value problem solving, strategic thinking, innovation. But to what end? Stood in the permanent exhibition, in front of me sat an array of chairs: Thonet, Panton, Rietveld. I had grown up learning about these design classics and I appreciated their ingenuity. And yet, at that moment, I couldn't shake the feeling that we, as a civilisation, pretty much have the chair problem wrapped up. Did I really want to focus all my efforts on such things when I'd seen so many other problems crying out for ideas?

My mind turned instead to those people I had seen on my way to the museum: huddled in sleeping bags or wrapped in blankets on the street. I decided that, even if I didn't succeed, trying to tackle some of the issues they face would be a better use of my training. But homelessness is a complex and human issue – it has no respect for professional boundaries, and unless we wish to sacrifice social change in the name of tackling only those problems which fall squarely within our traditional remit, neither should we.

1   In the early 2010s it was announced that the Revenue Support Grant would be removed entirely by 2020, with devastating consequences for public spending. This was captured by Newcastle City Council's budget report for 2017, which reads: 'The central Government grant which paid for bin collections, school crossings, trading standards, pest control, libraries, social workers, foster parents, street cleaning, tree planting, tourist information, road and pavement repairs, community centres, lunch clubs and much more, will [be] removed entirely. The Government has made it clear. After 2020 we are on our own.'

2   To date, councils have gone through an average funding cut of 40 to 50 percent and currently face a £7.8 billion deficit to keep services at current levels.

'WHAT WOULD HAPPEN IF ALL THE DETAILS WERE PUT BACK IN THE STORY?'

Interview with DAMON RICH

The city belongs to all of us, and yet not all of us have the tools or understanding to shape it. Through roles in local government, private practice, and as co-founder of the not-for-profit Centre for Urban Pedagogy (CUP), Damon Rich has sought to break down these barriers of expertise and access, embracing a diversity of perspectives that shape the built environment. In this conversation, Rich describes his work at the intersection of social, political, economic and material forces, showing how the things architects normally like to control can in fact be the key to a new kind of publicly-spirited design.

EDITORS   To start off, can you tell us what you studied, and how that might have shaped your way of thinking about architecture?

DAMON RICH   I grew up in the mid-century apartheid suburbs of Creve Coeur, Missouri, near Saint Louis, then lived and studied for two years at the student-governed Deep Springs College in eastern California, and finally earned an undergraduate degree in architecture at Barnard and Columbia College in New York City. Beyond looking for a new hobby to deal with a fresh heartbreak, I was attracted to architecture's critical and productive roles in the world as it is and might be.

In seminars and studio, we talked pretty abstractly about critical architecture as a tool to undo capitalism, humanism, and distracted habits. Meanwhile, outside, we saw the roles played by architects and their institutions in the development politics of mid-1990s New York City: supporting changes that others criticised as displacement, gentrification, and commodification of the city, and using the conjuring powers of renderings and archispeak to sell undemocratic development and legitimise spatial domination.

In design terms, a successful project at the time came with a narrative justification that cleverly resolved itself by recording a strictly limited number of facts and then responding with an equally taut set of design moves, bursting with intended meaning. That way, seven or ten stories could be told in a lecture. This faith in strong concepts was visually demonstrated by obtuse though succinct signs like Bernard Tschumi's three-layer Parc de la Villette diagram and Peter Eisenman's House X axonometric model. S,M,L,XL came out while I was studying, which seemed more connected to some kind of real world – at least planning got mentioned! OMA work from that time still often hung on these crystallised justifications like the Bordeaux House needs an elevator for a client that uses a wheelchair. Even though this way of talking about architecture reached out more, it still mainly steered clear of tensions, conflicts, and processes that drive site selection, land ownership, budgets, affordability, development regulations, and public approvals.

My closest comrades from that time and I wanted to see what might happen if all of the details were put back in the story? Looking to fill in these details about politics, materials, spiritual identities, construction work, legislation, financing, and maintenance led to a job working for the architecture office in the capital projects division of New York City Department of Parks and Recreation (NYC Parks).

EDITORS   It's interesting that you went to work in a public authority, rather than private practice, which is the usual route for an architecture graduate. What did you discover there? What did it teach you about who holds the power?

DAMON RICH   Both my experiences working as a designer in municipal government, at NYC Parks and the Newark Planning Office, have been the most educational times of my career, just trying to learn and operate the complicated human systems we've created to manage our habitat. They've been rewarding in that – whether you like it or not – these positions put you in the middle of a thousand conflicts that run through the built environment with real opportunities to make better, more interesting things happen.

Working at NYC Parks taught me about how the design process inherits, perpetuates, and alters all kinds of other political conflicts, in a way that does not easily fit into a studio presentation. Early in my experience, there was what we called the 'metal in the middle' episode, when we were preparing to rebuild a park in Queens that had four softball fields, arranged so the home plates and metal backstops were in the four corners, while all of the outfields merged together in the centre. When funding was allocated to the project, a council member showed up with representatives of the white, mainly Italian American softball league, carrying their strongly supported design to flip the fields 180 degrees to place the home plates in the centre. Thinking of how this would screw up the grading and drainage and why it was necessary, it took some time to uncover the scheme's main motivation: making it difficult for the neighborhood's increasing number of Latin residents to play soccer in the wide-open outfields of the current configuration. Even though not ordained by any law that softball should take precedent over soccer, the softball players got their way by using their privileges, institutions, and knowledge to shape this piece of public environment towards their desires and away from someone else's. Exposure to these infuriating micro-politics of public design helped break down my own sanctioned ignorance about the relationships between architectural ideas, implementation, and justification, and how it might work differently in the details.

> EDITORS   I can certainly see a line between this way of viewing the city and the organisation you would go on to found. Can you tell us about CUP? What is it? And what led you to set it up?

DAMON RICH   About to celebrate its twentieth birthday as a nonprofit organisation, CUP uses design and art to increase meaningful civic engagement, particularly among underrepresented communities. CUP staff work with other designers, artists, policy advocates, and community organisations to produce youth and community education projects addressing all sorts of public policy and design issues, from affordable housing and immigration to park maintenance and policing. Final products take form as posters, pamphlets, videos, websites, curricula, hands-on workshops, and more.

CUP began as an attempt to set up a different kind of institution for democratic development. I wanted to see how architectural tools and frameworks might remix some of the situations I saw at the NYC Parks department. Early CUP collaborators, co-founders, and board members brought aligned interests in architecture (Jason Anderson and AJ Blandford), graphic design (Stella Bugbee), political media (Josh Breitbart, Andrea Meller, Althea Wasow), and law and politics (Sarah Dadush and Rosten Woo). Together, we learned how to set up an organisation, apply for grants, and develop projects with partners including public high schools and advocacy organisations. After running things on a project-by-project basis for a few years, Rosten and I became the first full-time employees in 2004. I stepped down as executive director in 2007 to focus on being board chair, and later left the board to become a fan and cheerleader in 2015. CUP has been lucky to have many outstanding staff members and collaborators, as well as the last decade of leadership from executive director Christine Gaspar.

EDITORS   I'm interested in your use of the word 'pedagogy'. Who is doing the teaching, and who is learning?

DAMON RICH   Urban pedagogy meant paying attention to how designed environments teach us, how the materials of architecture and landscape embody and transmit social meaning. We wanted to learn how to teach architecture in the context of a new civic education, where democracy extends through the design of the physical world. I was also trained in techniques of popular education by the Queens Library Adult Learning Center as a reading and writing group tutor, where teachers and students work together to produce learning materials based on their own lived experiences. Teaching about the urban environment with humans of any age is definitely a popular education situation, learning together, unpacking identity, power, and space.

For an example of learning together, for CUP's 2002 project Garbage Problems, Andrea, Jason, Rosten, and I worked with teacher André Knights and students from the public alternative City-As-School High School to investigate New York City's garbage infrastructure, asking who makes decisions about it, and understanding how people are trying to change it. As a group, we interviewed waste management professionals, activists and entrepreneurs, visited sites of garbage activity, and discussed New York's many garbage problems to try and figure out what's at stake in the issues surrounding garbage.

Finally, we made things to communicate what we learned, from posters with death-metal illustrations of the related technical and social trade-offs of garbage technologies like incinerators and landfills. One student trailed their own garbage by skateboard like some kind of private detective, in order to draw a map of garbage movements within and beyond New York City. As a critical response to a public design competition to transform the city's last municipal landfill

Rich's current practice, Hector, works on a wide
range of projects across urban design, planning,
and civic arts, focusing on the complexities of

into a public park, we modeled a dark-humoured Garbage City resulting from an urbanism of increasing inequality and marginalisation, where students imagined residents restricted to making their living from unearthing the garbage of more affluent consumers.

Guided by traditions of popular education and critical design, working with high school students and others trained my imagination in how the work of design can be opened to more concerns and constituencies, and that this opening requires changing how we designers design the ways we learn about the world.

> EDITORS   One of the key long-term projects of CUP is Making Policy Public, the series of fold-out posters which explain complex spatial and policy issues. Where did that fit in?

DAMON RICH   Making Policy Public was a step forward in institutionalising CUP, where the organisation provides and maintains a defined project structure for staff to work with outside designers and advocates to produce a small well-designed and tested educational publication for a specific constituency. Interested advocates and design teams respond to separate rounds of requests for proposals, which created our best-defined 'front door' to date, and participants are selected by an external jury of designers and advocates along with staff. The design and testing process is iterative, and makes room for expertise without using it to draw lines: my favourite Making Policy Public experiences involved advocates with strong graphic design opinions, graphic designers who read the texts they design, and CUP staff who speak enough of both languages to keep the conversation going where it needs to go. All team members are paid, and the advocacy organisation receives a supply of the posters.

> EDITORS   It's an incredible project, and represents an important role of the architect, one where you step back and instead of making something, you listen, and provide the tools for others to articulate their issues.

DAMON RICH   I'm not mad about the elite celebration of the architect as advocate, which seems to have some renewed currency today. At the same time, I hope we are focusing on institutions that support and sustain this work, including critical reflection on the idea and limits of 'architect as change-maker.' Reforming our discipline to displace the idea of the architect as agent at the centre is more difficult than replacing the aggressive modernist hero with the considerate do-good designer as creative innovator. My experience at CUP gave me a more nuanced understanding of designing with other people's agendas in mind, how groups articulate their self-interest in the design process, so that the design can build in more shared understandings.

> EDITORS   I heard from Liza Fior that when you were awarded a Loeb Fellowship to Harvard in 2017, instead of taking classes in the design school, you went to the business school. Is that right?

DAMON RICH   I didn't abandon the design school, but like an electron was happy to zip through adjacent realms, like taking the law and business school foundation classes on architecture: property law and real estate development, where I learned that real estate is among the most tricky 'asset classes' because it is so illiquid! This helped prepare me to break down developer pro formas as I negotiated for more public design value as Newark's planning director.

> EDITORS   To jump now to your time working for the city of Newark, what led you into that role? Was it again about an awareness of those broader structures of decision-making? Of the tools that you might have at your disposal in a position like that to implement change?

DAMON RICH   I was first hired to be the planning department's urban designer, and later was promoted to planning director. My job was looking at the design implications of all the office's work in reviewing proposed development, writing zoning regulations, and managing public works. In many ways, this was my dream job after CUP, trying to implement what I had learned there at the scale of an entire city. Situated at the interface of private development and public democracy, with all these dramatic issues and hardball tactics, every day in the Newark Planning Office was a chance to tweak the city's system for designing itself, along with the designs that came out of it.

> EDITORS   And were you able to realise it? I imagine there is often a lot of resistance that comes from working within big bureaucracies of city government.

DAMON RICH   Having worked as a designer in city government before, I had a sense of what I was in for! And that's the craft of designing things and relationships around them to survive and thrive in the tenuous environments that architecture inhabits. So the big wins, like rewriting the city's zoning code for the first time in fifty years with basic requirements for design quality, or building a first section of riverfront park after three decades of resident advocacy and real estate fights, were like long noir novels with exhilarating endings. They required working with large and complex coalitions of constituencies, and using design throughout the process to make things bit by bit become real.

On the other hand, as a public official and a designer, you are usually not the most powerful player on the field, and you lose a lot in negotiations with private developers and other agencies. When I first became planning director, the trade-off between through-put and control felt like having a hundred basketballs shot at you and trying to tip as many as possible in a slightly better direction. Building a team system, cultivating political support, and learning to lose productively was the only way to survive and make any headway, as well as grab the true design opportunities that only appear when you are in the thick of things, in the conflict situation.

> EDITORS   With this book we are trying to shift the perspective on the role of the architect, from someone who imposes their own vision onto a place, to someone who operates more as an enabler, a negotiator,

or somebody who assembles a group around a table to achieve an outcome. It sounds to me like your practice falls very much within this second category, seeking to provide a framework for latent desires to be materialised, rather than directly shaping them.

DAMON RICH   I'll embrace that solidarity if we can hold onto the idea of increasing the recognised ways that things are shaped, partly by creating and maintaining more democratically responsive design systems. It's important for us architects to keep claiming our expertise in the materiality of human habitats, how we translate desires into construction drawings, even as we do the extra work of disassembling it for use by other people's agendas.

And alongside emphasising the strategic restraint of the designer, which keeps us architects at the centre, I'd advocate a relationship model for thinking about how we work with communities along with their latent and manifest desires. Students ask how Newark Riverfront Park's bright orange extruded PVC boardwalk emerged from the public engagement process, like who wrote it down and submitted the comment card. The answer is that no one asked for an orange boardwalk, it emerged out of a long process of building shared understandings and accountable relationships with organized communities built and tested over years. There is not a one-and-done checklist for accountable design, exactly because it has to live through organisations and relationships.

As an architect working with organised communities to translate complex agendas into concrete arrangements, you make lots of calculated decisions based on relationships and shared understandings. When you screw up and miscalculate, you risk losing part of your coalition. At Hector, we look for ways that a project can help people answer 'who put that there?' about things in the environment, as in, once the project is done, and people walk by and ask 'who put that there?' If the answer is 'well it's this architect who likes blue,' then it fails. Better results are stories about people's self-determination, about the complexities of democratically shaping a place.

EDITORS   You have mentioned your current work at Hector, where as a partner in a firm that practices urban design, planning, and civic arts, I assume you are now expected to be an author. How has being in a private practice changed how you work?

DAMON RICH   It's not typical that designers over here get treated as distinguished authors, though in the five years since Jae Shin and I launched the office, we've been lucky to work on projects that allow us to dig into design details while working with coalitions organized for parks, affordable housing, pedestrianizing public spaces, and more. We like doing the construction research and drawings ourselves, and helping create processes with more direct and interesting connections between these detailed choices and larger agendas. It's also a new challenge to try this within the general professional structures of contracts, budgets, and project timelines. Of course, there's less control over some things: instead of going into the mayor's office to pitch the project, we are often advising the people who are doing that.

Our favourite projects link different ways of practicing. In southeast Philadelphia, we've been working on neighborhood planning and redesigning a 120-year-old park with a coalition of groups including SEAMAAC (formerly Southeast Asian Mutual Assistance Association Coalition), Cambodian Association of Greater Philadelphia, and Bhutanese American Organization. As the communities represented by these organisations have developed since the 1970s, they have created agendas for improving the neighbourhood and capacities to make it happen. At each stage, more people and things enter into the design, materialising their mutual efforts and conflicts. These relationships allow us to design for organising, where each step builds the constituency and its powers. Looking forward from these 2020 pandemic days, we see all the ways we must learn to put ourselves together.

PUBLIC PRACTICE

FINN WILLIAMS

The idea that the discipline of architecture consists only of private practices is so common as to go unquestioned. But the horizon of possibility is much broader. Disillusioned by the working culture and lack of social purpose of private architectural practice, Finn Williams forged a career in the public sector. Now he has set up the social enterprise Public Practice to assist others to do the same. In this edited interview, we began by asking him what drew him to architecture in the first place, and how he got his start.

283

At an interview to enter architecture school in the late 1990s I remember being asked who my favourite architect was. I couldn't think of anyone other than Norman Foster. At the time, my idea of architecture was limited to 'iconic' projects by 'starchitects' being published on the covers of magazines. After graduating I did six months at OMA in Rotterdam, where I learned about the fallacy of the system of the 'starchitect' first hand. I saw the absurd economics of a model where you have hundreds of architects getting paid practically nothing to work round the clock on schemes that are often about making a few very wealthy people even wealthier. I learned a lot from that period, but it definitely turned me away from the idea of ever becoming an architect whose aim is to put their name on buildings that get on the front of magazines.

Over time, I became less interested in what architects were designing, and more interested in what they weren't. In the UK, architects only design around seven percent of new homes. Architects take up a lot of airtime in discussions of the built environment, but the reality is they have very little influence over the vast majority of what gets built. I started trying to learn out about the processes that shape the conditions architects work within, from procurement, to planning policy, to politics with a small 'p'. I came to understand that our built environment isn't formed by the vision of individual architects, but that it's the result of a much more messy process of creative compromise, negotiation, and ultimately getting on with people.

For my masters at the Royal College of Art I tried to create some semblance of this complexity by mirroring a real brief and using my project as an excuse to have conversations with planners, volume housebuilders and English Heritage. My final project was in such a close dialogue with the real version of events that it ended up being used by the developers to inform their approach to placemaking. That experience brought me into contact with the council, and made me realise the huge potential for creativity and influence of local government. It felt like if there was any form of practice that was ripe for rediscovery or reinvention, it was this kind of public service.

Meanwhile, it seemed to me that the agency of the architect was increasingly becoming flattened – literally – to designing either the facade of a building or the paving of the public realm. Many of the most strategic decisions were being made months, or even years, before an architect was involved. In fact, the more important the decision, the less design expertise seemed to be going into making it. I realised that there were plenty of brilliant architects, but not enough brilliant briefs. So I decided I needed to move further upstream, either by following the money into development, or following political power into the public sector. I was never particularly interested in or good at making money, so it was obvious which direction to take.

I was lucky enough to get a job in the Placemaking Team at Croydon Council in 2008. Croydon had a proud history of bold planning, an exceptionally talented Planning Department, and a great chief executive who understood the value of good urban design. It still does. Back then, the Placemaking Team at Croydon Council was led by Vincent Lacovara, who also had a background in architecture. For us, it was like building a small architecture practice, only better. We didn't have to bid for work, we had it on tap. So instead of chasing commissions, we had the luxury of really getting to know Croydon as a place, and its people. Instead of designing house extensions, we were shaping major masterplans and significant social infrastructure. And we weren't limited by briefs – we were writing them – so we didn't need to pretend that the answer to every problem was a building.

The wider context for public planning at that time wasn't easy. Austerity was hitting Council budgets hard, and a programme of deregulation from 2010 onwards made the planning system far more permissive and prioritised financial viability over social and environmental concerns. But we managed to piece together around £80 million of funding for a network of public realm projects across the town centre, commission some world-class schools and public buildings, and raise the standard of development across the borough – often far beyond the lowest common denominators of Government policy.

BEING ABLE TO VISUALISE AND SPATIALISE INFORMATION IS LIKE A SUPERPOWER IN LOCAL GOVERNMENT.

By 2013 it felt like Croydon was going to have a strong placemaking team whether I was there or not. So I moved to the Greater London Authority (GLA) to understand how planning worked (or didn't work) in other boroughs, and the picture was worrying. Between 2010 and 2017 local authority planning budgets were cut by 60 percent – proportionately more than any other service area. Planning departments understandably retreated to processing applications and producing policy, and stepped back from the non-statutory services that have the greatest influence on the quality of places; urban design, conservation, community engagement, public realm...
Just as problematically, when councils did have roles for built environment experts, they weren't able to attract enough good candidates. Every London borough told us they were having difficulties with recruitment. Finding the right people was actually a bigger barrier for them than finding the funding.

Of course, this wasn't a new phenomenon. Austerity had magnified a skills gap that had been growing for decades. Back in the 1950s, 1960s and 1970s, many of Britain's most talented architects were working in the public sector, often doing bold, experimental work with real social purpose.

In 1976 half of all architects worked in the public sector, but from 1979 onwards, a shift towards private enterprise meant ambitious architects were increasingly moving into private practice. By 2016, the proportion of architects working in the public sector was less than one percent. Given the scale of the housing crisis and looming climate emergency, it felt like the idea of architecture as a public service had reached its lowest ebb at a time when we needed it the most.

In Britain, where the planning system is based on negotiation, it's completely dependent on who is sitting at the table. So the huge imbalance of power between the public and private sectors has huge implications for how far new development is in the public interest. From the perspective of working for the Mayor of London, there was only so far the London Plan would be able to really change that. At Croydon we'd proved that good planners can work around bad policy. But the problem is good policy can't work around a lack of good planners.

That's how the proposal for Public Practice came about. On the one hand, it was clear that local authorities urgently needed to rebuild their capacity to plan proactively. In particular, they needed the kind of design skills, visual communication and place-based thinking that architects tend to be quite good at. On the other hand, I was aware that there was a generation of architects and other built environment practitioners who were increasingly frustrated by the commercial constraints of private practice, and had a real appetite to work in the public interest. They had gone into architecture or something similar because they wanted to serve society, but had ended up working on projects that were only benefitting a privileged few. Local authorities find it hard to reach or speak to these practitioners. At the same time architects and others can find it hard to navigate public sector recruitment processes – which tend to make the roles sound far more dull than they really are. Public Practice is a way of translating between the two.

I co-founded Public Practice with Pooja Agrawal, another architect-turned-public-servant, at the GLA. We secured the funding and support from the Mayor of London to spin it out as an independent, not-for-profit social enterprise in Autumn 2017. Public Practice recruits cohorts of built environment practitioners for year-long placements within public authorities. Within the first two years we've had nearly 1000 applications from architects, landscape architects, urbanists, planners, civil engineers, engagement specialists, data scientists, sustainability experts and surveyors at all stages of their careers.

So far we've placed 84 'associates' across 36 different authorities – including Outer London boroughs, council-owned housing companies, county councils, Transport for London and even Great Ormond Street Hospital. Almost every role is brand new – giving associates the license to do things differently, and work horizontally across departments. Not many of the roles involve architecture in the sense of designing buildings, but it's been fascinating to see associates using their architectural training to rethink spatial strategies, public services or planning policy. Being able to visualise and spatialise information is like a superpower in local government, where most people are used to seeing slides and spreadsheets. We've sent associates into authorities where they're the first in house design experts in living memory, and within a matter of months they've been working directly to the chief executive or leader of the council.

Architects who go on the programme often tell us they've felt more useful in their first few months than they had in the previous few years. In private practice, they might have been one of many architects working on one project for a long period. Through Public Practice they might be negotiating improvements to developments of thousands of homes, empowering communities to create their own social infrastructure, or rethinking the local economies of struggling high streets. They might be helping councils to build genuinely affordable social housing for the first time in a generation, or translating Climate Emergency declarations into real action. This is designing for everyday need, not privileged demand.

By this time next year we hope to have placed over 150 associates in the public sector. That's almost the same scale as OMA when I was there. The work of those associates may not make the covers of magazines, but it may well bring good design to a wider public.

PERSONAL-PRIVATE, PROFESSIONAL-POLITICAL

SHELLEY PENN

Where can you make the most impact as an architect? How might your skills and experience be applied to make a difference to the public at large? In a career spanning private practice, public sector, advocacy, and a look toward national politics, Shelley Penn has explored the various ways an architect can have influence. Roles in state government architect's offices in Australia opened Penn up to supporting the work of others, and shaping public policy. Through it all, she never lost sight of the gentle power of architecture, 'offering shelter, belonging, and meaning at the most intimate human scale.'

When I was 17, my school principal wrote me a note: *'may you give a lot, for you have a lot to give.'* The words struck my ego, but also drew out a serious desire to contribute. At that age, the idea of 'becoming an architect' seemed a way to do that, but it also suggested a wholesale transformation from one sort of person to another. My architectural journey has turned out to be more of a transformation into myself.

    I stumbled into architecture after vaguely thinking I'd do literature or photography. But three years into my studies, I was uninspired. A chance trip to Japan in 1985 and an encounter with Frank Lloyd Wright's Yamamura House changed that. It was under repair, wrapped in scaffolding, with doors and windows off their hinges, dirt everywhere. But the spatial arrangement and flow of volumes was intense. I was shocked to find myself in tears. So this was architecture!

    After completing my degree, and several years working for a small practice – loving it intensely, but repeatedly finding myself needing to wriggle free – I got registered and set up my own practice at the age of 28. In that period I was totally committed, and my love for architecture was perhaps most potent. Without realising it, I became quite bound within the idea of the architect. It was the Howard Roark model: the dedicated individual and the passionate, noble calling. I was serious and ambitious for my work. Inspired by contemporary and traditional Japanese architecture, by Luis Barragan, Carlo Scarpa's exquisite projects I'd seen in Venice and Veneto, and Le Corbusier's works which had led my recent journeys in France. I wanted to do something great and hoped I could if I worked hard enough and practiced with intent. My ambition was for visceral impact through spatial arrangement, proportional control, manipulation of natural light and a fluid relationship with landscape and context.

It was six years before I started to suspect it couldn't sustain me. It took another year to face the possibility of leaving, and to accept, with angst, the knowing that I needed to. In that process, I faced a loss of identity and feared a loss of credibility and purpose. Who would I be if not an architect? My work had gained recognition and I was proud of it, but increasingly I questioned its value. It felt self-indulgent: was another nice house really going to change the world?
I doubted it. If I kept at it, I figured my work would develop, and hopefully I'd earn a better living, but then... so what? Ultimately I followed my instincts, and the advice of a retired vocational psychologist I happened to sit with on a short flight one Friday afternoon. She offered two perfectly pitched messages: 'take your work seriously but not yourself', and 'test the alternatives.'

That encounter marked the beginning of a new phase. I moved to Sydney in 1999 and by serendipity was perfectly placed to take a great opportunity. I was appointed design director in the Office of the New South Wales Government Architect – a chance to work on public architecture, to contribute to something broader. In an office of 170 built environment professionals, I gravitated towards supporting quality in the work of others. I respected their knowledge and knew they were there for the long haul, whereas I was merely passing in this role. It felt more enduring and meaningful to help build the organisation's design culture rather than design a few projects myself. Then government architect Chris Johnson was instrumental in showing me that my abilities to read people and to communicate were strengths, and that what I knew of issues confronting the delivery of smaller projects was entirely relevant to larger ones. I discovered I could be effective as a champion for design excellence, and I was excited by the opportunity to engage with the making of public policy.

With the birth of my first son in 2001, I left. I'd swung from disillusionment with small practice to wariness about the workings of politics in government. A year with my son was another chance to reflect and, doing some collaborative residential projects, again, I returned to Melbourne and commenced what has become 20 years of hybrid practice, across small practice and the public sector, conducted in balance with raising two boys.

In my own practice I've continued to make architecture but choose to stay small. I only design houses, from my backyard studio, often in collaboration, and at a rate of perhaps one every four years. My pendulum of scepticism has been recalibrated, and I now recognise the value of each small intervention in the urban environment. I see the house as being at the symbolic heart of architectural purpose: offering shelter, belonging, and meaning at the most intimate human scale. Society as a collective… 'the public'… is made of thousands of individuals, each of us navigating the world through a rich and complex internal life, our experiences framed and affected by our environments. The human experience and the personal scale are *always* relevant to public architecture and public policy, however broad and high level. That awareness underpins every decent insight and every good piece of advice I've mustered in my public and private work.

At the same time I've worked extensively with government and private sector organisations – not designing at that larger scale, but supporting better outcomes for major infrastructure and public spaces through project procurement, governance and design policy, as well as consultant selection, design review and evaluation, and strategic and detailed initiatives to advance public outcomes at city scale. Advocacy for good design is central to all of my work. I've not met a person at any level who is actively seeking a poor project outcome, yet poor outcomes are abundant. There's no such thing as a perfect design solution. Every proposal can improve, and the focus for me is to help achieve something better. Understanding project drivers, respecting the client's constraints and needs enables identification of opportunities to improve project solutions that are achievable. This means places for people that are inclusive, safe, sustainable, fit-for-purpose, viable and enriching. Places that offer delight, beauty, connection and enduring meaning.

I've worked within government for periods of time in senior, influential roles such as associate Victorian government architect. I've chaired and sat on several government boards, led urban design evaluation on major public projects, advised private sector organisations including Universities and major infrastructure investment companies on design quality value and impacts. I've worked for the profession as a councillor and national president of the Australian Institute of Architects, and for other organisations as a strategic advisor and company director. In recent years my work is increasingly in directorship, governance and strategy, always underpinned by my sole-trader architectural experience.

In 2014 the relationship of my personal wish to contribute more broadly and my chosen professional pathway was brought into sharp focus. Until then I had only worked on the public service side of government, a place where I was valued for professional independence and apolitical expertise. I was then asked by a senior, former politician for whom I have enormous respect, to consider a political role. My journey so far had involved numerous shifts and tangential deviations but this represented a major change of direction. I had 48 hours to decide and, in huge trepidation, feeling humbled by an opportunity many others worked their whole lives for, I accepted. I was preselected as a candidate for the Australian Senate, some two years out from the next election. This felt like a chance to *really* make a difference through leading public policy, but the appropriateness of my character, skills and experience was less clear to me... was I smart enough? What did I know about politics?! I wasn't even sure what the job meant, especially in a time where politicians are maligned, sometimes with good reason. I interviewed several then-current and former state and federal politicians, advisors and others to try to understand what was involved. And the spectres of identity, credibility and self-doubt arose again... did I really have what it would take to be a politician?

Those considerations were not what led to my withdrawal a year later, but they were hovering unresolved. It was unplanned changes in my personal life and recognition that if I was elected, it would mean being absent from my sons' lives at a critical time. I couldn't do that. My decision was confirmed by a close friend and professional colleague who observed: 'the question is, where will you be most effective?' He was right, and the answer was obvious.

Again, it lay in that nexus of personal/private/professional/political… how could I be most effective in doing what I was passionate about while also protecting those I loved, and being true to myself? At that time, it was not to be through capital 'P' Politics.

I've practiced reflectively and have learned to accept self-doubt throughout my career. I recognise the importance of listening to my inner voice, accepting uncertainty, taking responsibility for my errors, staying open to opportunities, and not allowing fear to stop me. I have certain strengths and weaknesses, skills and inadequacies that I've learned to either hone or let go. An aesthetic acuity and love of language were there in my early and enduring interests in photography and literature, a tendency to the 'big picture', a fearlessness and ability to cut-through are countered by impatience, sometimes-insensitivity and a persistent failure to retain or focus on detail in any kind of sustained way. I've observed and am still learning the criticality of respect and listening well, the power of real leadership and good governance, the crude impact of hierarchy, and the right time for pragmatism. There's a great need to support more passionate, committed and capable architects to do more diverse, excellent work, and to recognise and honour what enables that. Of the people I encounter, I'm most consistently inspired by the younger architects I mentor.

Architecture has been a passionate pursuit and at other times an oppressive force in my life. Things are always in flux, but the constant for me is that it's all been personal and it's all been political, in that what I've done professionally has been shaped by my private world: who I love, what I value, my regard for others and the world I'm part of, my circumstances, abilities and limitations. That has been defining for me. I seem to be moving even further from the architectural norm right now, but I'm not sure that means I'm 'after architecture'. Perhaps I'm simply part of its redefinition.

ARCHITECTS FOR THE HUMANITARIAN SECTOR

SHAREEN ELNASCHIE, OFFICE OF DISPLACED DESIGNERS

How can architectural training be put to use in one of the most pressing challenges facing the world today? Shareen Elnaschie turned away from private practice to work on the front-line of the refugee crisis on the Greek island of Lesvos, where thousands of refugees seek entry into Europe. Struck by the experience and design talent among the refugees, Elnaschie set up the Office of Displaced Designers (ODD), an NGO which supports learning and professional opportunities for refugees in various design disciplines, helping people at their most vulnerable to reclaim their identity and self-worth.

I remember the strange frustrations I felt at having to design buildings as a student, the tension between process and aesthetic. After graduation, I spent a couple of years working for small practices before completing the Master of International Cooperation Sustainable Emergency Architecture at the Universitat Internacional de Catalunya. Then I undertook an internship with TAO Pilipinas, an inspiring women-led, grassroots architecture NGO in Manila, Philippines. They used to run training workshops to educate informal settler communities on building regulations and help them devise plans. In addition they also designed emergency shelters and supported rebuilding after Typhoon Haiyan. It was during this time that I met fellow outliers and my qualities of being a perceptive observer, an intent listener and someone who could empathise with multiple perspectives and make connections finally found space to grow.

In 2015 I started working with a small NGO based at Kara Tepe: a temporary accommodation site run by a special branch of the municipality on Lesvos, Greece. The following year, the EU-Turkey deal came into effect with the aim of stopping the migration flows moving through Europe. The borders were suddenly shut and the situation changed quite dramatically across the Aegean islands. People who were transitioning through the island for a night or two were now trapped in limbo for many months, years in some cases. It became clear that we had to start thinking long term, beyond basic programming.

To respond to the challenge we began by conducting an education needs assessment. Through that work, we met people with many different creative backgrounds – from landscape architecture, to graphic design and fine art – demonstrating the wealth of creative talents present in these camps and, by contrast, the scarcity of opportunities to support them.

At this point Kimberly Pelkofsky and I decided to found ODD and, working with partners including metaLAB (at) Harvard, Oxfam and local groups and individuals, we designed a series of intensive workshops for both the refugee and local community, as a way to bring them together.

OUR WORKSHOPS ARE DESIGNED TO HELP REFUGEES RECLAIM THEIR LOST IDENTITIES, BY USING THEIR SHARED INTERESTS TO CONNECT ACROSS BARRIERS.

Up until that point activities in the camps had mostly focused on language – German and English and later, when people started to register the reality of the new measures in place, also Greek. These courses targeted almost exclusively the 'most vulnerable': children, women, and people with underlying health or mental health issues. However, we could see that those who had pursued successful careers at home and who were considered most resilient in this context, particularly men, were in fact struggling. In the camps a person's value is a measure of their own personal tragedies.
Their vulnerability is often the primary filter through which they are assessed and through which they can access the services provided, from healthcare to education. In many ways people lose their identities, which is alienating and poses serious threats to mental wellbeing.

At one of the workshops, we asked one of the participants about his background and his ambitions.

Through workshops, construction training sessions and individual consultations, the Office of Displaced Designers helps refugees rebuild their portfolios and, with it, their identities.

The only information he shared was how long he had been in the camp and where he was from. When we enquired about his skills he replied: 'Oh, you know, nothing much'. By the end of the day we discovered he had 12 years media experience and some years training as a civil engineer. So, when we asked him why he hadn't shared that at the beginning of the day, he said that he didn't think we were really interested in that particular story. Our workshops were designed precisely to challenge this narrative and help refugees reclaim their lost identities, by using their shared interests to connect across barriers and mix with other nationalities.

The workshops were usually project-based and quite short, mainly because everyone's existence in Lesvos is so uncertain. There are last minute interviews, appointments and the looming possibility of being moved off the Island when you least expect it. Using sound mapping, documentary film-making and story-telling for example, the participants created really amazing work which they could use to start rebuilding their portfolio (which typically would have been lost) and, with it, their identities too.

One of the most successful initiatives was the Alternative Tours of the City workshop. Over the course of two weeks, we developed ideas for a walking photography tour exploring the edges of Mytilene and a social gaming tour of the city based around challenges, such as quizzes in relation to key places or monuments. We then invited members of the public to experience the tours and give feedback on how they could be developed further. The main goal was to encourage interactions and allow participants to form a shared mental map of Mytilene, as a record of their own spatial and social experiences. To achieve this we applied a design thinking framework to train people to work together, to troubleshoot as a group, to brainstorm and crucially to proceed by trial and error, or deal with failure or with the discomfort of not knowing something – a condition which can be quite challenging, particularly in certain cultures. Another successful example was the creation of social spaces on the Olive Grove site adjacent to Moria hotspot, delivered through community-led construction training sessions.

As the landscape of services available in the camps has evolved over the years, we have now stopped running these intensive workshops. We are constantly re-assessing and evolving what we do according to the needs, wishes and gaps of the refugees. Last year we focused our attention to provide a dedicated space for high level professionals supporting a smaller number of candidates on a more individual basis through one-to-one mentoring, the creation of an exhibition and portfolio material that can be accessed freely online, CV development and international networking. We are currently in the process of codifying many of those initial experiences, so they can be replicated in other contexts, thus allowing us to scale our impact and embed our values and approaches within the humanitarian sector more broadly.

There is much scope for those pursuing an architectural education to redirect their skills towards social enterprises. Architects like to investigate and uncover and are good at joining the dots. If we can set aside the ego that we are often trained to indulge in, and can develop collaborative rather than leadership skills, we would be well on our way to a truly social revolution.

THE FREE WORLD

ROBERT MULL

The refugee crisis is one of the most pressing
issues facing Europe today, with thousands
losing their lives in dangerous sea crossings,
and many more living in awful conditions in
refugee camps. This is clearly a spatial challenge, but what can architecture do to help?
Architect and educator Robert Mull has
established the Global Free Unit – an organisation which places architecture students
in difficult contexts of deprivation, displacement and political uncertainty, where they
structure and deliver projects. Mull's work,
and that of his students, is a challenge
to architects to get out of their comfort zone,
and to apply their skills where they are
needed most.

I am increasingly disillusioned with the values of architectural practice, so often dominated by self-interest, competition and mistrust. These values have now also permeated architectural education and change is urgent.

I have been involved in education, research and practice in areas of deprivation and political change since the 1980s, and, since 2015, I have worked in the refugee crises. Whether on the beaches of the Lesvos, the streets of Izmir, or within the Calais Jungle, I met people who had rejected the values of conventional higher education and challenged me to rethink how we deliver architectural education and the values we pass on to students.

Whilst architects were largely absent in these contexts, there were many individuals designing public space, making buildings, and planning small cities. One of these worked in the Calais Jungle. He was known as Posh Ben. Ben was on a gap year and had a place at university to study humanities. Armed only with a clipboard and a mobile phone, Posh Ben was responsible for receiving new arrivals, allocating sites and arranging for shelters to be built. Ben was in effect the Jungle's informal housing officer, chief planner and architect. That Ben had taken on this role without any formal training or architectural background was a challenge to my concepts of education and professionalism.

If architecture rather than architects was present in Calais, then design at all scales was also present. Design was present in the extraordinary interior of the church built by Eritrean migrants. It was present in the numerous self-build shelters, and in the complex details migrants used to stop the nails that secured the tarpaulin skin to their shelters from ripping the cover. As with all details there was a highly developed language.

Architects After Architecture

There was the multicoloured bottle top detail, the folded card-board detail, and the diagonal batten. Untutored, there were all the principles that dominate architectural education: typology, details, materiality, urbanity.

Of course, design was also present in less positive ways, as in the fake life jackets sold in Izmir which contained cheap packaging material that is absorbent, rather than the more expensive material used in real lifejackets, which meant its wearer would drown. It was present in the cynical pricing structure developed by the smugglers who controlled the sea passage from Izmir to Lesvos, which meant the price dropped as sea conditions became more dangerous.

THE INFORMAL ARCHITECTS AND DESIGNERS OF THE REFUGEE CRISES CREATED PLACES WHERE THE DIGNITY OF THE DISPLACED WAS RESPECTED.

So, architecture and design are present throughout the refugee crises, but architects and designers are not. When conventional practice does get involved the results are often impractical or dangerous. The infamous Ikea flat pack shelter, which won numerous design awards was uninhabitable in hot weather, dangerous in a fire, and creaked in a way that terrified children who had endured dangerous sea crossings. Other designers have made passport covers for people without passports, or coats that deploy into tents made out of the fabric of the boats they almost died in and want to forget.

In stark contrast the informal architects, designers and urbanists of the refugee crises created places where the identity and dignity of the displaced was respected and preserved. Even in the harsh conditions of the Calais Jungle there were informal schools, churches, shops, restaurants, laundries, libraries, hammams, theatres, youth clubs, a high street, and a radio station. The food in the famous Afghan Café on the Jungle's high street was amongst the best in northern France, and the art produced in the informal art school centred on the famous Blue House on the Hill built by the Mauritanian refugee and artist Alpha is seen as of international significance.

In all the places I worked the generosity, common purpose, collective action and mutual support I witnessed represented exactly the opposite values to those that worried me about architectural practice and education. Having experienced this alternative value system, many participants – be they refugees, migrants or volunteers – said how hard it would be to accept the values of conventional education again. Everywhere I went within the refugee crises, when people found out I was involved in education, I was asked the same questions: why can't what I am doing here be recognised as part of my education? And, how can you help me? I saw this as a direct challenge.

Since 2004 I have been leading a teaching initiative called the Free Unit. Initially based at the Cass Faculty of Art, Architecture and Design in London, where I was Dean, the Free Unit supported architecture students to structure and deliver projects in difficult contexts of deprivation, displacement and political uncertainty. Projects were identified by the students themselves and the brief recorded in the form of a contract between each student and the tutors they had chosen to assess the work. This system was designed to reverse the normal power structures of education, thus returning agency to the student and freeing them from the control and ego of the faculty or the school. For many students their projects formed the first part of their future practice, rather than the last part of their education.

By 2015 graduates of the Free Unit were distributed across the globe continuing initiatives they had started as students. In 2016 a beautiful drawing made by graduates of the

Free Unit captured this archipelago of practice and named it the 'free world', tracing a model for a new form of federated non-institutional education which was to become the Global Free Unit.

The Global Free Unit now works in live project 'classrooms' in areas of deprivation, conflict and political change across the globe. This includes ongoing work within the refugee crises, with community groups, with educational partners, NGOs and in prisons. These are some examples.

In the Greek Island of Lesvos and the neighbouring Turkish city of Izmir, the classroom partners with small NGOs supporting mainly Syrian refugees and migrants trapped in Greece and Turkey following the EU-Turkey deal that effectively imprisoned refugees and migrants in the Greek Islands and the Turkish mainland. Since 2016, the Global Free Unit has helped build small community buildings, proposed new economic structures, and brokered employment opportunities. Most recently the Global Free Unit has become part of a Global Challenge Research Fund project looking at wellbeing and housing in Basmane, the Syrian quarter of Izmir, and in the farm camps that surround Izmir where more than 20,000 Syrians work in appalling conditions and live in informal camps controlled by private landlords. The project and its four live project classrooms will produce written guidance for how camps and houses can be designed and built safely and cheaply and realise two demonstration projects.

In a very different context in rural Russia, the Global Free Unit has been hosted by Nikola-Lenivets Art Park, 200 kilometres south west of Moscow. Following the collapse of the Soviet Union and the closure of collective farms, the area around Nikola-Lenivets lost its economy and employment. Since 2000 the artist Nikolay Polissky has used large scale public art to provide an alternative source of employment and identity. The Global Free Unit has collaborated with Polissky to explore art as labour and the new forms of rural economy it sustains. The Global Free Unit has constructed summer and winter classrooms supporting the educational programme of the art park and the local villagers.

In the UK, the Global Free Unit has worked in a number of contexts including in Wetherby Young Offenders institution,

Mull has been involved with the refugee crises
across Europe, including the camp in Calais,
known as 'The Jungle'.

to provide education in architecture and design to young offenders aged 15 to 18. The 'boys' have measured, photographed, drawn and modelled the prison and the specific interior spaces they use. Through the act of recording and making they were able to communicate the complex physical, social and emotional conditions that govern their time in prison. The Global Free Unit has now received support to construct a freestanding classroom on an area of unused land at the heart of the penitentiary. The building will be designed by the boys and constructed with the help of prison staff and architecture students. Several of the boys who took part in the first classroom have been released and are now exploring employment opportunities with local businesses who supported their classroom, while those who are still serving their sentences will help choose boys for the next programme and then act as teaching assistants.

The Global Free Unit has other active classrooms including in Bosnia, working with the Most Mira project promoting post conflict reconciliation; Folkestone, on Britain's South Coast, working with the Kent Refugee Action Network; it also collaborates with others in Seoul, Sweden and Italy. Currently a new classroom is being developed in Colombia which addresses issues of displacement and identity in response to Venezuelan migration. In each of these contexts the Global Free Unit not only provides training to ordinary students, but also routes into education and employment for refugees, prisoners, volunteers or locals.

A number of the classrooms are supported by educational partners who validate their work and provide formal academic credit under the European Credit Transfer System. This allows students to accumulate academic credit as they attend different classrooms and carry that credit with them into formal education. This accumulated credit can then be bolted together to give them formal academic awards and professional registration. Similarly, the other participants can develop a portfolio that helps them enter formal education or employment through a progression agreement we have established with educational institutions.

The advantages of this itinerant, federated model are becoming clear. On a practical level it addresses the cost of education, debt, and fear of debt. Participants in the Global Free Unit are hosted by the classrooms and work within the economy of that classroom. So primarily they are volunteers, teaching assistants, builders, and many other roles, depending on the nature of the classroom and then the students secondarily. But in every case, they do not need to pay for the infrastructure of an educational provider. They do not need to pay fees to subsidise vice-chancellors' building projects, fund PR departments, cross subsidise research, or fund compromise agreements.

But perhaps more important than the practical benefits are benefits to student's wellbeing and sense of purpose. Those who participate in the Global Free Unit are able to connect their actions and projects to their own values and life circumstances. Education is no longer a rehearsal for future practice or a space apart from their everyday lives but a part of it. Whilst learning, students are making themselves useful to the wider society they are a part of.

The Global Free Unit is in its early stages and the forms of education and practice it promotes are seen as marginal. But the pressures under which it emerged are growing. The refugee crises are still ongoing and climate change promises to intensify migratory fluxes across the globe, posing challenges which will define our society in the years to come. Now more than ever, as the pressures on conventional forms of education grow, the lanyard tightens and students continue to suffer, it is urgent that we devise new ways to train the next generations of architects and designers with the humility and collective will to face these and other pressing issues.

OVERLEAF   In Izmir the Global Free Unit works with local partners to design and build new facilities for the large number of Syrian refugees trapped in Turkey following the EU-Turkey deal.

BIOGRAPHIES

MIRIAM BELLARD is the art director for visual development at Rockstar North in Edinburgh. She came to videogames after studying architecture in New Zealand.

HARRIET HARRISS is an architect and dean of the Pratt School of Architecture in New York. Her teaching, research and writing focus upon pioneering new and inclusive pedagogical models for design education.

RORY HYDE is the curator of contemporary architecture and urbanism at the Victoria and Albert Museum; adjunct senior research fellow at the University of Melbourne; and a design advocate for the Mayor of London. He is the author of *Future Practice: Conversations from the Edge of Architecture* (2012).

ROBERTA MARCACCIO is an editor and an educator at the Architectural Association in London. Her writings on historical as well as emerging modes of practice have featured in *Architectural Design, AA Files, Blueprint* and in the books *Real Estates: Life Without Debt* (2014) and *Erasmus Effect* (2014).

JOS BOYS is course director for MSc Learning Environments at The Bartlett, University College London. She was co-founder of Matrix Feminist Design Collective in the 1980s. Most recently she co-founded the DisOrdinary Architecture Project, bringing disabled artists into architectural education and practice to critically and creatively re-think access and inclusion.

JUSTINE CLARK is a Melbourne-based architectural editor, writer, researcher and critic. She is a former editor of *Architecture Australia* and the director and co-founder of Parlour: gender, equity, architecture – an activist group advocating for greater gender equity in architecture.

JUDITH CLARK is a curator and exhibition-maker based in London. She is also professor of fashion and museology at the London College of Fashion, co-founder of the Centre for Fashion Curation and visiting professor in the Dipartimento di Culture del Progetto, IUAV, Venice.

ANGHARAD DAVIES is an artist and architectural researcher based in London whose work focuses on urban subjectivity.

ANT FARM was an avant-garde architecture, graphic arts, and environmental design practice, established within the counter-cultural milieu of 1968 San Francisco by two architects, Chip Lord and Doug Michels, later joined by Hudson Marquez and Curtis Schreier. Known for their performances, media events and site structures, the group worked the fringe of architecture and art until 1978.

ARCHITECHIE is a social platform designed to help architects transition their careers to technology. Former architects Gavin Johns – a digital product designer at Opendoor – and designer/entrepreneur Blake Hudelson are Architechie's co-founders.

PEGGY DEAMER is Professor Emerita of architecture at Yale and a principal of Deamer Architects. In 2013, she founded The Architecture Lobby – a group advocating for the value of design and for fair working conditions in architecture.

SHAREEN ELNASCHIE is spatial designer, creative researcher and design educator. In 2016 she co-founded Office of Displaced Designers, a creative agency that utilises design to bring diverse people together.

LIZA FIOR is founding partner of Muf; professor of architecture and the built environment at Central Saint Martins; and a design advocate for the London Mayor.

FORENSIC ARCHITECTURE is a group of architects, filmmakers, coders and journalists which operates as a forensic agency to make evidence public in different forums such as the media, courts, truth commissions and cultural venues.

JANE HALL is a member of the multidisciplinary collective Assemble. She studied architecture at the University of Cambridge and the Royal College of Art, from which she received her PhD in 2018 after completing the British Council's Lina Bo Bardi Fellowship in 2013.

TAKESHI HAYATSU is a Japanese architect, founding director of London-based Hayatsu Architects and studio master at both Central Saint Martins and Kingston University. His research through practice and teaching focuses on craft, materials and building techniques for community engagement.

CHRIS HILDREY is the director of London-based Hildrey Studio, which deploys architectural skills to tackle complex social issues. In 2018 he set up the social enterprise ProxyAddress, to allow those experiencing homelessness to reconnect with support services.

INTERBORO is an urban design, planning, and architecture firm based in Brooklyn and Detroit. Founded by Tobias Armborst, Daniel D'Oca and Georgeen Theodore, their participatory, place-specific approach creates consensus around complex projects from buildings, parks, and open spaces to neighbourhood, city, and regional plans.

ANDRÉS JAQUE directs the Advanced Architecture Design programme at Columbia GSAPP and is the founder of the Office for Political Innovation – a New York/Madrid-based transdisciplinary agency that seeks to connect discussions of embodiment and queerness, with ecological, climate and environmental activism.

MATT JONES is a principal designer at Google's Research & Machine Intelligence division in London. He originally studied architecture and, before joining Google, was creative director for the launch of BBC News Online, worked at Nokia and co-founder of design studio BERG.

HOLLY LEWIS is co-founder of We Made That, an architecture and urbanism practice with a strong public conscience, focusing on urban research, area strategies and delivery of architecture and public realm.

KIMBERLI MEYER is an independent curator, cultural producer, writer, and designer based in Los Angeles. After studying architecture she became the director of the MAK Center at the Schindler House, and then of the University Art Museum at California State Long Beach.

ROBERT MULL is the managing director at Publica, professor of architecture and design at the University of Brighton and visiting professor at Umeå University. He leads the Global Free Unit with former members and teachers of the Free unit including Xenia Adjoubei, Catrina Beevor, Vernes Causevic, Karl Lenton and Tom Randall-Page.

ELSIE OWUSU OBE is a Ghanaian-born, British architect based in London, and the founding chair of the Society of Black Architects. Elected to the RIBA Council in 2014, she came second in the 2018 presidential election and, the following year, she initiated the Architecture:Incubator project to boost equality, diversity and inclusion in UK architecture.

SCOTT PATERSON is the founder of Adventuring Ventures. His expertise spans from a career in architecture to award-winning design consultancies Frog Design and IDEO as well as teaching at IESE, CCA, and Parsons.

SHELLEY PENN is an architect, educator, urbanist and built environment advocate, whose work combines architectural practice with senior roles advising government and the private sector. She is currently an adjunct professor and the university architect at Monash University, associate professor at University of Melbourne, and member of the Office of Projects Victoria Advisory Board.

DOINA PETRESCU is an activist, architect and educator dealing with commons-based resilience, feminist approaches and participative architecture. She is a founding member of the Paris-based Atelier d'Architecture Autogerée, and professor of architecture and design activism at the University of Sheffield.

PUBLIC WORKS is a London-based art and architecture practice which uses playful tactics to involve local users, residents and passers-by in the development of strategies for supporting social, cultural and other initiatives in both urban and rural contexts.

DAMON RICH is a partner at Hector – a New Jersey-based urban design, planning and civic arts studio, and adjunct associate professor at Columbia GSAPP. He has previously worked in the public sector and is co-founder of the Centre for Urban Pedagogy, a nonprofit that uses art and design to increase civic engagement.

ROTOR is a cooperative design practice consisting of a group of architects, designers and other professionals interested in material flows in industry and construction. They disseminate creative strategies for salvage and waste reduction through research and design, and also produce exhibitions, books, economic models and policy proposals.

PASCALE SABLAN is the 315th living African-American female registered architect in the US. She is senior associate at S9Architecture in New York and the founder and executive director of Beyond the Built Environment, a platform to support and encourage wider participation and representation within architecture.

JOEL SANDERS, FAIA is professor at Yale School of Architecture and founder of MIXdesign – an inclusive design think tank and consultancy that is a branch of his New York-based design studio JSA.

Sanders' writings and practice have explored the impact that evolving cultural forces (including gender identity and the body) have on the designed environment.

ALEX SCHWEDER is a New York-based artist using architecture as a medium. His installations explore human interactions in space and they have been widely exhibited internationally.

JACK SELF is an architect and writer based in London. He is director of the REAL foundation, editor-in-chief of the *Real Review* and master of Diploma Unit Six at the Architectural Association.

MALKIT SHOSHAN is a designer, researcher, and author. She is the founding director of the Foundation for Achieving Seamless Territory (FAST) – an architectural think-tank that develops projects at the intersection of architecture, urban planning, and human rights – and the head of Art, Design, and the Public Domain (ADPD) Master in Design Studies at Harvard GSD.

MATT STORUS is a senior design manager at Coinbase. After studying at Harvard GSD and working in various architectural practices, he left architecture to pursue his interest in digital product design and user experience.

STUDIO FOLDER is a Milan-based design and research studio founded by Elisa Pasqual and architect-turned designer Marco Ferrari. The outcome of their work spans across data visualisations, exhibition design, editorial products and digital platforms.

JEREMY TILL is head of Central Saint Martins and pro vice-chancellor of University of the Arts London, as well as a trustee of the New Economics Foundation. He is also a writer and an award-winning architect.

SIB TRIGG is an architect and community organiser at PEACH, the People's Empowerment Alliance for Custom House.

She is currently undertaking doctoral research titled 'Knowledge infrastructures in contemporary community responses to urban regeneration' at Central Saint Martins.

SARAH WIGGLESWORTH MBE is the director of the London-based practice Sarah Wigglesworth Architects, which she founded in 1994, and widely recognised as a pioneering influence in British design, particularly in the field of sustainability.

FINN WILLIAMS is the co-founder and chief executive officer of the social enterprise Public Practice as well as a visiting professor of practice at the UCL Institute of Innovation & Public Purpose.

WORKac is a New York-based architecture firm, which, through their projects, seek to reinvent the relationship between urban and natural environments. WORKac is led by founding partners Amale Andraos and Dan Wood. Andraos is also the dean of Columbia GSAPP.

ROGER ZOGOLOVITCH is the founder of the London-based independent development company Solidspace and the author of *Shouldn't we all be developers?* (2015). His career transformation happened over 30 years ago, when he left CZWG – the architecture practice he co-founded in 1975 – to become a developer, the career he continues to today.

IMAGE CREDITS

p.35-43	Sarah Wigglesworth Architects
p.49	Muf
p.55	TOP Photo: Dianna Snape
	BOTTOM Photo: Nina Hamilton
p.67	Project: DisOrdinary Architecture / Masashi Kajita. Photo: Jos Boys
p.69	Jos Boys
p.76-77	Photo: Miguel de Guzmán
p.80	Rendering: Design Distill
p.80-85	Interboro
p.95	JSA / MIXdesign
p.101-103	Public Works
p.119	Hayatsu Architects
p.120-121	Photos: Morley von Sternberg
p.123	Peter Barber
p.132	Photo: Philipp Ebeling
p.133	Assemble
p.148-149	Photos: Olivier Bréart
p.150	Rotor
p.152-153	Rotor/AA School Diploma 18, 2018-2019
p.161	Ant Farm / WORKac
p.169	Jack Self
p.175	Photos: Rory Gardiner
p.203	Forensic Architecture
p.209	Courtesy of the Dutch Ministry of Defence
p.213	Photo: Iwan Baan
p.217	Courtesy of the Beall Center for Art and Technology, UC Regents and Lauren Woods Photos: Will Yang
p.226-228	Photo: Clemens Klein
p.235	Courtesy of Rockstar Games, Inc
p.261	Courtesy of Scott Paterson
p.262-265	Photos and sketches: Dan Hill
p.266-267	Studio Folder
p.279	TOP Photo: Jae Shin BOTTOM Courtesy of Hector
p.291	Photo: Ivan Jones
p.301	TOP Photo: Brooj Al Ammari BOTTOM Photo: Bethany Williams
p.309-313	Courtesy of Robert Mull

INDEX

T - #0123 - 080121 - C0 - 229/152/14 - PB - 9780367441210